CURIOSITIES SERIES

D1319022

Indiana
CURIOSITIES

QUIRKY CHARACTERS, ROADSIDE ODDITIES & OTHER OFFBEAT STUFF

DICK WOLFSIE

SECOND EDITION

INSIDERS' GUIDE®

GUILFORD, CONNECTICUT
AN IMPRINT OF THE GLOBE PEQUOT PRESS

INSIDERS' GUIDE®

Text design by Nancy Freeborn
Layout by Debbie Nicolais
Maps by Rusty Nelson © Morris Book Publishing, LLC
Photo credits: See page iii.

ISSN 1932-7366
ISBN-13: 978-0-7627-4113-7
ISBN-10: 0-7627-4113-9

Manufactured in the United States of America
Second Edition/First Printing

Photo Credits

All photos by the author except the following: p. vii: Indiana National Road Association; p. 5: Chad Stevens and Skydive Greensburg; p. 11: Sandy Sheets; p. 23: Katie Murphy/KMPD; p. 47: Anthony Villainis; p. 54: Randy Chambers; p. 61: Kruse Automotive Carriage Museum; p. 70: Martin Marietta Aggregates; p. 85: Mary-Ellen Bertram; p. 89: People's Burn Foundation; p. 91: Myrtle Young; p. 95: Indiana State Museum; p. 97: Alice Stickler; p. 111: Layne Cameron; p. 112: Elkhart County Convention Bureau; p. 120: Tom Fisher; p. 125: Devon Rose; p. 130: Layne Cameron; p. 133: Jerome Bockting; p. 143: Zeormix LLC and Lucent; p. 155: Wilbur Wright Birthplace; p. 164: John M. Staicer, Historic Madison, Inc.; p. 170: Roselyn McKittrick; p. 183: John Kleinman; p. 189: Switzerland County Welcome Center; p. 210: Sharon Ivers; p. 218: Betty Bartley; p. 227: USS LST Ship Memorial; p. 232: John Baker sports; p. 237: Travis Bell; p. 239: Gary Keener; p. 245: Kenneth McFelea and Maxine Archibald; p. 247: Lake County CVB—John Dillinger Museum; p. 289: Lew Wallace Study and Museum; p. 294: Howard Van Doren Show, Paul A Myers, executive director; p. 295: Fair Oaks Farms; p. 303: Hesston Steam Museum; p. 308: Rogers Group, Inc.; p. 312: Steph Mineart; p. 314: Rod Stein, Red Crown Museum; p. 317: Steph Mineart; p. 320: T. J. Smith Studio; pp. 323, 324: John D. Wilson; p. 326: Monticello United Methodist Church; p. 333: Oxford Memorabilia; p. 352: Cherrie Lifonti.

INDIANA

Contents

In Celebration of the
200th Anniversary of U.S. Highway 40   **vi**

Introduction   **vii**

Greater Indianapolis (aka Indy)   **1**

Northeast Indiana   **53**

Southeast Indiana   **135**

Southwest Indiana   **197**

Northwest Indiana   **275**

Index   **345**

About the Author   **352**

In celebration of the 200th anniversary of U.S. Highway 40

In my travels, I spent a fair amount of time driving U.S. Highway 40, America's Main Street, but few places I visited along the route ended up in this book.

The reason is simple. The good people at the Indiana National Road Association who oversee the safeguarding of this national treasure have done an excellent job of preserving the structures and preserving the history of scores of places along the Historic National Road.

Every one of them, a treat.

But you don't need *Indiana Curiosities* for those sites—there are books, brochures, and maps galore to help guide you to the celebrated landmarks.

And so, if you decide to spend some time traveling this historic byway, put this book in your glove compartment. It's a good companion to have if you wander off the Historic National Road and see a few oddities and curiosities on the side, so to speak.

Have fun. Safe travels. And happy anniversary.

No matter how many times we say *historic*, it's never enough.

Introduction

After the first edition of *Indiana Curiosities* was published, I figured I was through with my compulsive search for oddball people and places. But the truth is I never stopped working on the book, even after it hit bookstores. Almost immediately, fans of *Indiana Curiosities* wrote, e-mailed, called, or left notes on my car windshield telling me about bizarro stuff I had missed—the people and places I had overlooked. More than a dozen people who had bought the book were traveling the state to get the signatures of everyone I had written about. And they were finding new stuff in the process.

I realized that within a few years there would have to be a new edition of *Indiana Curiosities*. I figured I'd take out a few places that had lost their luster and add maybe ten or twenty fresh ones. Okay, how about over sixty? It's hard to say "no" to an oddity.

This second edition is even better than the first. For starters, this book is bigger and thicker, just like the four-pound burger from the first edition that now weighs in at almost five pounds (see the Indianapolis chapter). And there's lots of really weird new stuff inside, like the Hair Museum in French Lick and the world's largest orchid. There are also a few sobering places, like the Holocaust Museum in Terre Haute. For you folks who like to walk and gawk, you just have to get your caboose up to the Monon Connection—my vote for Indiana's best new museum.

And so, once again, thanks to all who offered suggestions in helping compile this second edition of *Indiana Curiosities*, especially Layne Cameron, who helped me with several entries and let me yell at him on the phone. Oh, and I want to sneak in a thanks to Heidi Newman, my personal proofreader, who read every word in this book except this sentance.

I am very grateful. I couldn't have done it without you.

But the royalties are all mine.

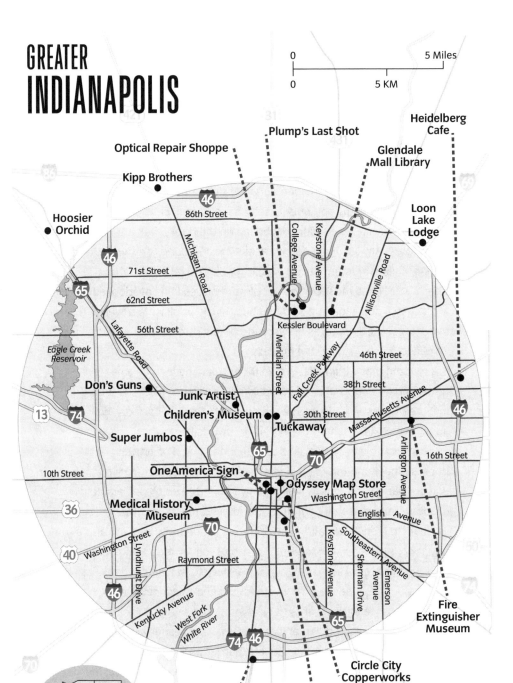

GREATER INDIANAPOLIS

0   5 Miles

0   5 KM

Optical Repair Shoppe

Plump's Last Shot

Heidelberg Cafe

Glendale Mall Library

Kipp Brothers

Hoosier Orchid

86th Street

Michigan Road

College Avenue

Keystone Avenue

Allisonville Road

Loon Lake Lodge

71st Street

62nd Street

56th Street

Kessler Boulevard

Lafayette Road

Eagle Creek Reservoir

Meridian Street

Fall Creek Parkway

46th Street

38th Street

Don's Guns

Junk Artist

Children's Museum

Tuckaway

30th Street

Massachusetts Avenue

Arlington Avenue

16th Street

Super Jumbos

OneAmerica Sign

65

70

10th Street

Medical History Museum

Odyssey Map Store

Washington Street

English Avenue

36

Washington Street

Lyndhurst Drive

70

40

Raymond Street

Keystone Avenue

Southeastern Avenue

Sherman Drive

Emerson Avenue

46

Kentucky Avenue

West Fork White River

65

Fire Extinguisher Museum

74 46

Circle City Copperworks

Adrian Orchard

Custom Phone Shop

Greater

INDIANAPOLIS

(aka Indy)

Because I live in Indianapolis, I figured after the first edition of *Indiana Curiosities*, I had pretty much found all the really unique stuff. Not even close. Since the last edition, Indy now has the only fire extinguisher museum in the solar system. I completely missed the 500-pound orchid, which is hard to do; and now you can read about a man who got rich bending pencils. Some of my favorites remain, so if you are in the market for 500 whoopee cushions, it's not too late. I kept in that four-pound hamburger, which is now almost five pounds. Sadly, a few things are gone, so hold on to your last edition . . . or I can sell you one really cheap.

Big Flower Lover

William Rhodehamel has a lot to brag about. He has the biggest one in Indiana—maybe the country. Heck, maybe the biggest in the world.

It weighs 500 pounds and it's 10 feet tall.

It's an orchid.

William Rhodehamel, starring in Little Shop of Orchids.

Yes, an *orchid*. An orchid so huge that Rhodehamel says it literally eats fertilizer.

You can see this monstrosity at Hoosier Orchid on the northwest side of Indianapolis. But that's not all you can see. You can see a room with 6,000 glass jars that contain millions of plantlets which will grow into thousands of orchids representing hundreds of species. The room looks like something from a sci-fi movie, the workplace of a mad scientist bent on creating a new life form.

Rhodehamel has been intrigued with the beauty and majesty of orchids ever since he was a young man, and his fascination has resulted in several hundred awards. He has written scores of articles about orchids and spends twelve hours a day in his greenhouse. A species of orchid—*Masdevallia rhodehameliana*—was named after him. Other than that, he's pretty normal.

Rhodehamel says there's a lot you may not know about orchids. For example, vanilla—a worldwide popular flavoring—comes from the seedpod of one variety of orchid.

Or this: Many orchids grow in the ground with two large tubers at their root. The word *orchid* is Greek for testicles.

Aren't you glad you bought this book?

Hoosier Orchid is at 8440 West 82nd Street in Indy (317–291–6269).

Distorted Thinking!

Tom Killion is not crooked, but his business is. He is the founder and creator of Bentcils, plastic pens and pencils that come in more shapes than you can shake a warped stick at. His Indianapolis company is unique in the world. Bic has tried to copy him, but they can't keep up. Maybe they should get the lead out.

Tom was an industrial arts teacher back in the 1970s when, after demonstrating to a student what happens to plastics when they are heated (they melt, of course), he started wondering what he could do with plastics if he could control the materials and the temperature. "If I could make a pencil that was twisted," he remembers thinking, "I would have a product that anyone, at any age, anywhere in the world, would purchase." Don't laugh. He was right.

It took a couple of years of trial and error, but by 1978 Killion was producing a half million Number 2 pencils. They sharpened like a wooden pencil, wrote like a wooden pencil, and looked like a wooden pencil, but they were plastic. And they were bent like a pretzel.

By 1983, Killion had about seven designs and remembers saying to his employees, "I think we've run out of shapes." Now, with over 1,000 designs, his products are sold all over the world through novelty distributors.

All the machinery in Killion's plant was designed by him and constructed right on the premises. The material is prepped by machine, but each pencil is shaped by hand using a kind of cookie-cutter die.

You can call Tom at (317) 271–4536. Better yet, here's the Web site: www.Bentcil.com. Go to it. Plug in a category, like dogs, or flags, or cars, or syringes (nurses love those), or toilets (a big hit with plumbers). The available designs come up.

Be creative. That's the whole point.

Never Too Late!

Want to jump out of an airplane for your sixtieth wedding anniversary—
or ride in a racecar at 180 mph for your ninetieth birthday?

Those are just two wishes granted by Never Too Late, a unique
organization located in Indianapolis. Founded by Bob Haverstick, the
organization's mission is to grant wishes to seniors nearing the end of
their lives, wishes that range from the banal
(go to Disney World with a great-
granddaughter) to the
bodacious (ride in a
dragster).

It's never too late . . . to do something totally nuts.

Haverstick founded the organization back in 2000 after seeing a local play, *Touching Lives*, which inspired him to see if folks in nursing homes had unfulfilled dreams. Most wish organizations are devoted to helping kids, so this was a senior twist on an idea already operating successfully all over the country.

One of Haverstick's earliest requests was from a senior who had retired from his farm due to failing health and wanted to return one last time and sit behind the wheel of a tractor. A wish like this is relatively easy to grant, but it made Haverstick realize that even the most modest request may require "connecting a lot of dots to make everything run smoothly." Haverstick and his corps of volunteers know how to pick up the phone and make things happen.

Ironically, Haverstick is dealing with a population that was brought up to be "selfless, not selfish," and the result is that many seniors have never thought about a last-chapter wish or are reluctant to express it.

Since 2000 Never Too Late has fulfilled more than a thousand wishes. Many are heartwarming, like that of ninety-eight-year-old Pauline who had not seen her institutionalized son for eighteen months. Bob arranged for Pauline's son to be relocated from Rockville, Indiana, to a nursing home four blocks away from Pauline's long-term care facility so they could see each other once a week.

Here are some of the more adventuresome requests Haverstick has received over the years:

- 84-year-old Mary Lou wanted to go rafting with her grandsons
- 94-year-old Ruth wished to ride a Harley one more time
- 79-year-old Bobby yearned to return to an old naval vessel from WWII
- 88-year-old Albert wanted to take his wife parachuting
- 78-year old Eloise dreamed of riding in a dragster
- 81-year-old Francis wanted to pet a wild tiger

- 87-year-old Louise wished to ride a railroad car
- 106-year-old Alvin wanted to be invited to a Colts cheerleader slumber party

All wishes but one were granted. Everybody survived. How cool is that?

Remember, this is a curiosity you can't get in your car and visit. With the price of gas so high, you'll be glad I wrote a few like this. But you can call: (317) 823–4705.

You're Fired

Randy Koorsen caresses a fire extinguisher like it was a fine wine. Many of his best vintages go back to the late 1800s.

Randy doesn't have a cellar for his treasures; instead the collection is displayed in an old credit-union building on the property of his sixty-year-old family business: Koorsen Fire and Security. Now it's starting to make sense, huh?

Koorsen's grandfather and father had dabbled in collecting, but Randy really caught the bug (which is not a good metaphor in the fire business) in the late 1960s.

Koorsen's collection grew over the years, but it was only recently that he thought his 700 copper, brass, and stainless steel works of art needed a real home. Wait a second. Did I say works of art? Yes, indeed. Many of the canisters boast ornate decoration and a creative display of the company name or city where it was manufactured.

Does this make them very valuable? To Randy, yes. But truth be told, Koorsen has been pretty lucky at finding extinguishers at garage sales and antiques shops at, well, fire-sale prices. "The people on eBay are starting to get smart," says Koorsen, "and at some of the antique fire equipment shows, they know me now, so that may drive up the price."

Most of the extinguishers look pretty shabby when rescued, but Koorsen knows several people who can restore them to their original look. The museum also has a few fire alarms, as well as a collection of grenades—glass bottles from the turn of the twentieth century filled with saltwater that you just threw at the fire. Now that sounds like fun, doesn't it?

Randy Koorsen and his distinguished extinguishers.

The museum is open to the public at 2719 North Arlington Avenue in Indianapolis (317–542–1800), but Koorsen says he seems to attract mostly firefighters. Well, go figure.

By the way. Do the extinguishers still work? Hard to tell. Does the airbag in your 1993 Taurus still work?

I hope you never have to find out.

Easy as Cake

For more than thirty years, people have stopped at the Heidelberg Cafe at 7625 Pendleton Pike in Indianapolis. Others have driven by the flamingo-pink building vowing to someday yield to their curiosity and venture inside.

Regulars know what to expect. It never changes. The Heidelberg is a bakery, a gift shop, a cafe, a restaurant, a video store, and a museum. And every inch of the place is a celebration of old Germany. Okay, there's a touch of Switzerland and Austria, too.

The owner is Juergen Jungbauer, known as JJ, a pint-sized pastry chef who packs a lot of personality and knows his whey around whipped cream.

JJ studied in Europe and was a master pastry chef by the time he was sixteen. He came to the U.S. while he was still a teenager and opened the cafe in 1968. Today, people come from all over to sit at the counter or at the tiny tables and have a piece of kielbasa, or some *mettwurst*. If you don't know what mettwurst is, you really *don't* know what you are missing. And don't forget the hot German potato salad.

The big draw, of course, is JJ's pastry creations—authentic cakes and tortes made right in the back every day. The chef bristles at my inquiry about pies. "You want pies?" he says, "go to a pie shop." The Black Forest cake, with a ring of chocolate buttercream, is his most popular item, but he refuses to sell to other restaurants. "I can't control the product," says JJ. "If they kept it in the fridge for a week with a catfish, what do you think it would taste like?"

The huge glass display cases in the store feature dozens of home-baked items, all of which can be purchased in individual slices for take-out. Once you've satisfied your sweet tooth, visit the bakery museum, featuring tools of the trade going back over a hundred years, including a coal oven and hand implements from the turn of the twentieth century. School kids like the museum. They like the chocolate fudge cake even better.

Inside you'll find German gifts, German toys, German magazines, German candies, and German T-shirts. And all videos are rated G (for German, of course!). Call the Heidelberg Cafe at (317) 547–1257. You can go to their Web site, but it doesn't smell as good as the shop: www.germanvideo.com/service_pages/heidelberg.html.

Picky, Picky

Geoff Davis hated the school where he was teaching. Then he found a better school. So he quit. Now he's singing a different tune. Some of those tunes are: *Five Foot Two, Chicken Ain't Nuttin' but a Bird,* and *I Like Bananas Because They Have No Bones.*

Davis is the founder of the Key Strummers, a band of pint-sized pickers who tour the country, bringing the plucky sounds of the ukulele to formerly grumpy people everywhere.

"We put smiles on faces 100 percent of the time," says Davis, who started the group after he began teaching at the Key Learning Community in Indy. A special program offered him the opportunity to teach something he was interested in. He was supposed to be interested in something to do with social studies. But he had a better idea.

A musician, Davis had once fiddled with the uke and knew it didn't require great talent to get started, just a little confidence and a sense of fun. "The problem with teaching musical instruments," says Davis, "is that teachers pick music kids don't enjoy. It's like learning to read with *Moby Dick*."

Talented kids, uplifting music, garage sale shirts.

11

Davis began with just a handful of kids and a bunch of silly songs, and before you knew it the band was playing not only at schools, but at retirement homes, picnics, and birthday parties. In recent years they opened for Garrison Keillor at the Indiana State Fair and played a memorial service for the late Governor O'Bannon, a big fan of theirs.

For the band members themselves, it's been a downright, down-home good experience. Before joining the band, many of Geoff's students (ages nine to fourteen) were headed for some serious problems in and out of school. "The band has given so many of these youngsters something to be proud of, something to look forward to," he says. Initially, the kids balked at playing for retirement homes. Now, says Geoff, the group is eager to get seniors in a toe-tapping, hand-clapping mood.

The group has also created an event called Midwest UkeFest, a yearly get-together of top ukulele players from around the country who come to Indy for five days of pickin' and strummin' every October.

It's unlikely that many of Geoff's kids will ever make a living playing the uke. But playing the uke has made living a lot more fun for everybody.

If this whole thing sounds like music to your ears, call (317) 226–4992 or visit www.keystrummers.org.

Scrapping It All

Ever since Bill Ryder was a kid, he loved taking things apart—like his father's Elgin watch and his sister's dolls. He loved to tinker.

Ryder attended art school but never finished, and ended up making a living as a graphic designer. In 1996, at the age of fifty-nine, he decided that before he junked the rest of his life, he would put life into junk. In the years since, Bill has taken tinkering to a new level.

Walk into his very modest home on the west side of Indianapolis and you step into a world of wires, bed frames, shingles, shower heads, springs, old keys, pots, car doors, street lights—just about anything you'd find (and ignore) in a junkyard.

Miraculously, as if a perfect storm blew the spare parts together, you'll come face to face with *Rusty Dusty,* a lady of ill repute created out of farm wire and metal wine barrel hoops. Her locks of hair are fashioned out of rusty chains, washers—and padlocks.

There's *Rahsaan*, a famous blind musician, made of copper and brass wiring gathered from an Indianapolis Power and Light plant. And *The Unknown Blues Singer*, whose microphone is a shower head and whose shock of hair is crafted from forks and spoons. The image of *Red Ryder*, Bill's father, is made entirely out of a metal bunk bed twisted like a pretzel. Awesome.

Miracle on Clifton Street: Garbage in, artwork out.

13

Bill admits he sells very few of his creations (they're not cheap), but it isn't about the money; it's about the quality of his new life—a humble one to be sure, but one where each day is filled with discovery and accomplishment.

He works tirelessly, twelve hours a day, seven days a week, often creating on his front lawn when weather permits, as he bends and breaks, solders, and shapes bigger-than-life expressions of his past experiences. You can see his creations as you walk by or drive by.

Or fly over. Several plane passengers have told Bill they can see his front-yard sculpture of Jesus from the air.

Ryder has no illusions of fame or fortune. "If I never sell a thing, that will be okay," he says. His joy comes from his occasional art shows and the respect and love people have shown him. "I used to have anger, but I don't any more. It's the happiest I've ever been."

Bill may be an unsung genius in the art world, but if you stop by and watch him work, you'll sing his praises as I have.

You can reach Bill at (317) 924–6168, or walk by the house (everyone else does) at 3417 Clifton Street in Indy.

Dino-mite

Most of the material in this book is hidden. Just like the subtitle says, we are talking about roadside oddities—stuff the average traveler might miss unless he knew what to look for.

This entry is a huge exception. And I mean HUGE. It's the long-necked dinosaur that seems to be bursting from the confines of the Dinosphere at the Children's Museum of Indianapolis's state-of-the-art addition at the corner of 33rd and Illinois.

The concept is unique in the world, although artist and designer Brian Cooley of Canada had created three-dimensional works of art for

twenty years, including an outdoor tableau of an *Albertosaurus* (that's T-Rex's cousin) chasing his prey at a nearby museum.

When the folks at the Children's Museum brainstormed ideas for their new wing, they had heard of Cooley and went to Canada to see his work.

In what must have seemed like eons of discussions, the idea of the dinosaur "escaping" the confines of the venue was born. "It was actually an idea my wife and I came up with," says Cooley.

But which dinosaur to erect? The museum folks did an informal survey of kids and found that the long-neck dinosaur was the most popular. When the choice was narrowed a bit more—although there is nothing narrow about this dinosaur—the museum opted for the *Alamosaurus*, which clearly had a presence in North America over sixty-five million years ago.

Breakthrough art from the Dinosaur Age.

15

Cooley and his company actually built the dinosaur out of fiberglass in Calgary; then it was transported to Indiana, a migration of prehistoric proportion. The dinosaur was built to scale, says Cooley. "There were some bigger and some smaller, but there was definitely one that size."

By the way, the project took a year and a half to complete—which is really not very long in dinosaur years.

To see the dinosaur, just get on Illinois Street downtown and drive north to 3000 North Illinois Street. If you don't see it, you shouldn't be driving. Call (317) 334–3322 or visit www.childrensmuseum.org.

Chalking One Up

Matt Lewis has a great attitude. After a grueling day at work, he just picks himself up, dusts himself off, and prepares for the next day.

He has to dust himself off. He's covered with the stuff. Red dust, blue dust, green dust—about forty dusty colors in all.

Matt is a chalk artist, one of only a handful of motivational speakers in the country who can create a 6-by-8-foot work of art right before your very eyes. (Caution: Your eyes may need Visine.)

Matt was a self-proclaimed nerd in high school, an awkward teenager who didn't fit in. Toward the end of high school he realized he had a knack for the dramatic and decided he wanted to spend his life in front of fans (preferably, adoring ones). He started a fledgling speaking career. But he lacked a hook.

One day at a conference, Matt watched another presenter, Ben Glenn, use chalk to create a beautiful image in fifteen minutes from a blank canvas. "I was blown away," says Matt. That's an odd expression coming from someone who works with chalk.

Ben took Matt under his wing, providing some instruction that summer, but Matt continued to hone the skill himself and now travels the

country spreading a message by spreading chalk on a canvas.

The messages are simple but important: Strive to be your best; Believe in yourself; Respect the power of choice. Depending on his audience, Matt picks a particular theme and then fashions his artwork to that concept. He works quickly, but methodically; his movements seem almost in time with the accompanying music. He sporadically blows the chalk dust from his fingers, swooping down to pluck a different shade of chalk from the myriad colors piled on the floor.

He seldom speaks while "painting." He doesn't have to. Even the roughest groups of kids are mesmerized by his technique and his talent. It's fun getting a standing ovation from teenagers. (I taught high school for ten years and never got one.)

The presentation is an hour, but the drawing takes a snappy fifteen minutes. During that period, you often think that the picture is finished, but Matt continues to add layer upon layer, fine-tuning the mural and the message.

Both Matt and his mentor, Ben Glenn, are hits wherever they go. The combination of talk and chalk is captivating. You can e-mail Matt at Mattlewis3@yahoo, call him at (317) 437–6756, or visit him online at www.mattspeaks.com.

Bonne, Michael Bonne

Michael Bonne once had a cookie-cutter operation. No insult intended. In 2001 he was the largest producer of copper cookie cutters in the world. From angels to apples, baskets to bows, pumpkins to pigs, he seemingly had every large and small cookie cutter you could imagine. He actually made cookie cutters for a famous person who spent some time in the slammer. We're not allowed to say who that was.

Bonne once housed the world's only Cookie Cutter Museum inside his Knightstown shop, with cookie cutters that went back hundreds of years. The display was on loan from cookie-cutter collectors all over the globe. But they called in the loan. That's the way the cookie crumbles.

When Bonne moved from his Knightstown location in 2003, he had to rethink and reshape what he was doing. Now located just east of downtown Indy in a small warehouse, Bonne's Circle City Copperworks is still the only real coppersmith shop in Indiana. And while his new place is smaller, it still shines.

Bonne currently specializes in birdbaths and antique-looking kitchen hoods, although he does sneak in a few cookie cutters now and then. He also makes weathervanes, napkin rings, jugs, whisk bowls, boilers, and dozens of decorative items. His retail shop, just inside his studio, is open to the public.

Some of Michael Bonne's work is for the birds.

Circle City Copperworks doubles as a museum, filled with antique tools and machines used in the 1830s that are still used by Bonne today to produce his wares. "They have never made machines that work any better, and I like the idea of crafting on the original equipment," says Bonne. Visitors can watch Bonne do his thing. It's a thing you won't see anywhere else.

Bonne's shop is at 614 East Ohio Street. His machinery may be old, but his Web site is new: www.circlecitycopperworks.com. Or call (317) 635–5880.

Free Ride

Don West is having a midway crisis. This is not about fast automobiles and beautiful women. It's about bumper cars and bearded ladies.

West is a collector of circus and carnival miniatures and models. His basement (he prefers "lower level") is eye candy for anyone who has ever ridden a roller coaster, seen a sideshow, or gone to a circus.

Don started out as a young man doing the traditional railroad collecting, but somewhere along the line he got off track. Ironically, it was after the change in direction that he learned circuses and carnivals ran in his family, way back to his great-great uncle and grandfather who owned a sideshow. "That's when I knew it was in my blood," he says.

His first carnival model was a small die-cast replica of a tilt-a-wheel, which is still his favorite piece. But now his basement—sorry, lower level—is filled with models of more than one hundred rides and attractions, virtually all in working order. There are tiny replicas of sideshows, food stands, fun houses, and circus trains.

He also has a workshop where he constructs his models from kits or, in some cases, builds from scratch, often combining parts from different sets. "It can take a hundred hours to build one of these rides," says

West, who enhances the final product by repainting each part to make it look even more authentic.

West loves the "wow" he gets when anybody sees his collection. Says Don, "It's the greatest little show on earth."

You can reach Don at ptbarnum@ptbarnum.us. If he doesn't reply, he may be down below, if you know what I mean.

Don West has a thing for bearded ladies. Doesn't everyone?

Picky Farmer

If an apple a day keeps the doctor away, George Adrian will never need an HMO.

In 1980, on an apple-crisp day in late September, Adrian picked 30,000 apples (that's eight tons, 365 bushels) at his orchard. And he became, according to the *Guinness Book of World Records,* the fastest apple picker in the world. By the way, that's 2,000 pounds an hour.

Adrian is a third-generation apple grower, and when he heard about the record in the late 1970s, he saw no reason why he couldn't break it. Working with only a ladder and a picking bucket, Adrian used both arms as he twisted and contorted his body for eight straight hours, stopping only for lunch. Not to be picky (which he was), but he beat the old record by twenty-four bushels.

Another Indianapples record-holder.

Adrian's record remains unbroken to this day, though more than a few have tried to outshine him over the years. Adrian claims that he has better technique now, but he has no interest in competing. "It's tough on the knees and the arms," admits Adrian, who says that after holding the record for so many years, he'd be happy to give it up to a new crop of record-holders.

You can find George Adrian at his orchard most days at 500 West Epler on the south side of Indy. For the best apple cider ever (made fresh at the orchard), drop by or call Adrian Orchard at (317) 784–0550.

Monkey Business

Walk over glass, stick a nail in your nose, eat fire, lay on a bed of nails!

Heck, that's just a day's work for Bart Simpson and the men of the Blue Monkey Sideshow.

These self-admitted masochists banded together in 1998, after doing a Halloween party and realizing the audience was tickled by anything that looked like it didn't tickle. "We realized that we were really doing a circus sideshow and the audience loved it. So we decided to develop some of those acts."

Simpson and his co-hurts researched the sideshow traditions, threw in a few of their own creations, and billed themselves as the Blue Monkey Sideshow. "The name lent itself to some great graphics," says Simpson, who can't wait to get up and go to work, assuming he can get up.

The Blue Monkey Sideshow has entertained (and grossed out) audiences all over the United States, but the group's home is in central Indiana, where they work out of a garage in the historic Fletcher Place of downtown Indianapolis. They claim to be the only such sideshow in the

Midwest and one of the few in the country, and you can see them at fairs, corporate functions, and colleges.

Two of the Blue Monkeys have master's degrees, and all of them love to live on the edge . . . and walk and sit on the edge, as well. "The Three Person Shrink-Wrap" is three guys sitting in a huge envelope of shrink-wrap while an assistant sucks the air out of the plastic material with a vacuum cleaner. The result is not pleasant to look at. Hey, it's a sideshow.

Bart Simpson also wants people to know that he is not related to the television character. Whatever that means.

Get more info by calling (317) 822–0802 or visiting www.bluemonkey sideshow.com. We suggest you eat AFTER you look at their Web page.

The Blue Monkey Sideshow wraps up another day.

Wood-Be Artist

If you want to speak to Chie Kramer, YOU HAVE TO YELL. Why's that? Because most of the time this guy is in his shed brandishing a chainsaw. AND WHAT'S HE DOING? Hold onto your headdress. He's making Cigar Store Indians.

While Kramer was stationed in the San Juan Islands in 1976, he watched the native Indians craft beautiful totem poles. Years later when he was in college, a business professor asked the students to investigate an enterprise that was not in the Yellow Pages. Kramer, who up to that point wouldn't have touched wood carving with a 10-foot pole, realized there was no listing for wood-statue makers.

Kramer made a quick statue for the class, then another for a neighbor, who paid him cold hard cash for the little wooden Indian. Kramer was hooked. He hasn't looked back since. But looking down is a good idea, especially when you use power tools sixteen hours a day.

Beginning with a chainsaw, Kramer carves out the basic outline in about an hour, then fine-tunes his Indian with hand tools and a power grinder. Indians are painted by hand, always with authentic tribal colors. Total time for carving, painting, and drying can be a couple of months. Prices begin at $250.

Today, more than 2,500 Cigar Store Indians later, Kramer is one of the few wood carvers in the Midwest with this specialty. His work has been sold around the country, often to people with an interest in Indian history or some connection with cigars or tobacco. "The Cigar Store Indian," says Kramer, "is a true American icon."

Kramer doesn't want people just showing up at his house, so check out his Web site at www.cigarstoreindianstatue.com. But if you are on the northeast side of Indy, you'll probably hear him.

Give Me a Sign

OneAmerica has the two most popular signboards in Indianapolis. No joke. Well, actually it is a joke.

The company's two signboards have been providing Circle City residents with a wealth of witticisms for more than five decades. They were the brainchild of then-chairman Clarence Jackson and have been inspiring people to chuckle, guffaw, cheer, and, on occasion, even snort coffee through their noses since 1958.

The OneAmerica sign—amusing Hoosiers, one-liners at a time.

Over the years, OneAmerica has steered clear of inspirational sayings, advertising, political endorsements, and, generally, anything that's "too preachy." It has, however, made an art of humorous briefs without crossing the line into insulting or off-color. "Since people are usually driving past, we don't want them to stare too long at our board," says Kyle Proctor, manager of creative services. "We go for ones that produce a groan or laugh on the spot."

Some of the highlights include:

- Puns—Why isn't *phonetic* spelled the way it sounds? Do horse breeders strive for a stable population? Cross a vampire with a snowman and you get frostbite.
- Definitions—Laughing stock: cattle with a sense of humor. Pacifier: Scream saver.
- Holiday Humor—Can't stop eating pumpkin pie? Try a pumpkin patch. Polite ghosts spook only when spooken to. Holiday blahs? Try Santa's elf-help tips.

Check out the signs at Vermont and Capitol and New York and Illinois, or visit the Web site at www.oneamerica.com. Select "About OneAmerica" and click on "OneAmerica Signboard."

IDDNAT INTRESTING

John Terhune is an Indianapolis chiropractor, and you'd better bone up on your pronunciation before you pay him a visit. Terhune has been listening to Hoosiers talk for ten years and is convinced that the people of Indiana speak a lean, economical language all their own, a language so simple and easy to use that it is destined for worldwide acceptance as "The New Global Language."

In his book, *Why Hoosiers Can't Pronounce "Indianapolis,"* Terhune treats readers to 263 pages of words and their pronunciations and definitions, Hoosier-style. In the book, you will learn, for example, that "Auzhusinkinat" is really "I was just thinking that." Yes, there are hundreds of examples like this, and just for the record, here is Terhune's list of seventeen different ways to say our capital city's name:

ANNAPLUS	INDYPLUS
ANYANAPPLES	INIANAPLUS
ANYNAPLUS	ININAPLUS
ENGINEAPLUS	INNAPLUS
INDIANAPLUS	INNUNAPLUS
INDIAPLUS	INNYNAPLUS
INDIANAPOIS	INYUNAPLUS
INDIANAPPLES	NNAPLUS
INDIANAPLUS	

Terhune also tells the reader which recognizable Indianapolis personalities are guilty of each of these linguistic massacres. His explanation for the wide variety of pronunciations? "Hoosiers have no use for a six-syllable word."

Don of Guns

For more than a quarter of a century, Don Davis has been trying to convince people that he doesn't want to make any money, he just loves to sell guns.

Well, that may be true, but that doesn't mean he hasn't made any money. In fact, Davis, a former Teamster, admits to becoming a millionaire in large part due to a silly slogan that began because all his Teamster buddies wanted a discount at his gun store. Davis told them that he didn't really want to make any money, he just wanted to give discounts to his pals. He took a sarcastic variation of that retort to the airwaves and soon became the best-known TV huckster in Indiana, maybe the Midwest.

He doesn't want to make money, folks, but he does. Lots of it.

When Davis first began in 1974 with a tiny gun and fishing shop, he had a couple of grand in the bank. "At that time, my goal was to clear fifty bucks a day and go fishing on Sunday," says Davis, who by the 1980s had two 10,000-foot gun ranges, a residence in Florida, a home and golf course in Greenwood, and assorted real estate. "I went from 300 a week to 300 an hour," notes the gun dealer, who has never made any apologies for his success. "In my wildest dreams, I never thought this could happen. Only in America."

Davis has not been without controversy. At first, TV stations shunned him. And when they finally did relent, they'd only put him on after midnight. He might be the first TV spokesperson to shoot a machine gun during his ads. He even performed in a rock band to stimulate gun sales. All that, plus more jewelry than a disco monkey, has made him a lightning rod for debate between NRA enthusiasts and gun control advocates.

Davis believes everyone has a right to own a gun but thinks people should be properly trained—and the gun registered. He's debated this issue on TV, radio, and college campuses. But it's no matter. He will always be known for that one slogan that turned him into an Indiana icon and a gazillionaire: "I don't want to make any money, folks, I just love to sell guns."

Don retired for a while, but he hated it. So now he's back at his one store just about every day. To make life interesting, Don stuck a seven-ton rock in his front yard and had the Second Amendment engraved in it. "Without that amendment," admits Don, "I'd be broke."

Most of his neighbors think the rock is cool. Some are a little chilly about it. Like he cares. Here's Don's number at the store: (317) 297–4242. You can say anything to him you want. There's that First Amendment, too.

Don's Guns is located at 38th and Lafayette, or check out www.dons guns.com.

Insane Museum

Okay, so you've just had lunch in downtown Indy and you have a choice. You can go see the best racecar track in the world, the best basketball stadium in the NBA, or the best minor-league baseball park in the United States. All within a couple of miles.

But why? Especially when you can visit Indy's best-kept secret: the nation's only remaining nineteenth-century pathology building.

Now remember, this assumes you've had your lunch. Because inside the Medical History Museum you will see diseased brains, kidneys, and livers. There are antique X-ray machines, old stethoscopes, and assorted quack devices. In total, more than 15,000 medical artifacts. You can also stroll through the lab or the photography department or sneak a peek at the extensive medical library.

The facility was built in 1896 on the campus of Central State, a hospital for the *insane*, to use the nineteenth-century term. It was the second freestanding pathology unit built to serve a mental hospital. Today, it is the only remaining nineteenth-century pathology building in the United States.

Want a creepy feeling? Walk into the amphitheater where more than one hundred years ago, medical students were lectured by professors who knew nothing of antibiotics or aspirin. They did know something about leeches. By the way, the first gallbladder operation was performed here by a Dr. John Bobbs in 1906.

The museum is at 3045 West Vermont Street (317–635–7329), or you can reach it at Edenharter@aol.com. The co-pay to get in is $5.00. I mean, the admission.

Party Time

You're planning that big surprise birthday bash for your wife and you need 200 whoopee cushions, and you need them fast. Who ya gonna call? Kipp Brothers, of course.

The Kipp brothers of Germany are long gone, but their more than one-hundred-year-old dedication to novelty items has never wavered here in Indianapolis. Having been housed in a number of locations in downtown Indy, the company recently moved from its historic building that stretched five stories up (and one below). That was six stories chock-full of every imaginable novelty item: Slinkies, paddle balls, canes, hats, party favors, sunglasses, mugs, Hawaiian leis, cameras, cap guns, and toys.

What could be grosser than a gross of whoopee cushions?

31

Need a yo-yo? Owner Bob Glenn can lay his hands on 4,000 dozen yo-yos without lifting a finger—except to his computer to see where they are in the warehouse. Huge quantities of items, most of them imported from places like China and Korea, are purchased in thousands of grosses to start.

Needing more room, in fact, was what prompted Glenn to move from the old location downtown to a new location on the north side of town. His new building is 100,000 square feet, containing 38,000 different items, all listed in a 250-page catalog. If you can't find what you want, they don't make it. And if they don't make it, Bob Glenn can probably get it made. But here's a warning: It will be cheaper if you order a couple million.

Of course if you need just one whoopee cushion, a scenario hard to even imagine, Glenn does have a retail shop where patrons can see the novelties in shiny glass cases before committing to any particular item.

Glenn ships coast to coast, often filling huge orders, like a recent request for 30,000 purple bears. "After 9/11, I bought over a million flags. I won't be stuck with them," he says. "Patriotism will be hot for a long time."

Glenn never asks what people are planning to do with some of their huge orders. "If it's legal, that's all I need to know," he says. "I mean, if you are going to rob a liquor store, you don't need 10,000 pairs of Groucho glasses."

Visit Kipp Brothers, just west of Michigan Road on Ninety-sixth Street, or contact them at sales@kippbro.com or (317) 814–1475. They'll send you a catalog.

Loony Restaurant

The Loon Lake Lodge is not a tribute to the movie starring Jane and Henry Fonda, but it is a tribute to the inventiveness of Chip Laughner, a local restaurateur, who dreamed of a theme restaurant to mimic the fishing lodges of the Adirondack Mountains. "We wanted to provide a northern woods environment where people could relax and relive some childhood fantasies."

Laughner tore down one of his former cafeterias in the Castleton area of Indianapolis and rebuilt it with the outdoorsman in mind, creating several rooms like The Porch, The Trophy Room, The Lodge, and The Cabin, all decorated to reignite "the woodsman in all of us." Well, most of us.

You can spot the lodge from blocks away by the hybrid Cessna airplane atop the roof, retrofitted with pontoons to add to the total fishing and hunting adventure. "We wanted to give the sense of people stopping

Plane on the outside. Wild on the inside. The Loon Lake Lodge.

at the lodge for a week or so, uninterrupted by the outside world," says John Ersoy, a partner in the business.

Once inside, your warm, cozy, safe feeling may be temporarily disturbed by the roar of a bear, the sound of birds, or the sight of a raccoon. Laughner installed state-of-the-art animatronics to delight kids and adults alike. "But we keep the effect subtle," says Ersoy. "We want you to enjoy the technology, but not have it disturb your meal."

The food is traditional, with a small part of the menu featuring exotic dishes like snake and elk. And if the wait is too long, there's always their retail store, an upscale shop where you can buy handcrafted hickory chairs or a chandelier made of elk antlers.

The Loon Lake Lodge is located at 6800 East 82nd Street. For details call (317) 845–9011.

Returning to the Mall

In the year 2005, 662,538 people went to one particular library in Indianapolis. But who's counting? Actually, a lot of people are. Why? Because the library's location is unique in the country.

This library branch—part of the Indianapolis–Marion County system—is probably the only full-service library facility operating inside a mall in the United States.

The idea began a few years ago with three local issues: a neighborhood library was too small with no place to expand; a nearby mall was in search of a marketing concept to make itself more user-friendly for local families; the mall's huge, empty spaces were begging to be filled.

Enter developer John Kite with an idea so simple it was pure genius: "Let's put your new library inside our mall."

Maria Blake, director of communications for the library system, remembers a great deal of skepticism on the library board's part.

"Library people are purists," reflects Blake, "so the idea of a library in a retail space took some getting used to."

Within just a few weeks of its opening, the Glendale Mall Library was the busiest library branch in the entire county, handling a couple thousand people a day and almost twice that on the weekends. Research showed that people who had not gone to the old library—and in some cases, people who had never been to a library at all—were going to the new library.

The library is open when the mall is open, allowing patrons to browse the shops for shorts or the shelves for short stories. The library has a full complement of computers, a Lego Mindstorm area for kids, a quiet reading room for adults, and a cafe for coffee and snacks. This is a long way from card catalogs and SHHH signs.

A final note if you're thinking of turning an old department store into a library. Books weigh much, much more than men's suits and ladies' dresses. So get a good structural engineer.

The library is easy to find. It's just south of 62nd on Keystone (317–269–1791). Check it out.

A library with a unique story. Read all about it.

LAWN DAY'S JOURNEY

Tom Abeel was so impressed with the 1992 Clinton inauguration that he became a chairman. No, not a chairman of the Democratic Party. A chair man for the Woodruff Place Lawn Chair Brigade.

It was actually Abeel's wife, Linda, who had attended the presidential festivities. She then reported to her husband about a rather odd aspect of the parade: a group of men marching in unison with lawn chairs. Abeel immediately had a vision he couldn't shake. He saw his neighbors in a similar posture, marching the streets of historic Woodruff Place in downtown Indy. Abeel had no trouble recruiting "soldiers" for his brigade, but at the time he saw it as little more than a publicity stunt for some of their annual neighborhood events.

The brigade consisted of nine men dressed in casual attire with folded newspapers in their back pockets and lawn chairs in their arms. The brigade marched and one leader, a former major in the U.S. Army, barked signals. Every once in a while, the parade would cease, chairs would be unfolded, and newspapers drawn from back pockets. Their slogan: When the parade stops, we sit.

Before you knew it, Abeel and his crew were getting requests to march in other parades. The first big march was in, what else, March, in the St. Patrick's Day parade, where Abeel was dumbstruck by the huge response his motley crew

The Lawn Chair Brigade. They're all chairmen, reigning on their own parade.

received when they
rounded the corner to the applause of thousands.

After that, the group got so busy, they hardly had time
to sit, I mean stand . . . whatever. They have performed in
the Indianapolis 500 Festival parade, July 4th parades, and
dozens of other events in and outside Indy.

The Woodruff Place Lawn Chair Brigade may be one of
only a handful in the entire country, a dubious honor to say
the least. But their motto says it all: Harmless Fun Since 1992.

Atlas Hugged Here

If you are looking for Tim Gravenstreter's store near downtown Indy and you can't find it, you may need a map. Actually, even if you can find it, you probably need a map. Because that's what Gravenstreter sells: maps.

In fact, that's all he sells, making his the only shop in Indiana selling just maps. Is this clear? Or do I have to draw you a map?

Gravenstreter, who used to build loft beds, had a lifelong love affair with maps. "Most boys my age looked at Mr. Atlas," says Gravenstreter. "I'd just look at an atlas."

When Gravenstreter opened the Odyssey Map Store in 1984, he had spent a sleepless week concerned that making a living selling only maps was "like opening a masking tape store." His fears were unfounded. "People came out of the woodwork," remembers the map purveyor.

Many of Gravenstreter's customers are vacationers planning a trip. Others are salespeople staking out territories, or outdoorsmen organizing a hike. Some are looking for antique maps for a collection. "There is no typical customer," says Gravenstreter.

Gravenstreter carries about 3,500 titles (maps), so he can usually accommodate a request on demand. "Do you want a map of Iceland? No problem," brags Gravenstreter. But sometimes he must order from map publishers, especially for very specialized areas. Topographic maps for some remote regions, for example, are not on hand, but Gravenstreter can put his hands on about 600,000 different titles if he has to.

Gravenstreter also sells rare, antique maps and can show you Indiana maps going back to the 1830s. But he can't accommodate everyone. "We get a few requests a year for maps of the human body. That's not us," says Gravenstreter. "We go a lot of places, but we don't go there." There's probably more to tell you about maps, but I'm tired of typing Gravenstreter.

The store is easy to find, even without a map. It's on the corner of 9th and Delaware, right near downtown Indy. Call (800) 972–1388 or you can e-mail tgravenstreter@ hotmail.com. By the way, Gravenstreter helped with the maps for this book. That's why he sells the book in his store.

Tim Gravenstreter. Lost in thought, but never lost in Indiana.

Optical Solution

Verner Mabrey is a humble man. He never makes a spectacle of himself. But he does make them for other people. Since 1979 Verner Mabrey has been the only person in Indiana to make a living just fixing eyeglasses.

His tiny store at 6021 North College Avenue in Indianapolis, the Optical Repair Shoppe, is a haven for people who have dropped, stepped on, or run over their eyeglasses. "Some people don't know which end to wear their glasses on," laughs Mabrey as he relates the number of people who have sat on their spectacles. "When asses meet glasses, I'm in business."

A sight for poor eyes. Indiana's only optical repair shop.

Mabrey has always been a tinkerer, repairing anything he could get his hands on. Looking for a new career in his late forties, he realized there was a niche for eyeglass repair. Most opticians didn't want to be bothered or the wait was endless. His tiny shop soon gained a reputation. And he got tons of referrals from the opticians because he did not sell glasses, only fixed them.

Mabrey fixes 4,000 pairs of glasses a year. The most common repair is a broken frame or temple. Many of his clients cannot afford two pairs of glasses, so they wait an hour or so for same-day service. "Some of my customers can't find the chair to sit down," says Mabrey, whose patented logo is a pair of specs held together by a safety pin, a nail, and some tape.

Mabrey charges a flat $22 for most repairs. He has no computer, no fax machine, no receipts, no help, no nothing. Just a knack for fixing and a love of people. "I always ask people what they do," he says. "I learn something new every day."

The Optical Repair Shoppe is at 6021 North College. Or talk to Mabrey at (317) 251–6629.

Rug-ged Cars

Is it just me, or is it hard to find anyone nowadays to Astroturf your car?

Of course, there's always Henry Pelc of Indianapolis, who claims to be a rug salesman, but his real passion is covering cars and vans with indoor-outdoor carpeting.

Pelc says that in 1982 he had a dream—which probably isn't in the same category as Martin Luther King's dream—but it did motivate him to completely cover his 1969 GMC van with Astroturf. Pelc won't describe the dream, but it was, well, auto-neurotic.

When others saw Pelc's finished product, his phone just rang off the hook. Okay, that's not exactly true, but he did have more than a few neighbors express interest in his concept. According to Pelc, folks like the idea because it protects the car if it's new and covers a multitude of sins if it's old.

Incredibly, the cars are covered in one piece of turf—no seams, just car doors and windows cut out. You pick your color as if you were in a carpet store.

Pelc has done cars, vans, parking bumpers, and the outsides of garages. He started charging $500 a car twenty years ago, but his prices have skyrocketed to $500 a car. "This is not for everybody," admits Pelc, whose latest design is a '97 van that was then airbrushed by a famous local artist.

And how do you clean an Astroturfed car? "Well, you can go to a car wash," says Pelc, "or you can vacuum it. Either way, it's a conversation starter."

You can reach Pelc at (317) 898–4295.

A Real Phone Card

So you have an old pair of gym shoes from 1984 and you just can't bear to throw them away. I mean, after all, you made three straight free throws in those high-tops. Don't toss 'em; make one into a phone.

Visit the Custom Phone Shop in Indianapolis (638 Virginia Avenue) and talk to Mike Irwin. He's the genius behind this unique concept. "I don't know of any place in the country where you can walk in off the street, hand a guy your old baseball mitt, and have it made into a phone."

When he first got into the business, he sold his products cheap, trying to compete with the mass-produced novelty phones, which were generally dull and uninspired. But when his creations started showing up in New York City art galleries, he knew he was onto something. "Our phones are functional art," says Irwin, who admits that many of his phones are often more conversation pieces than mouthpieces. And now assembly-line produced novelty phones are, more often than not, knockoffs of his earlier creations.

Irwin now does a big Internet business, catering to folks who want to create personal memorabilia or people in search of the perfect gift. Prices range from a couple hundred to $5,000. "That's if you want us to make a phone out of a diamond ring," says Irwin. "Of course, if you supply the ring, it gets a lot cheaper."

Irwin has made phones out of liquor bottles, softballs, golf balls, musical instruments, and stuffed animals. The hottest item lately is the baseball mitt phone, which was seen in several scenes of the movie *Fever Pitch* with Jimmy Fallon and Drew Barrymore. "It's been an incredible response," says Irwin. "Like Oprah holding up your book." His favorite: a phone made from the racing helmet of an Indy driver. There is no limit or restriction on what he can and will do, which is why some of his work cannot be legally displayed in the window of his store in the mall. But most of his stuff is in good taste. So can Irwin make a functional work of art out of your old gym shorts? Get on that old, dull, drab thing that you call a phone and call him at (800) 783–6385, or visit his Web site: www.customphones.com.

Is that your shoe ringing? Don't answer that.

Pleasantly Plump

To someone passing through the Broad Ripple area of Indianapolis (6416 Cornell Avenue), it looks pretty much like any bar and restaurant. Even the name, Plump's Last Shot, seems like some veiled reference to a guy's last drink.

But this is no ordinary restaurant. It's a testament to what can arguably be called the greatest moment in Indiana sports. The "last shot" refers to Bobby Plump's final toss of his high school basketball career. A shot that has made Plump a living icon for more than fifty years.

In 1954 the little town of Milan defeated the giant Muncie Central 32–30 at Indy's Hinkle Fieldhouse, in what has become the quintessential David and Goliath story. Not that the Milan kids were losers. They had gone to the Final Four just the year before, but the idea of defeating big, bad Muncie seemed a bit remote.

To make a long story short (something that Plump has been unable to do for more than five decades, to the delight of hundreds of thousands), there were only forty-eight seconds left in a tied game. Plump took the ball and held it for what must have been an agonizing half minute, then called time-out. Coach Marvin Wood gave Plump his final marching orders, commanding the senior to "hold the ball 'til there were five seconds left, then dribble to the basket or take a jumper." Plump complied, faked left near the foul line, and shot himself into legendary status.

Plump says that 90 percent of the people in Indiana either watched that game on TV or heard it on the radio. Or said they did. When the team returned to Milan from Indianapolis, there were 30,000 people there to greet them—not bad for a city of 1,000. "I never tire of telling the story," says Plump. "What a rare opportunity it is for someone to talk about their formative years and have so many interested listeners."

More than fifty years later, the remaining members of the original team still meet every year, and Plump is still asked to recount those moments from more than a half century ago. In case you've been living in a cave (or Muncie, where the tale doesn't have the same glow), the movie *Hoosiers* is based on this bigger-than-life story.

Oh yeah, and that restaurant. In addition to good food, it's packed with basketball memorabilia and there's even a video showing that final shot, faded and blurred though it may be.

Owner Bobby Plump is often there. But where would he be today if he had missed the jumper? The late curmudgeonly sportswriter for the *Indianapolis Star*, Bob Collins, said that Plump "would be pumping gas in Pierceville."

"I don't think so," says Plump with a smile, "but let's just say I'm glad I made the shot." Plump says he's seen quite a few bad calls in his day. Here's a good one: (317) 257–5867.

Meet Plump in person. Two shooters for the price of one.

RELEASING INFORMATION

In 1976 Bill Shirk, a thirty-year-old radio DJ from Indianapolis, went to Pamplona, Spain, strapped on a straitjacket, and ran in the streets. He was hit head-on by two bulls. It was all part of Shirk's master plan to become the best escape artist in the world. He soon became the best known, making it into newspapers throughout the world for his apparently reckless stunt. Then Shirk was off to Mexico, where he dove off a 150-foot cliff, again in a straitjacket.

His career had begun only a year or so earlier when he was supposed to chicken out of a stunt involving a straitjacket as a part of a radio promotion. But instead Shirk got hooked (or unhooked, I guess) on escaping and began a dedicated pursuit to learn more about the art of self-extrication.

Inspired by Harry Houdini, Shirk began developing more and more of his own escape tricks. Before long Shirk was hanging upside down or being buried alive in his straitjacket all over the country. In 1979 he hung from a helicopter in a straitjacket while ABC recorded his record-breaking escape. In 1981 he buried himself in the ground for seventy-nine hours with two tarantulas, a rattlesnake, and a 10-foot python. Hey, I'm not making this stuff up.

In 1991 Shirk spent fourteen days underground in a coffin. No food, just water, and a telephone so he could talk to reporters around the world. In 1993 Shirk was handcuffed, chained, and put in a Plexiglas coffin, then buried under seven tons of concrete. Can you imagine being married to this guy?

Age hasn't slowed down Shirk—he's always looking for another way to prove he's one of the best escape artists in the world. In October 2005 he escaped from a straight-jacket while hanging 20 feet in the air in front of a haunted house in Lebanon, Indiana. He did it in 7.9 seconds, about a half second faster than the previous record.

By the way, if you call Bill's office (he's president of a radio broadcasting company), his secretary thinks it's cute to say that he can't talk because he's tied up at the moment. It was funny the first time.

Bill Shirk is heels over head in love with Houdini.

Tuckaway

It would be hard to find a house in Indiana more steeped in mystery and more alive with history than a place called Tuckaway. If you want to know what life was like in the first half of the twentieth century, this is the place.

From 1910 through the 1940s, this forestlike bungalow was the home of Nellie Simmons Meier, a pint-sized patron of the arts with a penchant for palm reading, who hosted a throng of stars looking for a guided tour of their future. Nellie was not a psychic. She never claimed

Nellie Meier's house. Give her a hand.

to tell the future, but instead she made observations about the person after analyzing the lines on their palm, then combining that with research into the person's character and history. She was probably just as accomplished at reading people as she was at reading their palms.

Her client list was impressive: Walt Disney, James Whitcomb Riley, George Gershwin, Booker T. Washington, and Helen Hayes, to just drop a few names. Legend has it that Nellie pleaded with Carole Lombard not to board the plane that would eventually crash, a clear departure from her claim that she did not predict futures. Nellie even read the palm of Albert Einstein. Oh yeah, and Eleanor Roosevelt.

Walk into the massive drawing room with its 15-foot ceiling and gaze upon original autographed photos of past clients, each with appropriate thank-yous. The present owner, Ken Keene, an expert on the restoration of historic properties, has re-created the generation's mood with Persian rugs, Victrolas, a grand piano, fringed shades, and shaded lamps. Those who have been there say the entire atmosphere lends itself to conversation about this world and the next.

Tuckaway is not open to the public, but Keene does allow nonprofit organizations to hold fund-raisers there, in the spirit of Nellie herself who donated her palm-reading assets to charity. In addition, Keene will occasionally rent out to private parties. But for the most part Tuckaway remains unknown, though it's located just a block off the main drag of Thirtieth and Meridian.

Nearby residents can get a look via the annual neighborhood house tour, but for many reading this story (you may be one), you're learning about Tuckaway for the first time.

The home is not open to the public on a regular basis, but Ken does arrange tours several times a year through the Historic Landmarks Foundation of Indiana (317–639–4534; www.historiclandmarks.org).

Rodney, King of Sandwiches

Herb Howard has the biggest buns in Indiana, maybe in the whole country. He needs them. His restaurant, Super Jumbos, serves an almost five-pound hamburger—seven pounds when you add all the trimmings. The cost of this beefy delight is very reasonable: It's free. Providing you can eat it all by yourself in two hours. And the fries and a large Coke. Burp!

Food for thought. For people with lots to think about.

Howard, a former construction worker, claims he's had hundreds try and only a handful succeed. One 490-pound gentleman completed the task in forty-five minutes and vowed to be back the next day. "I haven't seen him since," says Howard, who now offers an additional $50 for successful completion of the Herculean task. "Everyone thinks they can do it, but I don't shell out many fifty-dollar bills," he says.

The burger, which is 12 inches in diameter, sits atop a specially made bun that the baker calls a UFO. Howard grills the burger in four sections so that families can share it. Average cooking time is just under an hour.

For most families, the patty serves four to six people, and it costs $24. Patrons can also opt for more normal-sized treats, and Howard is proud of his supersized tenderloins and Philly steak sandwiches. Everything is big but the shop; it's a former liquor store located on the corner of Lafayette Road and Kessler. There's also a new store at 1430 West Washington, next to the zoo.

Howard's business has boomed as word has spread of his free-meal deal. Says Howard, when asked to compare his product to the competition down the street: "If you want a snack, get a Big Mac."

For takeout call (317) 916–0379. Eat hardy.

NORTHEAST

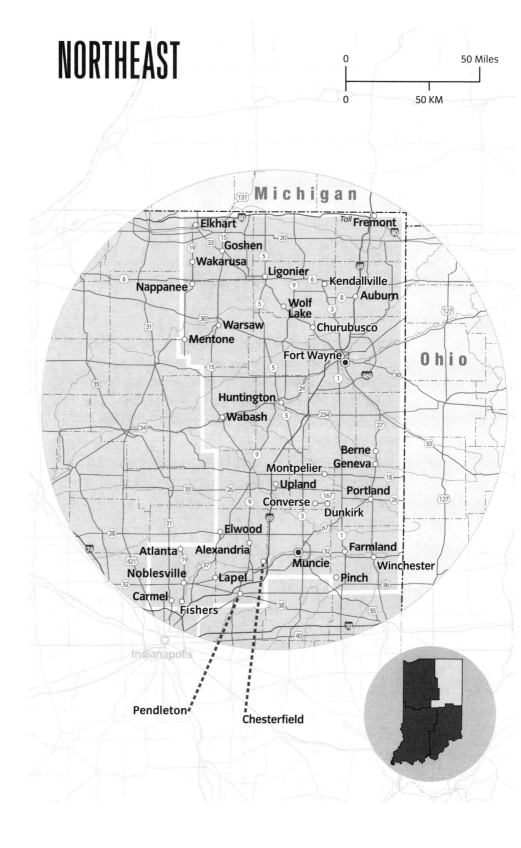

NORTHEAST

I don't know what it is about northeast Indiana that makes it so ripe for oddities. Maybe it's closer to New York. That paintball in Alexandria has almost doubled in size; the folks at a children's camp in Converse built an exact replica of Noah's Ark; and six not-so-young ladies in Farmland took off their clothes and posed for a calendar to raise money to save their courthouse. In Muncie, a guy runs a pumpkin-carving contest—*underwater.* And don't miss the biggest collection of fruit jars in the world. There used to be a barn in Bryant, Indiana, with 2,000 wrenches attached to it—but being in the last book drew too much attention, so they took them all down. Nuts.

Brush with Greatness

Alexandria

Mike and Glenda Carmichael have been married thirty-two years and still have a ball. In fact, they've had the ball for nearly thirty years. A paintball, that is.

It all started in 1977, when Mike and his three-year-old son, Michael Jr., painted a baseball. Mike, a painter by trade, thought it would be a fun pastime for his family to continually repaint the ball to see just how big it could get.

A brush with greatness.

Fast forward almost three decades and more than 20,000 coats of paint later. Now you have a 550-pound sphere of paint, the size of a huge beach ball. Yikes! And there is no end (or circumference) in sight.

Mike has the paintball safely tethered to the top of a barn that he built just for the ball. The sphere sways ever so gently as neighbors come by to apply a fresh coat. Mike keeps a log of all visitors and carefully tracks how many coats of paint have been applied, as well as the specific colors used. "We've had people from all over the country and even a few foreign visitors," says Mike, who's not sure how people find out about his oddity. No doubt being in *Ripley's Believe It or Not!* is part of the explanation, and of course it's hard to keep something like this quiet. That's why Mike has found himself on the *CBS Morning News* and the Discovery Channel. And partly because of the publicity from the first edition of this book. Did I get a thank you? Actually, I did.

Glenda, herself, is responsible for more than 9,000 paint coats, a feat for which she is openly proud. "It's more fun than vacuuming and you feel like you have accomplished something." You have?

Mike is a pretty friendly guy, but don't just drop in. You can call him if you're up in Madison County, near Alexandria (765–724–4088). You might or might not get the brush-off. By the way, Mike's enterprise is now sponsored by Sherman Williams. You may think Mike is crazy, but he's not stupid.

Frog Man
Alexandria

The Midwest's only frog jumping championship used to be in the tiny town of Orestes, but now things are really hopping. The good people at Red Gold now sponsor the annual competition and have moved it to Alexandria. These things do better in a booming metropolis.

Every summer scores of people arrive for the festivities, either "renting" or bringing their own bullfrogs for the big competition. Winners are automatically entered in the international championships in Calaveras, California—a contest after which Mark Twain named his famous short story. The winner there can take home five grand. The losers get green with envy.

Finally, things are jumping in Alexandria.

Contestants have thirty seconds to nudge their entries into the hopping mode. Then judges record the total of three jumps. "If your frog goes backwards, you're just out of luck," says Rob Williams, one of a small list of licensed frogmeisters in the Midwest. (I'm not making that up.) Winning frogs usually manage to hop about 10 to 12 feet. "We've lost a few," says Williams, "but trained frog wranglers scoop up the frisky escapees." This is more confusing than cricket.

Participants range in age from eight to eighty (people, not frogs), and kids too squeamish to handle their own frogs can enlist the help of frog jockeys to place the feisty contestants into position.

By the way, the contest is held at the County Fair. And guess what the big food delicacy is each year. Pork chops! Scared you, didn't I?

For more information call Red Gold at (765) 754–8415. Don't ask them how to become a frogmeister. They don't know. They just make tomato juice.

Smell of Success

Atlanta

Judi Peters spent much of the year 2000 sniffing around the French Riviera. She was unhappy with the perfume choices in Paris that summer and traveled to the tony resort area to visit a shop where customers could create their own aromas.

Intrigued with the concept, she attempted to bring the idea back to the U.S., but the French were stubborn (does that smell familiar?) and didn't want to release the idea to the U.S. market.

Peters's persistence paid off, but the company required her to go through a rigorous training process under a Nose. Yes, a Nose—one of only a handful of true aroma experts who had to ensure that Judi had the right "equipment" to run a perfume shop. Could she, for example, recognize fine distinctions in fragrances? Yes, she passed her test. Ah . . . the sweet smell of success.

In 2002 Peters opened Le Studio des Parfums in Atlanta, Indiana, a kind of experimental lab where clients can create their own personal aromas by mixing and matching some 127 different fragrances. Crafting a perfume is like creating a new recipe. Just like anchovies and ice cream don't make a pleasant concoction, there are certain scents that, well, don't make sense. To ease the process, customers are given a kind of manual of guidelines so that there are no inexcusable faux pas, like combining peach with a sea scent. Oh, yuck.

Judi's customers are buying more than a fragrance: They're buying memories. "People want smells that relate to their growing up, their courtships, or unforgettable vacations," she says.

Perfumes cost about $60 for 50 milliliters, or about $20 per ounce. But according to Peters, it's worth every scent because when you splash on that special fragrance, your eyes light up, you get a rush, and it's positively rejuvenating.

Okay, fine. But I'm still an Aqua Velva Man.

Atlanta is north on U.S. Highway 31 to 296th Street. Turn right, stick your nose out the window, and start sniffing. The shop is located at 165 East Main Street (765–292–2059).

Auto Exotic

Auburn

This museum is a duesy, no doubt about it. It's the Auburn Cord Duesenberg Museum in Auburn. Just drive your pathetic 1994 Ford Taurus
to the intersection of State Road 8, 20 miles north of Fort Wayne and 35
miles south of the Indiana Toll Road, and you're 98 percent of the way
there.

Once inside this 1930 art deco building (the former headquarters for
the Auburn Automobile Company), prepare to drool over the world's
most glamorous automobiles—including the Auburn, the Cord, and the
Duesenberg. But this museum does more than display pretty cars. Its
mission is to take these icons of the classic car era and beyond and put
them into historical perspective. Cars are displayed in galleries that
help the patron understand the impact that luxury motoring had on the
automobile industry and the nation as a whole.

The cars were more than fashion statements, however. They were
supremely crafted engineering feats that allowed the driver to go 125
miles per hour while the lady in the back applied her makeup before the
built-in vanity.

There are more than one hundred cars to look at, cars owned by the
richest and most famous people in the world. See what Gary Cooper,
Greta Garbo, and Clark Gable paid up to $20,000 to drive. Look at J.
Paul Getty's 1932 Duesenberg J. Torpedo Convertible, the same type
car driven by author John O'Hara. Over the years, the museum has featured cars owned by Elvis, John Lennon, Frank Lloyd Wright, and the
Smothers Brothers.

A favorite is the Cars of Indiana Gallery, featuring autos of the past—
manufactured in, of course, Indiana. Cars like the Revere, the Haynes,
the Premier, and the Stutz, just to name a few of the more than 150 different brands produced in the Hoosier state.

Labor Day weekend is the Auburn Cord Duesenberg Festival, a collector and tourist favorite, and the largest event in Indiana outside of Indianapolis. Each year at this time, thousands of cars are auctioned off to hungry enthusiasts eager to buy a piece of history. In the past, autos belonging to Michael Jordan, Clark Gable, and even an armored car once used by Princess Diana have all been sold, commanding huge prices. Even the Batmobile from the 1995 movie *Batman Forever* changed hands to some caped collector for his cave. Also part of the festival is an antiques sale, quilt show, decorator showcase home, and downtown cruise-in.

So bring your cameras to 1600 South Wayne Street in Auburn. The museum has virtually no restrictions on picture-taking. Lots of Dues, very few don'ts. For information call (260) 925–1444 or check its Web site: www.acdmuseum.org.

Heaven on wheels. Go to the museum, because you can't afford to buy one.

Arms Place

Auburn

The American Heritage Village in Auburn, Indiana, is really a *museum* museum. Why? Because inside the 200,000-square-foot building are five different venues, each featuring truly unique items—stuff you won't find anywhere else.

The Kruse Horsepower Museum takes you from the world of true horse power—antique carriages and stage coaches—right through the world of Indy racing. Stop in between and see Howard Hughes's Rolls Royce or Elvis Presley's Mercedes. There are two winning cars from the Indianapolis 500, along with two pole cars.

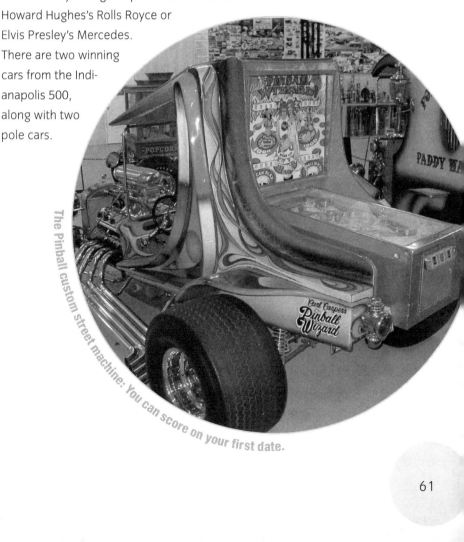

The Pinball custom street machine: You can score on your first date.

How about Fonzi's motorcycle from *Happy Days*? Thumbs up to that. And our favorite: a car created by auto designer Carl Casper made from a pinball machine.

The Northeastern Indiana Racing Museum celebrates the birth of racing from midget cars to stock cars, while the Northeast Indiana Baseball Association's Hall of Fame provides a nostalgic look at the roots of baseball in the Hoosier land.

There's the Philo T. Farnsworth Center for Television History, an incredible collection of TV memorabilia in honor of the man generally credited with inventing television. There are antique TVs, a complete collection of *TV Guides* (count how many times Lucy is on the cover), and an entire display of Howdy Doody memorabilia from the 1950s.

Finally, the WWII Victory Museum is believed by many to be the finest display of military vehicles and motorcycles in the world. Most of the collection comes from a museum in Messancy, Belgium, but other artifacts have been donated or placed on loan. You can see General Patton's armored jeep or one of Eisenhower's staff cars. A rare portrait of Hitler and what is probably the world's largest collection of German WWII vehicles are highlights of the museum. This part of the village is 80,000 square feet, so don't expect to breeze through it. Every stop will give you pause.

Auburn is north of Indianapolis on Interstate 69, about twenty minutes from Fort Wayne. And it's worth a tank of gas just to see some of those tanks. Check out their Web sites—www.wwiivictory.org and www.kccmuseum.org—or call (260) 927–9144.

Ace Is Not the Place

Auburn

The really cool thing about Auburn City Hardware is that Abraham Lincoln could have bought an axe there. He didn't, but he could have. Why? Because Auburn City Hardware is more than 150 years old—the oldest continually operating hardware store (in the same location) in Indiana.

yes, they have it—but can they find it?

Founded in 1850 as Pioneer Hardware, the store has had about a half-dozen owners. The building was destroyed by fire in 1868 but was soon rebuilt. In 1932 E. L. Kokenge bought the nuts and bolts operation and in 1952 passed it on to his son.

Now, more than fifty years later, Robert Kokenge is still the crusty old proprietor of a store that can only be described as a step back into the past, and often a step back into a pile of sheet metal, leather straps, and antique rakes. "We do things the old way," brags Kokenge, who claims that if you want just one of something—like a battery—they'll break open the package. "'Course then we have to charge you for our time."

Inside the store is a range of products that spans pretty much the period between the Civil War and noon today. While modern appliances are readily available, you can also find a hundred-year-old meat grinder, pipe threaders, glass-cutting tables, belt-making machines, and canning jars. There are rocking horses, old trunks, and fifty-year-old cans of paint. "We don't do dynamite anymore," sniffs Kokenge. "The government thinks we shouldn't sell it, and they know best." He was gritting his teeth when he said that.

There are no computers in the store, just a hundred-year-old National Cash Register and an adding machine. "I've been here more than fifty years," says Kokenge, "and nothing has changed." He was smiling when he said that.

There are other hardware stores in town, but eventually customers end up at Auburn City Hardware at 203 South Main Street (260–925–3610). A place where Ulysses S. Grant could have bought a hammer. He didn't. But he could have.

Pressing Information
Berne

When William Hauenstein emigrated to the United States from Switzerland in 1856, he had no plans to build the world's biggest cider press. But he did, in 1864, and it's still the world's largest. The press beam of this mammoth contraption is 30 feet long, hewn from a single, giant, white oak tree—a tree that was probably a sapling when Columbus arrived in the New World. Hauenstein used only hand tools, an axe, chisel, and hammer to fashion his creation.

The contraption weighs in at two tons and can turn thirty bushels of apples into one hundred gallons of cider with one cycle. Layers of straw are used to siphon out skin, seeds, and stems after the apples have been cut by the grinder wheel. Nowadays, the apple mush is siphoned through a type of cheesecloth, but the concept is similar.

The press worked on and off for more than one hundred years at its original forest site in Huntington County. Beginning in 1972, the building that housed the press fell into disrepair and the unit sat unused.

In 1992 the Amos Schwartz Construction Company dismantled, restored, and reassembled the press in the Swiss Heritage Village in Adams County, where it now churns out delicious apple cider for the annual Berne Heritage Festival. The barn was also restored using much of the original timber, furthering the feel of nineteenth-century America.

You can see the press and enjoy the festival at the Swiss Heritage Village in September each year. The village is open May to October with fifteen restored buildings re-creating life in Adams County at the turn of the century—not this past one, but one hundred years ago. During special events, trained docents guide visitors through the village, where they may meet a variety of living-history interpreters going about their day-to-day activities as if you'd come to call in 1900.

If you like Conner Prairie in Indy, you'll love this place. Call for more info at (260) 589–8007 or visit www.swissheritage.com. Berne is at the junction of U.S. Highway 27 and State Road 218.

Small-Time Art

Carmel

If you say that Doreen Squire Ficara is the executive director of the world's smallest children's art museum, she'll correct you. "It's not a museum, it's an art gallery," says the British-born Ficara, who is very particular about the issue.

She should be. The *Guinness Book of World Records* has deemed her establishment in Carmel the "world's smallest children's art gallery," and she's got the certificate to prove it.

The museum, I mean the gallery, is about 9 feet by 15 feet. But there can be no "abouts" about it, so a city engineer measured the gallery, just to be sure.

Each month the gallery features student artwork from different local schools. Art teachers select the pieces and design the four tiny walls. The gallery is booked at least three years in advance.

A couple thousand people visit each year, but needless to say there is a high concentration of parents and grandparents eager to see their loved ones' first "showing."

Every young exhibitor receives a certificate authenticating and confirming their work was displayed at the world's smallest children's art gallery.

Ficara had researched the issue before approaching *Guinness*, only to discover there was only one other children's art gallery in the country listed in the record book. And that one went out of business. Which means that the gallery is also the biggest children's art gallery in the world.

The Children's Art Gallery is at 40 West Main in Carmel. It used to be at 30 West Main. They moved the building 50 yards. Really! You can call Ficara at (317) 582–1455.

Well Wishing

Carmel

For more than one hundred years, the people of Hamilton and surrounding counties have come to 116th Street near Gray Road in Carmel to get a jug, a jar, or in some cases, a barrel of the crystal clear (usually) H_2O that gurgles out of a standing pipe within eyeshot of the main road.

Free water. No wading.

Historians say the well was first discovered in 1903 while surveyors and excavators were looking for natural gas. As far back as anyone can remember, residents were convinced that the artesian water not only tasted better, but also had curative powers. Talk to people in line at the well and they'll tell you the water helps cure arthritis, eases back pain, prevents headaches, and soothes sore throats. And it tastes pretty good, too.

No one knows for sure where the water originates, though the best guess seems to be somewhere in the northeastern part of the state. "We really don't know," admits John Duffy, director of Carmel Utilities, "and that's part of the mystery, part of the charm."

The well has flowed almost continuously for a century with the exception of an unexplained slowing down in the 1960s and a complete stoppage for a while in the mid-1970s. The well attracts an estimated 5,000 people a month. Why not? It's free.

In the 1990s the immediate area became a park, a project spear-headed by local resident Gil Kett, who had also been instrumental in moving the well from across the street, where it had posed a traffic haz-ard. Then a quaint little shelter was built to protect people from the rain while they were getting their water. Huh?

During an evaluation and cleaning in 1999, complaints, uh, flowed in when the pipe was turned off. Residents, convinced that the well's water could cure even cancer, panicked when the well ran dry.

The well opened months later to long lines of thirsty residents who apparently not only drink the stuff, but also wash their hair and bathe in it. "My mother drank from it and my grandmother drank from it," said one woman, "and they both lived to be ninety. That's good enough for me."

And it's cheaper than Perrier.

Farewell, Fido

Carmel

If you told someone that the first freestanding pet funeral home in the country was in Carmel, they'd probably say: "Yeah . . . only in California."

No, we're not talking the left coast here. We're talking Carmel, Indiana.

The Pet Angel Memorial Center is the creation of Coleen Ellis, a former pre-planner in the human funeral business, whose grief over her own lost pet made her realize there was a need for a full-service pet funeral home. Of course millions of people have lost their pets over the years, but apparently no one else thought of this until Coleen did. Hard to believe.

Coleen walks people through the process from the first phone call about a pet's death to the burial or cremation. Pet Angel picks up the pet at your home or the veterinarian's office, wraps it in a blanket, and brings the pet to the funeral home, treating the death with dignity.

Then it can get pricey.

Urns run anywhere from thirty bucks to several thousand, and caskets can get pretty costly, as well. The facility performs actual services, where the animal lies in repose while family members and friends speak, recalling fond memories of the pet. But if the dog dug up your rose bushes or chewed your lawn hose in half, you tend not to show up for the event.

Coleen has arranged funerals for cats, bunnies, and even a rat. She gets calls for horses all the time, but all things being equine, there's no way to cremate or bury a horse very easily.

Part of Coleen's service is to honor personal requests, like the woman who wanted to re-create her dog in a life-sized bronze statue. No problem, said Ellis. Next!

By the way, on the Pet Angel Memorial Center Web site (www.pet angelmemorialcenter.com), Coleen claims to offer same-day service. Sounds like a good idea to me.

The facility is in Carmel, just north of Indianapolis at 172 East Carmel Drive (317–569–6000).

Rock Concert
Carmel

When John Schuler, an executive for a major aggregate company (they pulverize stone for construction), had the unenviable job of creating some positive publicity, he knew he had his work cut out for him. "Most folks don't want an eighty-acre hole in their community," notes Schuler.

Underground music? Yes, it's the pits.

As luck would have it, Schuler was also elected to the board of the symphony in Carmel, a bedroom community just north of Indianapolis. Schuler, who admits to an occasional offbeat notion, decided to combine his two missions. The result was America's first true rock concert, a full symphony orchestra playing from the very bottom of a huge limestone quarry.

Schuler admits to some skepticism by musicians and townspeople alike, but after a well-orchestrated PR campaign, he had the symphony playing his song. Musicians and patrons were bused to the bottom of the cavern, about 220 feet, where food and wine were served. Choirs sang, fireworks popped, and the symphony played. It gave a whole new meaning to orchestra pit.

The acoustics are good, it's nice and cool, and it's a great fund-raiser. But in 2002 it seemed to take a geologic era for the food to reach the bottom of the quarry. Some said the food tasted good, but the service was the pits. Very funny.

Will the event continue? They're looking over the situation. You can look at the hole anytime at 1980 116th Street. Call Martin Marietta Aggregates at (317) 573–4460 for information on the next concert.

CANDY LAND COVERAGE

For those of you who plan on traveling the state and visiting all of the places in the book, we thought we'd list a few places you might stop when you need the occasional sugar fix.

David Alan Chocolatier (1700 North Lebanon Street, Lebanon; 800–428–2310; www.davidalalchocolatier.com). When David Alan Honan visited Switzerland, it changed his life. He found his true calling. Summiting the Swiss Alps? No. Making chocolate.

Upon his return home, the Lebanon resident began making his own delectable truffles. The tasty treasures consist of a chocolate shell (milk, dark, or white) and a chocolate center or "ganache." (Yum . . . chocolate wrapped in chocolate!)

David Alan also makes snappers—his variation of turtles—and orange, raspberry, hazelnut, coffee, and mocha trufflettes. And to keep all of his candies family-friendly, the chocolatier never adds a drop of alcohol, an ingredient sometimes used by fine candy makers. Sometimes they use it after they make the chocolate. Not David Alan.

DeBrand Fine Chocolates (10105 Auburn Park Drive, Fort Wayne; 260–969–8333; www.debrand.com). Cathy Brand started making chocolates when she was eight years old. She started eating them when she was even younger. Over the years she has added two letters to her last name, opened four candy stores, and has become one of Fort Wayne's most famous sweet makers.

DeBrand's chocolates have been called "visually stunning" and "exquisite to taste." I'd just call them "darn tasty" (no need for formalities when we're talking chocolate). Along with the four DeBrand Fine Chocolates stores—all located in Fort Wayne—the company also has a booming mail-order business.

Ghyslain Chocolatier Inc. (350 West Deerfield Road, Union City; 765–964–7905; www.ghyslain.com). At Ghyslain Chocolatier, the candy is as much decor as it is delicious. The hand-painted chocolates are creations of Ghyslain, the international award-winning chocolatier, and the president and owner of the Union City company.

Offerings include Coffee Bean—dark chocolate ganache infused with espresso and cinnamon; Raspberry Mousse—bittersweet chocolate ganache infused with fresh raspberry puree; and Caramel Walnut Horseshoe—signature caramel and roasted walnuts in a French vanilla ganache.

Centerpieces highlight hand-painted pumpkins, snowmen with babies, and holiday logs, which range in price from $20 to $45.

Martinsville Candy Kitchen (90 North Main Street, Martinsville; 317–342–6390). Martinsville was originally owned by a man named Jimmy Zappapas who, in the 1920s, began making his famous hand-twisted candy canes. Today, the store makes twenty different flavors of canes, from peppermint to blueberry. While the kitchen has switched owners, the sweet-tooth tradition carries on. In addition to candy canes, the new owners also make ninety different candies. For a different twist on Valentine's Day, they bend their canes into heart shapes.

Mundt's Candies (207 West Main Street, Madison; 812–265–6171; www.mundtscandies.com). Fish candy? It may sound like an oxymoron, but in Madison it's a long-standing tasty tradition.

The fish candies first began hitting the streets in the mid-1800s. Traditionally they were made in November and December and were handed out as gifts during the holidays. Some say the fish honored the town's ties to the Ohio River, while others say the fish was a symbol of Christianity.

CONTINUED

Today, Mundt's still makes fish candy in the same building overlooking Main Street. (Thankfully, they make the candy year-round.) To locals, the historic building is known simply as the candy store. And if fish candy is not what you're looking for, they also have fine chocolates, ice cream, and more.

Plyley's Candies (P.O. Box 8, LaGrange, IN 46761; 260–463–3351; www.plyleyscandies.com). In 1917 Rilla Plyley set out a plate of fudge in the family store in LaGrange. Little did she know that that plate of goodies would set in motion a thriving family business that she would have a hard time recognizing today, even though it bears her name.

That's because today, Plyley's Candies can churn out around twenty-five batches of hard candy a day, each weighing eighty pounds. The candies come in cinnamon, sweet clove, rum and butter, wintergreen, fruits, and even sugar-free flavors. They also make creamy chocolates, nut clusters, butter creams, maple creams, coconut squares, and cherry cordials.

The business, which originally started as a candy and soda fountain, moved into a newly built factory in 1971, just a few blocks from their original store. Tours are available, and from what I hear, they are "scent-sational."

Schimpff's Confectionery (347 Spring Street, Jeffersonville; 812–283–8367; www.schimpffs.com). With Schimpff's being so close to the Ohio River, it is no surprise that the confectionery's most famous treat is fish candy. Maybe it was inspired by the fact that Schimpff's building has been flooded out by the Ohio on three occasions. Or maybe founder Gustav Schimpff simply thought it was a good way to lure more customers to his store.

Along with making its dandy candies, Schimpff's serves sodas, sundaes, shakes, sandwiches, and soups. The establishment also has the distinction of being designated one of Indiana's Hidden Treasures. Sightseers and confection consumers are always welcome.

As if candy isn't enough to lure you in, how about a candy museum—one of the few in the country. Within a single room you'll find plenty of candy tubs, tins, crates, barrels, jars, and boxes once filled with candy (some actually have the original contents); there's also an old-fashioned wrapper collection, and vintage toy cars, boats, and planes—trinkets once stuffed inside boxes of Cracker Jacks. Some of the museum's larger artifacts include an antique popcorn machine, a roasted peanut "street cart," and a wooden vending machine, circa 1928.

There's also a demonstration area that's an extension of the museum. There visitors can see a late nineteenth-century water-cooled table, an early twentieth-century stove, copper kettles, and numerous brass drop rolls on the wall. These aren't static displays, either. This is equipment that's still used nearly every day.

Zaharako's Ice Cream and Confectionery (329 Washington Street, Columbus; 812–379–9329). Columbus's version of Willy Wonka's chocolate factory is Zaharako's. Though it doesn't have Wonkavision, the historic building does have two Mexican onyx soda fountains purchased from the St. Louis World Expo in 1905; a 1908 pipe organ; large glass candy cases; and plenty of oak and mahogany woodwork.

Along with a wide assortment of candies, Zaharako's dishes out homemade ice cream, sodas, sundaes, sarsaparillas, and phosphates. The restaurant also cooks up some tasty cheeseburgers—with melted cheese and chili sauce.

Out of This World
Chesterfield

It would be hard to find fifty acres in Indiana more steeped in mystery than Camp Chesterfield. For more than 125 years, this enclave in Madison County has been the home or the stopping place for thousands of spiritualists—men and women who believe that while life on earth may be temporary, you live forever in the spirit world, which is only a séance away.

While skeptics may mock the supernatural aspect of the camp, Chesterfield attracts thousands of visitors each year—people who hope to reestablish contact with long-lost family and friends or just learn about the psychic world. Year-round there are educational programs open to the public, as well as demonstrations for curious visitors and passionate believers.

On any given day, séances are conducted throughout the grounds, always by personnel who have been personally tested by the Camp Chesterfield Board and judged to be competent in various aspects of the supernatural and spiritual world. Mediums, for example, might be tested in the area of Séances and Trances. Now that's an SAT exam.

While a visit to the grounds is free, a one-on-one consultation with a medium is charged accordingly. Whatever your thing, be it psychic phenomenon, handwriting analysis, astrology, or faith healing, there is an opportunity to take a class or have a private consultation with a staff member.

Other attractions include the large busts of the gods (Christ, Buddha, Mohammed, etc.) and the stone cave where you can pray or commune. There's also a large totem pole to celebrate the spirit world of the American Indian.

Want to stick around for a while? There's a cafeteria, a campsite area, and a hotel on the grounds. Yes, a world of activity, as well as other-worldly activity. To learn more, call the camp at (765) 378–0237 or see its Web site: www.Campchesterfield.net.

By the way, when I called Camp Chesterfield to update this entry, I asked the hotel manager if anything had changed. "Not in 125 years," she told me.

Shell-Shocked

Churubusco

They call it Turtle Town, this tiny village just 20 miles northwest of Fort Wayne. It has a rich history and its own version of the Loch Ness monster. Even the town name is steeped in folklore. A century and a half ago, local residents sparred over what to name their city. A fuzzy history says the name came from a city in Mexico where the Americans had waged a successful battle in the war with that country. Regardless, myth has it that even the people who picked the name had trouble pronouncing it.

Despite the tongue-twister name, Churubusco residents take great pride in their city, and they bask in the myth of the giant turtle that put their town on the map. The turtle was first sighted in 1898 in a lake belonging to one Oscar Fulk. Fifty years later, in 1948, when local farmer Gale Harris owned the lake, he claimed a similar sighting. Soon reporters and news cameras infiltrated Churubusco. Harris even drained much of the pond in search of Oscar (named after the turtle's original "founder"), but no luck.

How big was he? Some say as big as a tabletop (but people have different ideas of how big a table is); others say at least 500 pounds. Still others scoff at the notion that such a turtle ever existed. The skeptics are usually from Fort Wayne. A few people in Churubusco still claim to have seen Oscar, also dubbed the "Beast of Busco," but these people are usually drinking a Budweiser and winking at you.

Oscar and Churubusco will always be linked. And every June since 1980, this town has honored its hard-bodied friend with four days of music, dancing, turtle contests, food, laughter, and a parade.

Churubusco is easy to find. Just head north on U.S. Highway 33, about twenty minutes out of Fort Wayne. No rush. Everyone is on turtle time. I'd go in June. Not a heck of a lot going on otherwise.

Arks and Recreation
Converse

No, you haven't had too much wine. Yes, that does look like Noah's Ark, just west of the County Line Road in Converse, Indiana. But why is it there?

That's Rainbow Christian Camp, a year-round facility for young and old alike. And right smack in the middle of the camp is a quarter-scale replica of Noah's Ark. Maybe the only one in the country.

The ark was constructed on-site, after a previous attempt to build an ark at another church in central Indiana ran into some zoning problems. Rainbow Christian acquired the storybook ark but wanted to completely rebuild it so it would be more authentic. The final structure was to be based on the research of the late amateur archeologist Ron Wyatt, who claimed to have found remains of Noah's craft in Turkey.

The Rainbow Christian Church took the Wyatt plans to their own arkitect, who produced the final blueprints for the woody mammoth. With the help of campers and volunteers, the ark was built in two years, but work continues as they strive to make the inside of the facility even better suited for classroom activities.

While the outside of the edifice replicates what Noah's Ark may have looked like, Rod Cameron, who helped spearhead the project, explains that windows and emergency doors have also been installed. "Noah did not have to deal with a fire marshal," says Cameron. We should also add that the ark has real bathrooms, which would have made Noah green with envy.

Cameron believes that the ark is an inspiration to his campers, helping to instill a better understanding of the Bible's accuracy and helping demonstrate the Christian belief that we originated from a common ancestor. That would be Noah.

You can see the ark from the roadway, and many people passing by wander into the camp to ask about the unique structure.

"We encourage visitors," says Cameron. "We especially welcome couples."

For directions call (765) 395–3638 or visit their Web site at www.rainbowcamp.org.

Just like the real Noah's Ark, but with toilets.

Multi-Faceted Jay County
Dunkirk

The slogan for Dunkirk should be: Eat Here, Get Gas. And Glass. This tiny town in Jay County was considered by many to have been the glass and gas capital of the world—and in some ways it still is.

The city's population peaked in the 1890s because natural gas was free. Yes, free. A geological dome in the area actually trapped the precious substance, making it so plentiful that glass producers flocked to the Dunkirk area for the gas they needed for manufacturing purposes. At the turn of the twentieth century, there were more than a hundred local glass manufacturers in east central Indiana; a handful still remain, with two still operating in Dunkirk: Indiana Glass and St. Gobain.

But the town's big attraction is the Glass Museum, a two-story building filled with 6,000 pieces of glassware from 110 factories (past and present). Glistening from cases are leaded lamps, glass canes, chandeliers, bowls, bottles, stemware, vases, and candlesticks. Glass specifically from the Great Depression is of special historical significance because of its beauty and rarity. And, of course, the big favorites are pieces made by the Indiana Glass Company, still firing away just minutes from the museum.

Curator Mary Newsome is especially proud of the Vaseline glass, produced by Albany Glass, in a factory that burned down in 1929. Another favorite: a set of candlesticks surrounded by crystals worth about $10,000. And there's a Belgian glass basket made with one piece of glass. "I'm not sure what it's worth, but it's the only thing that the last curator ever locked up during the winter," says Newsome.

Visitors from all over the world come to the Glass Museum, 15 miles northeast of Muncie on State Road 167 (765–768–6872). The museum's hours are 10:00 A.M. to 4:00 P.M. Tuesday through Saturday, and Sunday by appointment. If you don't love the place, keep it to yourself. You know what they say about people in glass houses.

Recreational Treks

Elkhart

Question: When is a museum not a museum?

Answer: When it's a filing cabinet.

That might be a bit of an exaggeration, but Carl Ehry, president of the Recreational Vehicle/Manufactured Housing Museum, confesses his museum was pretty much that up until 1994.

From 1972 until 1990, historical information about RVs and manufactured homes was either archived in Washington, D.C., or being shuttled around in those filing cabinets. Then a group of suppliers, dealers, and manufacturers pushed for a real home in Elkhart, which is home to

Honoring RVs for providing safe recreational treks.

more than one hundred RV and MH manufacturers, including Coachmen, Jayco, Monaco, Holiday Rambler, Carriage, Skyline, Patriot, Liberty, and Fairmont. Half of all recreational vehicles on the road come from the Elkhart area.

The new 50,000-square-foot RV/MH Heritage Foundation headquarters is dedicated to preserving the history of the industry, celebrating the positive aspects of the lifestyle, and honoring the people who have made lasting and creative contributions to recreational vehicling (which isn't a word, so don't look it up).

Inside the Hall of Fame Museum, you can saunter through a parklike setting among the twenty-five vehicles representing the history of RVs. You'll see a 1913 RV, possibly the oldest still in existence, as well as the first Coachmen and an early Winnebago. Also displayed are 300 portraits of pioneers and inventors who made lasting contributions to the industry, as well as artifacts and memorabilia going back more than ninety years. Like to read? You can peruse the 10,000 volumes of RV research, magazines, newsletters, and manufacturers' catalogs. We'd rather go to the snack bar.

The museum, located just off exit 96 on the Indiana Toll Road, is open 9:00 A.M. to 4:00 P.M. Monday through Friday, and from 10:00 A.M. to 3:00 P.M. on Saturdays in June, July, and August. Need a place to stay? There are hotels, but most people who dig this stuff already have a place to sleep. Call (800) 378–8694 or check out its Web site: www.rv-mh-hall-of-fame.org.

Influence of Sphere

Elwood

If you wander into the Spencer Lapidary (at the intersection of State Roads 13 and 37 in Elwood, or online at www.spencerlapidary.com) and the owner, Mark Bennett, isn't there, take a peek in the back room. If you didn't know better, you'd swear you walked into the laboratory of a mad scientist.

Mark Bennett is not mad, he's just mad about rocks. It doesn't matter the size or shape. When he is through with them, they will be spheres—perfect spheres, in fact.

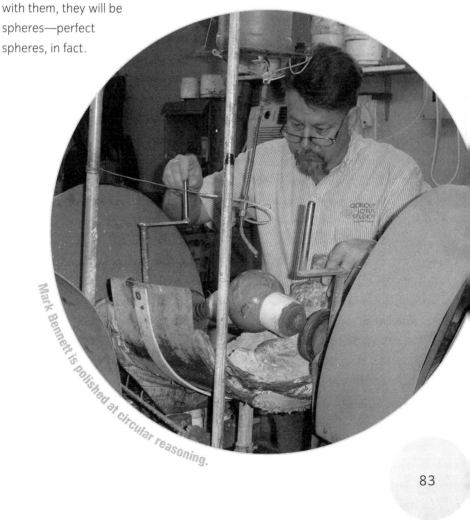

Mark Bennett is polished at circular reasoning.

Mark learned this craft from former owner Glen Spencer who used to brag, "We put bowling balls to shame." Spencer's fascination began more than forty years ago when he and his brother, Orville (how can an idea not fly when your brother is named Orville?), were collecting rocks in Oregon. Upon returning to Indiana, Spencer decided he wanted to turn those rocks into decorative globes. But how to do it?

Spencer masterminded, created, and rigged equipment to grind and polish jagged pieces of beautiful rock into priceless, perfectly round works of art. The machinery looks almost like a Rube Goldberg arrangement, and the result is a process that has fascinated people for more than thirty years. Gotta see it. Can't explain it.

So unique were Spencer's machines and his methods that he is recognized as one of the master sphere cutters in the United States. The Fermi Atomic Laboratory in Chicago asked Spencer to make a machine that could produce perfect spheres for research into the origin of the universe. Mission accomplished.

Bennett claims he can make a sphere out of almost any kind of rock, but the highly polished luster that attracts customers is difficult to create unless the stone is dense. Favorites include obsidian and septarian nodules. But you probably knew that.

Mark and his wife, Tina, also sell one-of-a-kind jewelry that they make in the store, as well as dichroic glass pendants. I don't know what that is either, but it's gorgeous. Classes in glass fusing, dichroic glass jewelry, silversmithing, and cabochon stonecutting are also taught.

And who would want these spheres? People who just enjoy their beauty, or those who believe, as did the Greeks, that spheres have a magical power. Whatever your reason, be prepared to pay anywhere from fifty bucks all the way to $5,000. Those are just round numbers, of course.

Diana Collins, Tina's sister, is always there to show you their beautiful work. But if you want to see Mark and Tina in action, call or e-mail first: (765) 552–0784 or info@spencerlapidary.com. They are always busy.

Court Dates

Farmland

In 2006 the six ladies of the Farmland Bridge Club (known as the Bridgettes) put their cards on the table. And their bodies on a calendar. Sleepy Farmland will never be the same.

With the popular 2003 movie *Calendar Girls* as their guide, the seven seniors (all but one was north of eighty) decided something had to be done to prevent the proposed demolition of the Randolph County Courthouse. The result was the 2006 Court House Girls Calendar, a tasteful journey through the year that reveals,

The Randolph County Courthouse—where briefs take on a new meaning.

among other things, a city's commitment to older structures, if you know what I mean.

The idea first bloomed at a brainstorming meeting to save the courthouse. Mimi (who was destined to become Miss October) was asked if the ladies of the bridge club would be willing to show their support for a fund-raiser. "Show" was the operative word here. Support also became an issue.

Mimi asked her bridge buddies to join her, and all happily consented—once everyone had agreed they would be in this together, in case they really ended up down at the courthouse.

Using replicas of the courthouse to protect their dignity, the images by photographer Mary Ellen Bertram are truly elegant. Even Iraida's (Miss December) husband was thrilled. "I want an 8-by-10 glossy," he told his wife. "Buy a calendar like everyone else," Iraida told him.

Five thousand calendars have been sold, but they have raised more awareness than eyebrows. Larry Francer, who helped spearhead the project and sells the calendar at his gift shop, Tangle Vine Crossing in Farmland, says, "We got calls from all over the world." Francer responds to the occasional critic by saying: "The real embarrassment is tearing down this fabulous courthouse." Francer admits the calendar idea was not unique—other calendars of this sort have been done—but he believes that the Bridgettes are the oldest bevy of beauties to make such a courtly gesture. You be the judge.

Will there be another calendar? At press time, the ladies had not shown their cards yet. Stay tuned to see what they *do* show.

Oh, Mrs. Wilson

Fishers

Marcia Wilson's business is mushrooming.

Technically, that isn't true because "mushrooming" is going out and looking for mushrooms, and Marcia doesn't have to look for them. They're all in her barn. Tons of them.

The idea for her business first sprouted when she attended one of those "earthy" conferences where people were pushing the advantages of fresh, local produce. When an acquaintance agreed to teach her the mushroom-growing business, Marcia, who was selling specialty beer at the time, decided that mushrooms and brew was a good combo. "I figured it was the yeast I could do." Very funny, Marcia.

Marcia had a barn at her house overflowing with her next garage sale, so she decided to turn the place into a mushroom moneymaker.

But it's not easy growing mushrooms.

Giant pods, about forty of them, are suspended from the ceiling and make her barn look like a scene from the movie *Coma*. They're actually huge blocks of sawdust "fertilized" with mushroom spores, various grains, and cotton seed hulls, then packed in polyethylene bags. If you ever visit this place, expect major nightmares later that evening.

Hamilton County's growth is mushrooming.

87

FIRED UP FOR SAFETY

In the early 1990s a group of firefighters were in search of a better way to get across some lifesaving messages to kids. "Standing up in front of kids in a tie and jacket and passing out equipment just wasn't cutting it," says Chad Abel of the Fishers Fire Department just outside of Indianapolis.

So Chief Phil Kouwe, a firefighter with both a passion and a song in his heart, decided that music was the way to capture the imagination of the elementary school kids. Lucky for Kouwe, he was not the only frustrated musician in the fire department. In a flash, the station had written a series of songs like "Stop, Drop and Roll," "Don't Play with Fire," and "Smoke Detector Blues."

With some makeshift musical equipment and a mascot named Sparky (a firefighter in shag), the new group, known as MC Axe and the Fireboys, began visiting local schools. The response from the public was okay, but they needed to spark more attention.

Things have heated up the last few years. Now known as MC Axe and the Firecrew, the group is now made up of firefighters from all of central Indiana, as well as a few volunteers from the DNR. Members perform voluntarily, often traveling on their days off and during vacations. Booked months in advance, the act has made its way from coast to coast.

Now operated by the People's Burn Foundation, the "Crew" is spreading the word like wildfire, fielding requests from schools and state fairs across the country. In addition, their audio equipment is

MC Axe—unmatched in educational entertainment.

state of the art and their 35-foot RV is hard to ignore as it rolls into town with its safety message onboard.

A black Lab named Kasey is also part of the team, performing some of the maneuvers, showing kids how to stop, drop, and roll during a fire. MC Axe and the Firecrew has reached more than two million kids. Songs are based on popular tunes and include "The Heat is On," "Matches and Lighters" (to the tune of "Runaround Sue"), and the "Seat Belt Song" ("Me and Julio Down by the School-yard"). In addition to three CDs, they have a music video.

How long will the group continue to sing? "We're hot," says Jeff Owens, the chaplain, "and we have no intention of cooling down."

Check out their Web site at www.peoplesburnfoundation.org or call them at (877) 814–2024.

To achieve the optimum temperature in the barn, Marcia jerry-rigged a system so she could manually control the climate. Local building contractors would not assist Marcia in a more high-tech approach because to meet the required specifications for growing mushrooms, the conditions would, they said, "result in mold." DUH!

The mushrooms, both oyster and shiitake, burst from their pods somewhat *spore*-adically, at which time Marcia pulls them from the pods, packs them, and delivers them to local restaurants, usually within twenty-four hours. During a good season, you get a crop about every ten days. Of the two varieties, the oyster mushrooms are a dollar cheaper at six dollars a pound. Hey, shiitake happens.

There are a few other people in Indiana who grow mushrooms like this, but we picked Marcia for the book. We're not sure her mushrooms are necessarily the best, but her company has the best name: Fungus Among Us. You can e-mail Marcia at wanderw@iquest.net.

Salt of the Earth
Fort Wayne

Myrtle Young loves potato chips. She doesn't eat them though. She collects them. "I have more than 400," says the eighty-something Fort Wayne native. "I have hearts, butterflies, cartoon characters, and many profiles of famous people."

No, she hasn't been sniffing snack fumes. Other people can see the resemblances, too. In fact, her lauded collection—the only known one in the world—has taken her around the globe.

Late-night television fans may remember Young's 1987 appearance with Johnny Carson. As she was showing off her chips, a loud crunch was heard. Had Johnny eaten one of her prized chips? Young grasped her chest, shocked that Johnny would do such a dastardly deed.

Johnny then revealed a bowl of chips he had stashed under his desk. *TV Guide* voted this classic Carson gag as television's funniest moment. "The editors of *TV Guide* told me that I was in the top fifty," says Young. "When I bought the issue, I just kept turning the pages and turning the pages to find out where I was listed. I was surprised to see that Johnny and I were number one."

Young has chips that look like George Bush, Rodney Dangerfield, Yogi Bear, and Snoopy. But her most famous chip has an uncanny resemblance to Bob Hope. When word got back to Hope about the caricature chip, he sent an autographed picture to Young signed, "So you'll remember what I really look like. Keep chipping away."

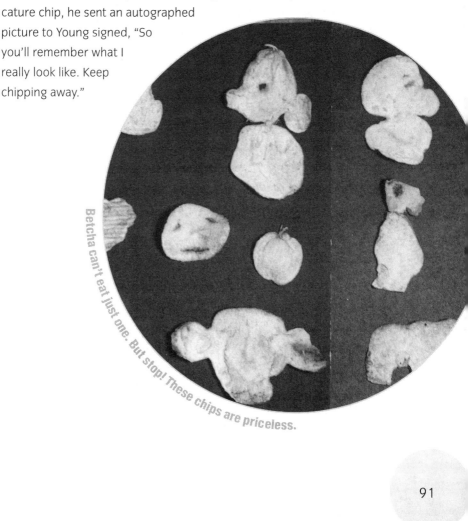

Betcha can't eat just one. But stop! These chips are priceless.

And she has. Young has displayed her collection in Bali, Japan, Hong Kong, and London. The chips always travel first-class—packed in cotton batting and always in carry-on luggage. They have been viewed by international television audiences, Princess Diana, and the Queen of England. Such acclaim has prompted the Indianapolis Children's Museum, Ripley's Believe It or Not, and the Smithsonian to express interest in purchasing her collection.

Young plans to pass on her collection to her children—chips off the old block.

You can't visit Young, but buy an old video of *The Tonight Show* and you'll see her.

Buffaloed
Fremont

Heard of buffalo? Sure you've heard of buffalo. But what about a buffalo herd, 200 of them, right here in Indiana? Just roam over to Fremont, in Steuben County, and you'll find the third largest private herd in North America and the largest in the state. The preserve, opened in 2001, was the dream of Dr. John Trippy, an Ohio-based surgeon whose visit to Yellowstone National Park as a small boy made a huge impression.

Trippy opened the park to "honor and preserve the land, the buffalo, and the people." Combine the buffalo herd with a bed-and-breakfast and a gift shop and you have all the makings of a unique attraction. Visitors to the preserve—whether they opt for the bed-and-breakfast or not—are taken on a truck or wagon tour that allows up-close viewing of the buffalo. "People are not allowed out of the truck," says Gerry Shiley, the preserve manager. "These are wild animals, and you are invited into their family to visit and to learn."

Along with the tour comes a brief lesson on the impact of the buffalo on American history. The gift shop sells Native American jewelry, buffalo hides, head mounts, frozen buffalo meat, and knives, as well as books and tapes further recounting the story of the American bison. You can even buy canned roasted bison. Yum!

Those who purchase the overnight package can enjoy a buffalo breakfast, which includes buffalo sausage or a buffalo casserole. Those with heftier appetites can hold out for the buffalo steak for dinner, which is less fatty and more nutritious because the buffalos at the preserve are grass fed and free of steroids and antibiotics. Even ostriches are jealous.

By the way, dinner is available to the public June through September on Wednesday nights, but the preserve is open all year-round and lunch is always available.

The Wild Winds Buffalo Preserve is located next to the Indiana Turnpike in the heart of the tri-state area bordered by Michigan and Ohio. Call (260) 495–0137 for more information and exact directions. Check out the Web site: www.wildwindsbuffalo.com. You'll find a range of information.

Limberlost

Geneva

Why would anyone want to take farmland and turn it into a swamp? Ask Ken Brunswick, a man whose mission is to do just that. Brunswick and his associates want to re-create the historical setting of one of America's most successful authors, Gene Stratton-Porter.

Geneva Grace Stratton, born in Wabash County in 1863, moved to Adams County with her husband in 1886. Here they built a more-than-modest fourteen-room Queen Anne home, where Mrs. Stratton-Porter wrote many of her novels and poems. Eight of her books ultimately became motion pictures.

Her inspiration? The nearby Limberlost Swamp, once described as a "treacherous swamp, quagmire, filled with every plant, animal, and human danger known." But Stratton-Porter, who prided herself as a naturalist, wanted to instill her love of the earth in her writing. And she just loved that swamp, like only a mother could.

By 1913 the swamp was ditched and drained. Stratton-Porter moved to northern Indiana where she built another home near Rome City (Noble County), known as Wildflower Woods. Visitors marvel at the two-story cabin with exterior cedar logs, the magnificent fireplaces, and furnishings and memorabilia belonging to the Porters.

But back to Geneva, where hundreds of acres of that original swamp are in the process of being restored. Visitors with a love of literature and the wild can hike the area and see mallard ducks, bald eagles, sandhill cranes, and tundra swans, all the result of restoring the swamp. If you want to visit the restored area, your best bet is to visit the Loblolly Marsh Wetland Preserve, located 3 miles west of Bryant on State Road 18, then one-half mile north on Jay County Road 250 W. Spring and fall migrations are fantastic. Brunswick, who started the project in 1993, is removing the hundred-year-old drainage hardware.

"When they began this in 1888, they said they were reclaiming the land. But they never had it to begin with."

Whichever Stratton-Porter historical site you visit, you'll enjoy a walk back in time. But many prefer her first home next to Limberlost. Let's just say it's a "swamp thing."

Limberlost is located at 200 East Sixth, one block east of US 27 in Geneva. The home is closed Mondays and Tuesdays and from mid-December through March. Call (260) 368–7428 for exact times. The Rome City home is northwest of Fort Wayne, just north of U.S. Highway 6 on State Road 9 (1205 Pleasant Point). If you're swamped and don't have time to visit, check out Limberlost at www.limberlost.net or the Rome City home at www .genestrattonporter.net.

Mrs. Stratton-Porter lived near a swamp only a writer could love.

Flight Action Camera
Goshen

Stuart Meade, of Goshen, is an unlicensed pilot. He admits it. And his clients don't seem to mind—even when he takes his hands off of the controls to snap a few photos during their flights.

Of the Remote Control Aerial Photography Association's 739 members, Meade is number 41, and the only one in Indiana. Traditional aerial photography can be a bit pricey. Meade doesn't offer snacks during flights, but thanks to remote control technology, he only charges peanuts for his service.

His flying wing, *ShutterHawk,* has a 6-foot wingspan, runs on a twelve-volt battery, and weighs a scant four and a half pounds, including camera. He built the plane and taught himself to pilot it. *ShutterHawk*'s inaugural flights were purposely scheduled in winter, when the ground was covered with a soft layer of snow. Meade substituted a weight for the real camera until he could get the plane's payload balanced correctly. "Until I got the center of gravity right, I crashed it into the snow the first couple of flights," he admits.

It takes 200 feet of runway to get the flying wing airborne. With remote control in hand, Meade maneuvers the plane over his target. With special Bond-like glasses, he sees what his camera sees. He relinquishes the controls momentarily to an onboard, computerized co-pilot, and via remote control, takes a number of digital shots.

Meade has three simple goals—have a successful takeoff, take great pictures, and land his plane safely. His company is only a few years old, yet land developers, roofing companies, and campgrounds have already sought out his services. "Everyone loves aerial photography, because it gives them a different perspective of something they see every day," Meade says.

Sky-high photos and down-to-earth prices—now that sounds like a business ready to take off.

BURSTING WITH PRIDE

Huntington County is not embarrassed by the fact that its most famous resident was a total bubble brain. Eiffel Plasterer had a passion for ordinary and not-so-ordinary soap bubbles, and he fascinated children and adults with his demonstrations for almost a century.

Plasterer was a man of both religion and science, a bit of a conflict in the 1920s when he attended DePauw University. Here he became especially intrigued with bubbles and began working on the perfect bubble solution (a concoction of liquid soap, water, and glycerine) as part of a lifelong attempt to produce an almost unbreakable bubble.

Plasterer blew bubbles at schools, church meetings, conventions, and banquets and on street corners. He wrote scientific articles and lectured in schools and universities, all the time blowing his own exquisite bubbles. Bubbles within bubbles, bubbles on top of bubbles, bubbles, bubbles, bubbles.

And he blew those bubbles on more TV shows than you could shake a wand at: Letterman, Tom Snyder, and Dick Cavett. Plasterer also holds the record for bubble longevity, capturing a bubble inside a mason jar to protect it from air currents and keeping it intact for one day short of a year. Longer than most gerbils live.

Plasterer believed you never outgrew the joy you could get by blowing bubbles, and he preached that philosophy up until he was almost ninety. Eiffel Lane, named after the famous bubbleologist, now runs through Hiers Park in Huntington. Plasterer's words still ring loud and clear as a bubble. "Our hopes and dreams are the bubbles of life we are blowing. They do not all have to break."

Eiffel Plasterer: all dressed up with someplace to blow.

Vice Squad
Huntington

It's a museum for politicians. But they claim to be nonprofit and nonpartisan. Already the whole thing seems a little suspicious. But it's true. The United States Vice Presidential Museum at the Dan Quayle Center is the only vice presidential museum in America. It started out in 1993 just honoring Dan Quayle, but Quayle himself was uncomfortable with the sole spotlight and encouraged the board to turn the old Christian Science building into an educational facility featuring all the number twos. It has paid off. The museum greets thousands of school kids each year.

Indiana claims five vice presidents and three also-rans and is second only to New York in the number of native-born veeps. And so—being second to New York—the Hoosier State is the perfect place for a shrine to seconds. The museum has artifacts representing all forty-six vice presidents, as well political buttons, political cartoons, books, and other memorabilia.

But Quayle does have the most space in the museum, an entire floor all to himself. In the display you can see everything from his report card to his dog-chewed high school diploma. There's a letter that the vice president wrote to his father during the 1989 invasion of Panama and a photo of James Danforth, the World War II soldier killed in action for whom Quayle was named. An entire section is devoted to newspaper and TV coverage of Quayle and the sometimes unfair treatment by the press. One display details the Murphy Brown speech and the ensuing media blitz.

The museum is at 815 Warren Street in Huntington, just minutes from where Quayle grew up and right across the street from the elementary school where he learned to spell potato . . . or potatoe. Whatever.

The museum is open Tuesday through Saturday 9:30 A.M. to 4:30 P.M. Closed Sunday and Monday. Information is available at (260) 356–6356 or www.quaylemuseum.org.

Milling Around

Kendallville

The windmill museum in Kendallville, Indiana, may be the only one of its kind in the United States. But it's the perfect place for it. According to Russell Baker, of the local historical society, seventy-eight windmill companies surrounded Kendallville in the early 1900s.

Baker started the project a few years ago to create a tourist attraction in Noble County. His interest was further piqued when he discovered that his own great-grandfather was a windmill builder. The mills, constructed to pump water, were built on-site following the digging of the well.

Admission is free . . . as free as the wind.

Baker and his associates purchased some land, and then refurbished a barn for use as a museum. Before long the museum founders brought in old windmills from all over the country, restored them, and put them on the museum grounds. One, a replica of the first windmill in North America, is known as the Robertson Windmill. The original was brought from England and erected on the James River in Virginia.

With more than fifty windmills on the museum grounds, and plans for another fifty or so to come, the Mid-America Windmill Museum is unique in its mission to educate people on the history of wind power. Windmills here rise as high as 55 feet, although most are in the 25-foot range. All the windmills work, and a handful are connected to underground wells.

Inside the museum, patrons can see old photographs, models, and exhibits. A nine-minute video tells the history of wind power from the Persians (around A.D. 300) through modern times and hydroelectric power. The last weekend in June is festival time, celebrated with historic windmill exhibits. As a highlight, museum employees drill a well, erect a windmill, and by the end of the weekend it is pumping water.

Admission is free, but the museum is open only during the summer from Memorial Day through Labor Day. Kendallville is on US 6 about a half hour northwest of Fort Wayne. You can reach Russell Baker at (260) 897–9918 or try the Web site, www.midamericawindmillmuseum.com. When we were there, most locals had no idea how to find the place. So just keep looking. Up.

Willow, Not Wicker

Lapel

Greg Adams doesn't claim to be the only willow artisan in the Midwest, but he may be the only one crazy enough to open an entire shop selling willow furniture. "Most willow guys just mess around in their garage," says Adams, "but I figured I'd do it right."

Adams, a social worker by day, spends his weekends in the 1,500-square-foot studio (a former grocery store from the 1890s) where he caters to a largely urban clientele looking for a rustic touch in their homes. He displays several dozen pieces that range from a simple wreath for a couple of bucks to a majestic, canopy willow bed that you can get into (and under) for $600.

Greg Adams is bent on crafting unique furniture.

His willow mania began on a fishing trip in the early 1980s when he couldn't catch any fish, but his imagination captured something else. Surrounded by willow branch saplings, Adams wondered if he could make baskets like the Indians. Through trial and error, he branched out and taught himself to make wreaths, trellises, arbors, headboards, plant stands, and screens. Walk into his shop and you feel like you're in a tropical rain forest. Oh, and it smells so good.

Adams has another passion: He travels the rural highways of Indiana looking for . . . well, he's not sure what he's looking for. "I'm a student of the back roads. I get in my car and just drive. I like finding roads that I've never seen before. In the process, I'll be scouting for some willows."

His shop, Willow by Greg Adams, sits on the main drag of Lapel. Take State Road 37 from Indianapolis to State Road 32, then east to State Road 13, then turn right and go 5 blocks to 702 Main Street. He's open on weekends, but call first to make sure he's not out driving around: (765) 534–3009. You can also make an appointment. By the way, Adams hates the word *wicker*. He likes the word *willow*. You don't want to make that mistake with so many wickets around.

Noble Museum
Ligonier

Bored with your DVD? You might want to hearken back to the days when you could just get into your BVDs and listen to the radio. No better place to hearken than Ligonier, Indiana.

When the Indiana Radio Historical Society was founded in 1972, its first display was atop the Auburn Car Museum. But an old filling station in Ligonier caught its eye and soon became one of the few freestanding museums in the country dedicated to the history of radio.

Inside the museum, thousands of visitors each year see about 400 radios, a few dating back to 1899. Each radio is tagged with a bit of history. Also displayed are vacuum tubes invented in 1906, still in their original boxes. You can see novelty radios in the shapes of food products, as well as radios used during wartime. Also inside are cathedral and tombstone radios, telegraphy, crystal sets, and horn and cone speakers.

The museum has a small transmitter that plays radio shows, and museum-goers can actually fiddle with an old-time radio dial to simulate how listeners from the 1920s and '30s tuned in their favorite shows. Kids especially enjoy the old-time telegraph keys or making their hair stand on end with a Van der Graaf generator.

In 2003 a new low-power station, WNRL 105.9 FM, was installed. The station plays 1940s, '50s, and '60s music for people who are in their seventies, sixties, and fifties.

Information about the Indiana Historical Radio Museum at 800 Lincolnway South in Ligonier is available online at http://home.att.net/~indianahistoricalradio/index.htm. During the winter (November 1 through March 31) the museum is open only on Saturday. April 1 through October the museum is open Tuesday through Saturday from 10:00 A.M. to 3:00 P.M. For more information call (888) 417–3562.

Beat the Cluck

Mentone

You probably don't know this—or care—but there is a raging controversy over where the world's largest egg is. Neither side has cracked; both maintain they harbor the biggest. The folks in Winlock, Washington, have one that's 12 feet long and 1,200 pounds; it sits on a steel pedestal, atop a pole. The sign next to it says: WORLD'S LARGEST EGG.

But Hoosiers disagree! In Mentone, Indiana (Kosciusko County), sits an even bigger egg—maybe. This egg weighs 3,000 pounds and is 10 feet high, so it's definitely heavier. But is it bigger?

Kosciuskoans (if there is such a word) say, YES! Mentonians agree. Mentone has been a center of egg production for more than a hundred years. By the turn of the twentieth century, Mentone chicken farmers were bringing their eggs by covered wagon to the train station for delivery throughout the Midwest. There were even judges who assessed the relative eggyness of the farmers' products.

Two huge egg producers still ship from the Mentone area, an area with far more chickens than people. Mentone's annual Egg Festival in June celebrates the area's rich egg history with music, food, a parade, a 5K run, and, of course, an egg toss. There's also a group of performers called the Hen House Five. Fortunately, we have no photo of this.

But the real excitement is the big Chicken Drop event. Chickens are placed in cages where the floor is marked with a series of numbers. Then the audience places bets on where . . . you know. I don't think we really need to explain this.

Mentone is on State Road 25, southwest of Warsaw. The Mentone Egg Festival is usually the first full weekend after the first of June, but call the Kosciusko Convention & Visitors Bureau at (574) 269–6090 or visit the Web site, www.mentoneeggcity.com, to check. Sometimes it isn't.

Standing Room Only

Montpelier

The 60-foot fiberglass Indian chief that sits (well, stands) in the middle of tiny Montpelier can be seen by everybody—no reservation required. Montpelier, a city that boasts a rich and somewhat saucy history of murder, brothels, and drinking, has calmed down quite a bit in the last hundred years. But the mammoth presence of Chief Francois Godfroy, the last war chief of the Miamis, is a pretty good reminder of the rich Indian heritage in Blackford County.

The statue was originally located at a Pontiac dealership in Indy, then moved to the Turtle Creek Museum. They were going to ship the Indian to the new Eiteljorg Museum in 1985. When those plans were nixed, the chief's great-great-grandson Larry (how many Indians do you know named Larry?) arranged for Montpelier to display the icon in the center of town, provided that the statue would be placed at the entrance to any future park in the city.

Is that a huge Indian? And how!

So far, no park. In the meantime the chief keeps watch over the city's quaint shops. Or should we say paint. The stores are actually painted on stone walls, the kind of busy main street that might have existed in another place or time. Ken Neff, former mayor, had seen the concept in his travels and brought the idea back to Montpelier where a local artist sketched in the outline and volunteers then painted by number.

Although all the stores represented, like Neff Realty, Neff Insurance, Walker Glancy Funeral Home, Grandma Joes, and Frosty's, really exist in the city, but are somewhat less idyllic in real life.

Montpelier is on State Road 18, just west of where it intersects with State Road 1, about a half hour east of Marion.

It's not real estate; it's fake estate.

Putting a Lid on It

Muncie

Rev. Philip Robinson can't keep a lid on his enthusiasm. But he can keep lids on some 4,000 fruit and canning jars in his museum in Muncie.

It was a single lid, in fact, that Robinson found more than thirty-six years ago while cleaning up an abandoned lot that led him to create his nationally known collection. He became intrigued with the abandoned top, curious to know what kind of a jar it came from. After years of searching, he finally located the lid's mate at a flea market. Both the lid and the glass container said "Hoosier Jar." The glass jar, he learned, was made in Greenfield, Indiana, in 1882. Robinson paid $700 for the jar. He could have sold the lid for $100.

Having a ball . . . with jars.

In Robinson's museum, a building just outside his home, the jars are arranged in a very scientific manner. "If it fits on the shelf, that's where I put it," says Robinson, who has jars as old as 1849 and as new as "just made yesterday." He's got jars from scores of foreign countries and in dozens of different colors. And if the jar lid is missing or broken, he makes a new lid—just like the original—down in his workshop.

Robinson's attitude toward some of his priceless possessions is, well, priceless. He encourages people to pick up the jars, touch them, feel them, enjoy them. "If one breaks, it breaks," he says. "I lived without them before, I can survive without them now. And they're all paid for." He even feels that way about his most valuable collectible, a nameless $7,000 jar. "If you start to worry about whether it's going to break, it's no fun anymore."

No charge to see the jars. Just stop by 1201 West Cowing Drive in Muncie, but call first: (765) 282–9707. Robinson wanted me to know that his wife is the president of the National Jelly Jar Collectors. And now you know, too.

Thank God It's Friday
Muncie

Ball State University has a costumed character who boosts campus spirit—and it ain't Charlie Cardinal.

While the university's official feathered mascot appears mostly at sporting events, this caped crusader speeds through campus on an electric scooter once a week. His trademark, "Happy Friday!" echoes off buildings at lunchtime and gets even the most stoic, book-bound students to smile.

The site of Happy Friday Guy brings students running to catch an up-close glimpse of the scooter-riding superhero. Some students, groupies if you will, actually congregate along his usual route through the heart of campus in anticipation of his weekly wail.

Meeting him up close doesn't disappoint. He never adjusts his volume while indoors, as he greets all with a hearty "Happy Friday!" He wears an old kickboxing helmet, ski goggles, kneepads, a Happy Friday Guy shirt, and an HFG cape. "It all pretty much came from Goodwill," he admits.

Like all superheroes, he has a secret weapon. If HFG's boisterous greeting doesn't brighten people's faces, his utility belt, filled with treats, does the trick. "I enjoy lifting people's spirits and making them smile," he says. "Friday on its own can do that, but this just enhances it. Like salt to a fine dish, I'm salt to Fridays." People on salt-free diets listen to him, too.

Happy Friday Guy's identity is known to but a select few who have pledged to protect his anonymity. He keeps a lair near campus to assume his HFG persona and perform necessary repairs to his scooter, which carries him on warm sunny days as well as wintry rides when the wind chill is in the teens.

Endorsement deals, say from a particular restaurant chain, seem like a perfect fit. But as of yet, HFG has received no corporate proposals. "People have, however, asked to be my sidekick," he laughs. "And girls have even asked to marry me, among other offers."

But this is a family book, and Happy Friday Guy is too clean-cut to tell such seedy stories. So until next week, it's up, up, and away—Haaaaaappy Friday!

Jack-o-Lantern the Knife!

Muncie

Tom Leaird hosts the oldest pumpkin-carving contest in the state of Indiana. Every year, from ten to twenty-five of his friends gather near his Muncie home, select a pumpkin, gut it, and grab a rock to keep it from floating.

Oh yeah, did I forget to mention: It's an *underwater* pumpkin-carving contest?

Leaird was one of the first divers in the state to be certified by the YMCA in 1960, just one year after the national certification program was launched. And let's face it, when you've made more than 2,600 dives and trained more than 4,000 students, you're looking for anything to keep diving interesting.

Leaird has gone scuba diving in the United States from Texas to Connecticut, and from Hawaii to Tennessee, as well as in Greece, Spain, Indonesia, and many times in the Caribbean. Leaird is always looking for new twists on his favorite hobby. So since the late 1970s, he's been hosting the annual Halloween dive in Muncie quarries.

Once divers select their pumpkins (and a rock), they find a "bench," or a rock outcrop, about 15 feet below the surface. With their dive knives or coping saws, they cut away on their creations. "Some of them have used moss for hair," Leaird says. "Others have decorated their pumpkins with a pair of glasses or false teeth they found on the bottom of the quarry."

Regardless of the air temperature, the dives go on as scheduled. "It doesn't matter how cold it is outside, because the water temperature is always the same," he says. During the fall and winter, water clarity is usually better. Another popular event, which happens only sporadically, is the Christmas tree decorating dive. But that's a story for another day.

Maybe it's the cookout that accompanies the Halloween dive that

Serious art with a little cutting up.

keeps it going year after year. Maybe it's that the winners get home-made pumpkin pies baked by Tom's wife, Bobbi. Or maybe it's because Bobbi doesn't force them to eat her tasty pies underwater.

In the unlikely event you'd like to "get down" with Tom, call him at (765) 288–8144, or reach him online at www.leaird-scuba.com.

Easy as Pie

Nappanee

Dwane Borkholder at the Dutch Village Craft and Antique Mall will not swear he makes the biggest apple pie in the world, but we don't have the time to call every bakery. So here's the recipe:

> 326 pounds of apples
> 94 pounds of pie crust
> (the rest is a secret)

The world's largest apple pie—not just another half-baked idea.

NORTHEAST

The idea began to cook in the late 1970s when Ron Telschow, formerly of the Lovin' Oven, started creating his gargantuan pies for the annual Nappanee Apple Festival. With the help of a 7-foot specially made pastry tin, he baked the pie in a huge Reel oven (that turns like a Ferris wheel) in about two hours.

A few years ago he passed on the core of his secret process to Borkholder, who still thinks it's the biggest pie around, but adds the caveat, "the biggest baked in an *oven*."

This eliminates all pies built over a campfire.

The pie takes a day and a half to cool before the hungry patrons at the Nappanee Apple Festival gobble up the 800 pieces in just a few hours. While waiting, there's an apple-peeling contest, baking contest, pie-eating contest, and a crosscut saw competition. There's also a classic car rally, an antique fire truck show, and a parade with floats—and some of the floats don't even have apples. And there's no charge for any of this.

To get a piece of the action and a piece of the pie, take US 31 north from Indy to US 6. Then US 6 east into Nappanee. You can also call (800) 860–5957 for more information. By the way, Borkholder claims the pie is not just big in size, but big in taste, noting that many folks say that their grandmother's apple pie just doesn't stack up to his.

Duck, Duck, Spruce

Noblesville

It looks like a duck; it walks like a duck; it quacks like a duck. But it may not be a duck. It may be a Bundy Decoy, probably the finest decorative duck decoys in the United States. And made in Indiana, just north of Noblesville.

Okay, they don't walk and quack, but they are realistic enough that John Bundy sells a bunch (flock?) to nature lovers and even some to hunters. But Bundy Decoys are largely for show, and quite a show they make.

Bundy purchased a few unfinished decoy ducks back in the 1970s and painted them, discovering that by using the natural grain of the wood he could create unique and beautiful designs. Soon he was duck-hooked.

Bundy purchased a spindle carver so that he could craft about twelve duck bodies at a time by guiding the rotary spindles along the blocks of wood. The ninety-minute process takes great touch and feel. One mistake is twelve mistakes and a great deal of wasted timber. Then his wife, Valerie, in a process labeled top secret, paints each duck by hand. The Bundys turn out 4,000 collector ducks a year, each one different, each one sold and certified for posterity.

Bundy's tiny showroom, at 1605 Strawtown Avenue in Noblesville, is not easy to find, but if you want to see the finest hand-painted decoys this side of Lake Michigan, it's worth the waddle. It's open 9:00 A.M. to 4:00 P.M. Monday through Friday. Call for directions (800–387–3831), or visit the Web site: www.Bundyducks.com.

Making exquisite decoys—and ducking responsibility.

Getting in Stride!

Noblesville

Tim Fleck is one of the nation's leading adjusters. No, not insurance. Horses. Make no bones about it, lots of people (even some fellow veterinarians) think that anyone who thinks this kind of thing really works lacks any horse sense. Which is kind of funny, since the horses seem to not only love it, but to benefit from Tim's experienced touch. Or in some cases a pull, a twist, or a shove.

Tim was influenced by his dad, also a vet, who was intrigued with the holistic approach to treating animals. He passed his enthusiasm on to Tim, who got a leg up on the process by taking a few courses in the subject back in the 1980s. Then Tim fell off his own horse and his experience with a human chiropractor really kicked his interest into stride. (Are these horse metaphors driving you crazy?)

Since the early 1990s, Dr. Fleck's veterinary practice has combined both the traditional and holistic approach to medicine, so don't be surprised if you walk into his clinic in Noblesville and see a Pekingese with pins in him: that would be canine acupuncture.

Dr. Fleck's real passion is for Arabian show horses, a hobby he shares with his wife, Rebecca. Fleck is so hip to the problems that these horses can have with gait and stride that he is often hired to fly to ranches around the country to lay on his hands. Watching Tim do an adjustment is quite a treat. And in some cases you can actually hear the "crack" that most humans associate with a successful adjustment.

"I really don't adjust the horse," says a modest Fleck. "I put the horse in the right position and he adjusts himself." Maybe, but the horse doesn't get paid. Tim does.

The Noblesville Veterinary Clinic is open to the public by appointment. Of course, you could just walk in . . . but watch how you walk. Everyone else will.

P.S. The folks at the clinic just loved that last joke, but they do want you to call: (317) 773–3283.

Dumplings without a Peel
Pendleton

Glen Grabow is an engineer. He's got a degree from Marquette University. He worked on the Polaris Missile and the Hubble Telescope. This is big stuff. Now he makes apple dumplings for a living. He's never been happier.

When Grabow retired in 1989, he bought an apple orchard in Madison County and decided to add a small bakery to the operation. His apple dumplings had gained a bit of a local reputation over the years, so when the Food Channel was looking for a feature segment on orchard/bakery combos, they picked Grabow's.

The segment aired in January of 2001, and things haven't been the same since. "I answered the phones and took orders for ten straight hours," says Grabow, whose success created a major problem: How do you ship a product like this and keep it flaky and tasty?

Grabow looked at it like any good engineer and created a "kit," which could be sent to hungry customers. Inside the box, dumpling lovers will find the uncooked dumpling, along with special sauce, glaze, instructions, and a comment card. We hope McDonald's doesn't steal this idea. The secret to these dumplings is, well, it's a secret. But if you want to try dumplings at home, Grabow strongly advises coring, peeling, and slicing the apple. "And keep the crust thin," he says.

You can buy the dumplings fresh at his Grabow Orchard and Bakery for a couple of bucks each by taking I–69 to exit 14, which is State Road 13. Turn left toward Lapel, travel 1 mile, and look on the left. Call if you get lost: (888) 534–3225. If you want to send dumplings to your sister in Denver, you're talking seven dollars each. And she has to bake them herself. Only Glen Grabow could have engineered that.

Glen has a peachy Web site at www.graboworchard.com. I'd call first because it's not easy to find. Okay, big shot, here's the address: 6397 South State Road 13 in Pendleton. But it's not really Pendleton, it's more like Lapel. Just call, okay?

Giant Savings
Pendleton

Vic Cook has no desire to live like a pioneer, or a groundhog for that matter, but since the early 1980s this high school teacher and musician has lived underground. He's no hermit. In fact, his home is open to the public. You may feel his home is beneath you, but it's worth lowering yourself—about 22 feet.

It all started in the late 1970s when Cook bought some land and began work on his vision. He wanted a home that was environmentally loving (friendly is not a strong enough word), but at the same time very high-tech. He wanted to blend science, art, and nature. The house was completed in the early 1980s and opened to the public in 1986.

The underground fortress, known as The Giant, was built with Cook's own hands, using fallen trees and a backhoe. The house has seven levels and uses the energy from the surrounding woodland, energy from the sun, and geothermal energy from the earth. Cook spends not a penny on public utilities, but he can chill a beer in his hollowed-out beech tree refrigerator faster than an Amana. The secret: special insulation and underground air currents.

Thousands of students visit the 7,000-square-foot home each year after a thirty-minute trek through the surrounding forest, led by Sue Blakely, president of Cook's foundation. Inside, guests marvel at a high-tech music studio, a big-screen TV, two computers, and a washing machine. Cook runs it all for less than a buck a day, powered by six storage batteries charged by solar panels, with a back-up gasoline generator. His toilet is a composting unit, which is probably more info than you wanted, but that's what all the kids ask.

You can visit The Giant by reservation only. For more information call (765) 778–2757 or check out the Web site: www.giantearthship.com.

In a Pinch
Pinch

The town of Pinch has no city hall. It has no downtown. Or uptown. Suburban sprawl would be putting up its first traffic light or constructing a second home. There goes the neighborhood!

Welcome to Pinch—the Hoosier State's smallest town. Its population of three suits Shirley Fisher just fine. That's because the two other residents live with her, and she's the town's self-appointed mayor. "I'm the mayor because I was born on this corner," she says with a laugh. "My husband, Tom, is second in command, and my son, well, he works just beyond the city limits so I don't know what his title would be." We'd suggest "outsider."

The triumvirate—and the entire town, for that matter—can be found in Randolph County at the intersection of 900 West and 400 South. There are three buildings: an abandoned seed/feed store, Shirley's ceramic shop, and the Fishers' home. And since the city limit signs are planted in their front yard, the Fishers can take an out-of-town trip by simply climbing over their fence.

Pinch hasn't always been this small. In the late 1800s the town was called Good View and bustled with an estimated population of twelve. The boom years ended, though, when the railroad bypassed the town, slowly derailing the population and inspiring a name change. "The story I heard is that everyone in town pinched their pennies," says Shirley. And the name has stuck ever since.

The tiniest town has had its share of media attention. Newspaper reporters, TV hosts, and even a New York fashion magazine stopped by for a spell. That just goes to show you that everyone needs a little Pinch now and then.

Pinch is located 22 miles northeast of New Castle and 14 miles southwest of Winchester. You can't miss it. Yeah, right.

Two out of three people in Pinch are Tom and Shirley.

Uniform Approach

Portland

Old soldiers never die, they just go to the Museum of the Soldier in Portland, one of the only museums in the entire country dedicated not to the artifacts of war, but the people behind them. One of the founders, Jim Waechter, has been a collector of military history for fifty years. Brian Williamson also started at an early age. All the board members share this passion.

The museum, a former Coca Cola plant, is 26,000 square feet, and while Waechter admits he hasn't filled all the space yet, he's optimistic about the future. "We've filled about 9,000 square feet right now, and we have many collections we can use as the building expands."

What makes this museum so different is that virtually every piece of military equipment is linked to a specific person. Each item, whether donated or purchased, is accompanied by a bio and photos of the person it represents. When pieces are acquired without that information, Waechter and his volunteers become amateur sleuths, going to local and national archives, checking any available records. "It's painstaking, but our people are very good at it," he says.

For background information, unidentified trappings may be displayed in the museum, but featured items always have that personal touch. In one case, museum researchers traced a uniform based on a name scribbled on the inside pocket. The owner of the uniform was so thrilled with the discovery that he happily supplied all the accompanying material.

The museum features all wars and armed conflicts including Desert Storm, the conflict in Bosnia, and the ongoing war against terrorism. And while the displays are probably a little Hoosier-heavy because of location, the exhibit features soldiers from all over the country.

Waechter plans extensive education programs with school kids, convinced that most fathers and grandfathers talk little about their war experience. "Kids will come to the museum, not realizing their own relatives were in a particular war. We want the kids to walk out with a feeling for the person behind the rifle, of the nurse who was in the uniform, as well as those who supported us back home."

The museum is located at 516 East Arch Street in Portland. Take State Road 67 northwest from Muncie, go east on State Road 26 to Portland, then follow the signs. Call for info at (260) 726–2967.

A-mazing Grace
Upland

Wouldn't it be great if there was just one place in the entire United States where you could play a round of golf and then walk into a labyrinth? You're kidding! You've never thought about it before? You don't even know what a labyrinth is? Thank goodness for this book.

A turf labyrinth is a pathway in the ground whose winding course leads inexorably to the center. Unlike a maze, there are no tricks, no cul-de-sacs, no wrong turns. This is called *unicursial*. Like you didn't know that. The idea is to think introspectively as you meander—instead of worrying whether you can find your way out.

Labyrinths like this go back thousands of years in Europe and Asia, but they are virtually nonexistent in America. Randy and Sara Ballinger changed all that when they built a labyrinth right next to their golf course (Club Run) in Upland, Indiana. They made it to honor Randy's great-grandmother who was born near Hanover, Germany, home of one of the world's most famous turf labyrinths: The Rad, circa 1500. Randy re-created The Rad here in hope that it would generate interest in the former abolitionist community of Farmington, where his golf course now sits. Here, too, is the historic Israel Jenkins House, an important part of the Underground Railroad network in pre–Civil War Indiana.

The labyrinth is 105 feet in diameter, the paths 18 inches, and the journey to the center is just over 1,400 feet. The labyrinth opened for the millennium, and while Randy knows it is not exactly a tourist magnet, he did think that a place for meditation might sit well with golfers who wanted to prepare themselves for a good round or needed solace after a bad one.

From I–69 take exit 59 (Upland and Gas City exit), go a quarter mile east on State Road 22, then a mile north on Road 700 East, then a half mile east on Road 400 South to the Club Run Golf Course entrance (800–998–7651). Remember to let faster meditators pray through.

A labyrinth to de-stress golfers. No carts allowed.

LET THERE BE LIGHT

Here's a trivia question designed to stump the experts. What was the very first city to be lit by electricity? New York? Nope. Los Angeles? Sorry. Chicago? Try again.

No, the answer is Wabash. That's right, tiny Wabash in northeastern Indiana made world headlines in 1880 when four lamps were hung in the dome of the courthouse, each facing in a different direction. Powered by a threshing machine steam engine, the lights (3,000-candlepower each) were turned on at 8:00 P.M. and dazzled the city for several blocks. Most people were stunned at how far the beams reached. From this one central source, people could read their newspapers at night as far away as 6 blocks. Folks in nearby cities saw the eerie glow around Wabash.

But why Wabash? No one is quite sure, except that Wabash was clearly in the market for a cheaper way to light homes. Gas was expensive, so town leaders approached Charles Brush, inventor of the arc lamp (a lamp ignited by jumping an electric charge between two poles), who was eager to show his invention to the world. The city had a little incentive money and a courthouse on a hill, two good reasons for Brush to test his creation in Wabash. Thomas Edison, we should mention, had invented his incandescent light (made with a filament) just a few months earlier.

But Brush's lights needed constant replacing, while Edison's longer-lasting design allowed cities to light streets and homes individually. Eight years later, the Wabash Electric Light Company replaced the Brush lights with the more modern Edison equipment. In any case, Wabash was the first electrically lighted city, and today's visitors to the courthouse can see one of the remaining arc lights in the lobby. A friendly janitor let me climb up (and boy, did I climb) to where the original four lamps were installed in the dome, but this area is not officially open to the public, so don't say I sent you.

To get to Wabash go fifteen minutes north of Kokomo on US 31, then east on State Road 115.

Rose-Colored Houses

Wakarusa

Devon Rose is never insulted when people accuse him of thinking small. Rose, a retired draftsman, started thinking tiny in the early 1960s while working on a model railroad set with his kids. After constructing a miniature feedmill, he began whittling, shaving, and cutting, creating exact replicas of other buildings in his hometown of Wakarusa. Now, more than forty years later, Rose's life's work is displayed in his basement—arguably one of the premier miniature displays in the country.

After completing all the buildings in the Wakarusa business district, Rose then went on to replicate at least one building in each city of Elkhart County. In the past several years, he has expanded his work and now has more than 200 buildings from more than twenty-five surrounding counties.

Devon Rose, thinking small in Wakarusa.

The work is meticulous, often requiring hours and hours of painstaking attention to detail. "I got thirteen pieces of wood out of one toothpick," says Rose, "and I still threw some of the stick away." A typical building could take more than 1,000 hours to complete. Rose sees no end in sight (we wonder how he can see at all), although Linda, his wife, sees the project getting too big for the basement.

Incredibly, Rose's scale is 1 inch to 5 feet, making his pieces far smaller than a typical dollhouse or miniature collection. In one part of the display, Rose has a lake stocked with tiny fish. At night, the entire project is lit with thousands of "stars." The sound of cats fighting and church music add to the realism of the work.

Rose loves to show his work, and for a nominal fee you can visit him at 325 South Elkhart Street in Wakarusa (take State Road 19 for 5 miles north of US 6). Call and talk to Linda for more information: (574) 862–2367.

Hanging It Up

Warsaw

Business at the 12,000-square-foot Party Shop in Warsaw, Indiana, hangs by a thread. And it has for more than thirty years. In the back of this somewhat traditional store is a one-of-a-kind showplace: The Hallmark Ornament Museum. There you can see over 3,000 Christmas ornaments made by the Hallmark people since 1973. It's the most complete collection in the world. And 20,000 people a year come to gawk at it in this tiny Indiana town.

According to the owner, Dorothy Snyder, the museum attracts families each year who browse the store, then stop and reminisce about Christmases past as they eyeball the vast array of Christmas bulbetry (which is not really a word, but it should be).

The ornaments bring back wonderful memories, unless, of course, you got stiffed a lot on Christmas morning. The collection itself is not for sale, but hundreds of other unique ornaments can be purchased for your own tree. Don't settle for simple glass balls. Instead look for motorcycles, NASCARs, reindeer on surfboards, and, maybe someday—tiny laptop computers? There are trains, penguins, Wizard of Oz characters. You name it, and they can reach for it.

Although there are about five or six people in the United States who also have all of the ornaments, The Party Shop is the only place they can be seen all at once on display. In fact, even the visitor center in the Hallmark headquarters at Kansas City, Missouri, only displays about 1,200 of the ornaments.

Dorothy Snyder says that Hallmark makes 300 new ornaments each year, so her collection, housed in spiffy Amish-made shelving, grows every year as well.

It doesn't cost anything to get into The Party Shop, but chances are it will cost you to get out. Prices for ornaments start at just a few bucks and can take off like Santa's sleigh. Merry Christmas!

Warsaw is southeast of South Bend, take U.S. Highway 30 to State Road 15 south. Then ask. The store is a bit out of town (3418 Lake City Highway), so give them a call at (574) 267–8787. And they have a Web site: www.thepartyshop.com.

Biblical Seeds
Warsaw

Would you be inspired if you walked through a garden filled with *Anemone coronarias* or *Anthemis nobilis*? Maybe you'd like to sit and reflect under an *Albies concolor* or lounge by a *Buxus sempervirens*?

You would probably find all this very relaxing (although it did drive Heidi, my proofreader, a little crazy). That's because all the plants listed above are also mentioned in the Bible. You can look it up.

You can also see all these plants and trees up close and personal by visiting the Warsaw Biblical Gardens. The garden was created by Sara Lee Levin in the late 1980s using land that had once been a family scrap yard. When the business relocated, her husband, Howard, erected a fountain on the property to honor his parents. Years later, Sara Lee was fascinated by a biblical garden she saw during a visit to New York City. She brought the idea back to Indiana, where she built her biblical garden around the fountain. Later she added an arbor, as well as an area just for trees.

Tours can be arranged, or you can just walk the three-quarter-acre facility and educate yourself using the signage that provides the scientific name of the plant or tree, the common name today, and the biblical reference (where the vegetation is mentioned in the Old or New Testament). In many cases, the biblical name is different than it is today. Thus, an *Anemone coronaria* is a windflower in today's parlance, but was called a Lily of the Fields in biblical times.

Some biblical flora cannot grow in Indiana, so the master gardeners who volunteer on the grounds often seek to find a strain of the plant or flower that can thrive in this climate.

According to Carmen Lock, who helps conduct tours between April and October, people come from all over and use the gardens for meditation. "We also have regulars," says Lock. "People who come every single day." Several marriage ceremonies have been performed in the garden as well.

There are guidelines for behavior. On rare occasions, Carmen finds some inappropriate conduct going on amidst the plants. But she makes it clear that the garden requires reverence.

"There's no skateboarding in the garden," says Lock. "There was no skateboarding in the Bible."

Warsaw is southeast of South Bend. Take US 30 to State Road 15 south. Warsaw Biblical Gardens is located at the corner of Canal Street and SR 15 North. For more information call (574) 267–6419 (Warsaw Community Development Corporation) or visit www.warsawbiblical gardens.org.

Coin-a-Copia
Winchester

If you're looking for a nickel tour in east central Indiana, stop by Winchester's Silvertowne. If you're lucky, the owners may even show off their quarters, dimes, and gold doubloons.

Leon and Dave Hendrickson are the father and son team of numismatists (coin collectors) who own Silvertowne, Indiana's largest, and one of the nation's leading, coin shops.

Their building has ten times more security than the town's bank. On a typical day, visits by Brinks trucks outnumber UPS trucks. Behind the bulletproof windows, they've got silver dollars by the bucketful, silver certificates by the shelf-full, and enough coins to make a mint manager envious. "Any U.S. coin ever made we've had in this shop, or we can get it," Dave proclaims.

Their shop draws all types—from kids looking to complete their state quarters collection to baby boomers looking to bankroll their retirement in gold coins. "We treat them all the same," Dave says. And with good reason. One transaction with a nice, older lady netted a handful of ordinary coins and one worth $50,000. Another interesting story involves a haggard-looking Harley rider who eventually bought $7.4 million in gold coins. "When he wrote a check for the coins, I said there's no way you're just going to walk out with these coins by writing a check," Dave recalls. "Needless to say, I was a bit surprised when the bank called and told me the check had cleared."

Equal treatment for each customer comes, in part, from the shop's humble beginnings. In 1949 the shop was no more than a collection of loose coins in a cigar box. Leon kept the box in his Winchester eatery (the Rainbow Restaurant) and sold the coins to patrons. Over the years the box

Going through the change of life in Silvertowne.

expanded into his basement, and later its contents filled an entire store. "In 1966 my dad sold $120,000 in coins," Dave says. "The next year, he sold the restaurant, went full-time into coins, and sold more than $100 million that year."

The businessman who bought the restaurant from Leon began making pies full-time. Seeing that both men went on to run profitable operations, the pie maker coined one of Dave's favorite phrases: "Well, it looks like we're both still in the dough business."

And Silvertowne is definitely getting its fair slice.

Visit Silvertowne at 120 East Union City Pike (800–788–7481) or online at www.silvertowne.com.

Noble Cause
Wolf Lake

When Shirley Hile and her sister, Mary Ellen, of Wolf Lake, Indiana, purchased an old, dilapidated hospital building a couple of years ago, they got *luckey*.

The Luckey Hospital, to be exact.

The hospital had played an important role in this tiny Noble County community, serving patients from the 1920s up until 1956, when the hospital closed. The first-floor clinic remained open until the mid-1960s, when the facility shut its doors for good.

The hospital was founded and literally built by Dr. James Luckey and his two sons, Harold and Robert, who were also doctors, but docs with a flair for mechanics as well as medicine.

Shirley and Mary Ellen are descendents of the medical trio, and they were particularly troubled as they watched the building morph over the years into everything from a video store to a Laundromat to low-rent apartments.

And so the enterprising sisters, both former nurses, bought the structure with the idea that they would be saving a piece of family history and also have a place to store some of the medical artifacts and memorabilia they had collected over the years.

When the Noble County Tourism Board saw the extent of their collection, they suggested a museum. A medical museum housed in an old hospital may seem like a no-brainer, but there are only a couple in the entire country.

The museum is a real step back into history, filled with some items that date back as far as the late 1700s. But the overall decor is Luckey Hospital as it looked in the 1920s.

You can see the surgical suite, the examining rooms, and the doctors' offices. And just like in the old days, you can get in with a minimum of waiting.

Before you have lunch, look at the bloodletting devices, aptly called *scari*ficators, the iron lung machines, or the trauma kits. Surgical saws and scalpels are everywhere. "I don't think we realized how much stuff we had," admits Shirley. "Some of it was stored in our friends' basements."

But the nostalgic favorite is the big collection of starched-white nurses' uniforms and hats, reflecting a time when "nurses looked like nurses," notes Shirley in an editorial observation about health care today.

By the way, there are still hundreds of people in Noble County who were treated by the Luckey doctors. All these people are in their eighties and nineties, a real living testimony to Dr. John Luckey and his sons.

The Luckey Hospital is located at 1397 North US 33. Call (260) 635–2214.

WEIRD TREES

The tulip tree has been honored as Indiana's official tree. Sycamores have been heralded in the song "On the Banks of the Wabash." And now, thanks to the Division of Forestry, weird trees are finally getting the attention they so rightfully deserve.

And as it turns out, these mangled maples and demented dogwoods are generating as much interest in Indiana's forests as the stateliest sycamores ever did. "We never received much media attention from our Arbor Day promotions," says Sam Carman, Indiana Division of Forestry's education director. "We wanted to come up with a better way to pass on the importance of Indiana's trees."

Forestry officials sparked some interest when they solicited Hoosiers to submit pictures of the biggest trees. Branching out to request the weirdest trees, however, has proven to be a "tree-mendous" success. "We received nearly 200 submissions for Invasion of the Weird Trees," says Carman. "I'm amazed in the interest it has generated."

"Mono Epidemic Linked to Kissing Trees!"

The submissions can be found on the forestry Web site (www.in.gov/dnr/forestry). Select "publications" and scroll down to the bottom of the page. One tree in Brown County has a large branch that shoots back into the ground and looks like a letter of the alphabet, "Give me an H." Another in Fountain County, which has two trees hugging, is entitled "Arboreal amour."

Carman's favorite entries are trees that have grown together or ones that are puzzling from a biological standpoint. For instance, one tree in Northern Vanderburgh County looks like two camels kissing.

The Web site proves that Mother Nature does have a sense of humor. Just ask a duckbilled platypus.

SOUTHEAST

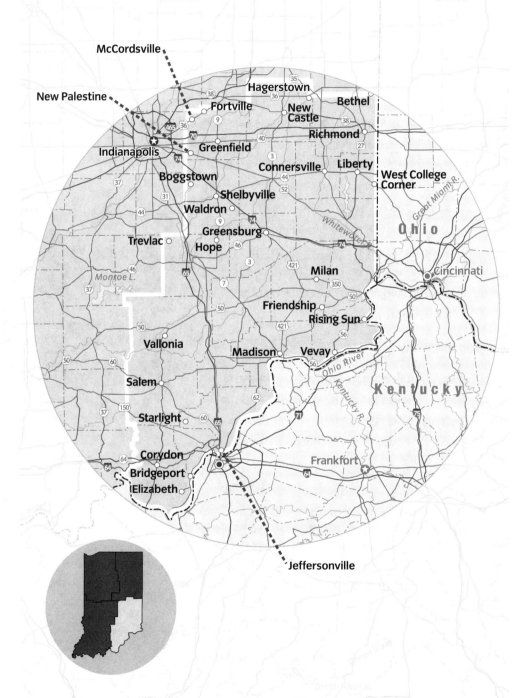

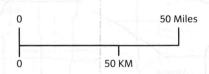

0   50 Miles

0   50 KM

McCordsville
New Palestine
Hagerstown
Fortville
New Castle
Bethel
Indianapolis
Greenfield
Richmond
Boggstown
Connersville
Liberty
West College Corner
Shelbyville
Ohio
Waldron
Trevlac
Greensburg
Hope
Milan
Cincinnati
Monroe L.
Friendship
Rising Sun
Vallonia
Madison
Vevay
Ohio River
Salem
Kentucky
Starlight
Corydon
Frankfort
Bridgeport
Elizabeth
Jeffersonville

Whitewater
Great Miami R.
Kentucky R.

SOUTHEAST

There's plenty to do in this part of Indiana, a region rich in history and easy to navigate. Many tour books cover it, and we've kept in a few favorites from last time, like the world's second biggest clock, the Howard Steamboat Museum, and the guy who blows up hot water bottles. But there's lots of new stuff, like a barber shop inside a train caboose and a man who got bored, so he built a covered bridge—that doesn't connect anything. There's a lady who rehabs turtles, and they actually come when she calls them. I also tossed in the Indiana Basketball Hall of Fame—my choice for the best museum in Indiana. If you don't know what I'm talking about, you're really not a Hoosier.

On Top of the World!

Bethel

It's the highest point in Indiana. My son said it was the lowest point of our vacation. But there it was, in Wayne County, just north of Bethel. We'd tell you more, but half the fun, actually ALL the fun, is finding it.

The map said we were 1,257 feet above sea level, but you can't see the ocean. You can't even see Interstate 70. And you wouldn't even know from the drive you were going uphill. But, yes, this tiny off-the-road spot, just a few yards north of some hay rolls and fieldstones, is the loftiest place in Indiana.

Some people apparently get a high from this kind of stuff. There are even Highpointer Clubs, groups of folks who want to climb to the tippy-top of every state. It's easy to do this in Indiana, where the climb is officially listed at 20 feet. It's tougher in Alaska, which is rated a ten on the toughness scale and requires a 24,500-foot climb.

Indiana is ranked the sixth easiest high point to climb in America. It would probably be considered the easiest if it weren't so hard to find and you didn't have to jump a fence to get to it. We'd give you the directions, but listen to my son. It's not worth it.

Okay, okay. Here they are: From Bethel go north to State Road 227 for just over a mile to Randolph County Line Road (Bethel Road). Go west 1 mile and turn south on Elliot Road, then about a quarter mile to an access road. Park and hike back a few hundred feet. You should see a sign. I'm telling you again, it's not worth the trouble, except then you can say you did it.

Alone at the top. Not for social climbers.

UNION PROBLEMS

Historians seldom refer to it and the details are a bit murky, but Boggstown seceded from the Union in 1861. Here's what we do know. Shelby County had voted for Stephen Douglas instead of Honest Abe in the election of 1861. Turns out that Boggstown had more than a few Southern sympathizers, which led to a local resolution stating that if the nation were to divide, Boggstown would attach itself to the Confederacy.

Some called this a big PR move by the area's accomplished debaters, and it is believed that putting Boggstown on the map, not removing it from the Union, was the big motivation. For when Fort Sumter was fired upon and Lincoln called for a Union army, Shelby County residents responded, raising two full troops. Boggstown didn't offer a peep in protest, despite its resolution that is—believe it or not—still on the books.

Nowadays Boggstown is known more for its cabaret than its tie to the Confederacy. For rip-roaring entertainment with songs you'll remember, call the Boggstown Inn and Cabaret on London Road (800–672–2656). If you don't remember all the songs, you'll not forget Queenie Thompson, now almost ninety years old, who plays the piano not just with her hands, but her feet as well. And then there's Vivian Cox, probably the only female rhythm and bones player in America. Take Interstate 74 to the London exit and stay on London Road until you get to the Boggstown Inn. If you miss the inn, you have also missed Boggstown and a great show.

They've Got Game

Bridgeport

The largest gaming vessel in the world is in landlocked Indiana. Don't believe it? Look it up in the *Guinness Book of World Records*. It's called *Caesars Indiana* and it has all the grandeur that was Rome. With a few more slot machines. This mighty riverboat is four stories high, 100 feet wide, and 450 feet long. That's how big you have to be to hold 2,400 slot machines, 140 gaming tables, and seven themed casino areas.

Ready for an exciting ride down the Ohio River? Don't bet on it. While the ship is seaworthy, neighboring states don't cotton to gambling, so ships stay close to shore and within a dice toss of Bridgeport, in Harrison County. Nevertheless, the riverboat is certified and manned by a full crew, including a ship's captain. They just don't go anywhere. Is that is a dream job or what?

There are actually ten riverboats in Indiana, but *Caesars* is the biggest. And most dramatic. Inside are magnificent Roman columns, gold-leaf molding, and the biggest chandelier in the world. One of the themed casinos depicts the burning of Rome. That's just to get you in the mood. For what, we don't know.

Take a chance on having a good time by calling (888) ROMAN–4–U. *Caesars* is geared to high rollers or low rollers. Bet a nickel at a time or throw in a $500 coin (two at a time, if you have the nerve). It's major Las Vegas. Name a game, you can play it. And they'd like you to play it, again and again.

Bridgeport is on the Ohio River in Harrison County, 13 miles west of Louisville on State Road 111.

On Track

Connersville

When Maurice Hensley retired from the U.S. Postal Service, he did what most people do. He took up a hobby. The eighty-something Mooresville resident has collected more than a hundred railroad lanterns and has driven his train more than 500 times—and never tires of operating it. "Railroadin' just gets in your blood," says Hensley. "You feel like you're accomplishing something when you're handling a trainload of passengers." Passengers?

Hensley doesn't operate toy trains. He is one of thirty-five engineers of the Whitewater Valley Railroad—the longest steam railroad in Indiana. The train he typically operates is a 1948 "Alco," an American Locomotive engine that pulls vintage open-window coaches and a woodside caboose. After eight days of training and working a couple of years as a brakeman, he finally got his chance to take the controls. After fifteen years, he has no plans to retire.

From May to October, Hensley drives to the WVR station in Connersville so he can shuttle sightseers down to Metamora and back, and he knows every rise and fall of those tracks. "I'm kinda getting on to it," he says. Familiarity of the run has not led to boredom, though. Hensley spots deer nearly every trip. And he's always striving to make the perfect run, a nice smooth trip absent of jerky stops.

Hensley's love for trains has led to a second career track. He doesn't get paid for operating the Whitewater Valley train, but the experience earned him a part-time job running a freight train from Connersville to New Castle. It looks like his training finally paid off.

The Whitewater Valley Railroad leaves Connersville at noon on weekends from May through October. There are also special weekday and holiday trips. For more information call (765) 825–2054 or visit www.whitewatervalleyrr.org. To get to Connersville take U.S. Highway 52 from Indy, then State Road 44 from Rushville.

Peep Show
Corydon

Ever ask yourself where you could get a good piece of glass in southern Indiana? I'm going to tell you where to find it. Although at first blush, you'll think you've come to the wrong place. If it's 392 Valley View Road in Corydon, it's the right place.

That's because the building where Kerry and Bart Zimmerman produce their world-renowned glass masterpieces in Corydon looks like an outdoor storage place for your lawn mower and old tires. It's a 60-by-40-foot steel corrugated building, and it sits just where it sat when their grandfather started the business in 1962.

The brothers, who took over for their father after his death in 1982, are self-admitted good ol' boys who pride themselves on not having e-mail, fax, or an answering machine. "We just finally got rid of our rotary phone," brags Kerry, who then casually mentions that his family's glass can be seen in the Museum of London and the Chicago Art Institute.

Despite an international reputation, the Zimmermans have never advertised. "It's all word of mouth," says Bart. "We don't want to be on the Internet. We would have to hire a third person."

Despite a ringing endorsement from glass collectors, the paper-weights, glass vegetables, doorstops, pencil holders, vases, and bowls average only about $40 each, much less than you would expect to pay for comparable glass items in a retail store. And, by the way, finding Zimmerman glass in a retail store is hard to do, since the brothers do not actively wholesale their items. If you want Zimmerman glass, ya gotta go to Corydon or call them on the phone. And I'm gonna give you that number. Ain't this book great?

You can also watch the brothers in action during regular business hours. Buses roll in—one day with filled with fourth graders and the next day with senior citizens. "The kids visit the old State Capitol in

Corydon, then they come see how glass used to be made the old-fashioned way. It's all part of Indiana history," says Kerry.

By the way, what they do is glass sculpting, a process that uses the pressure of steam trapped in the glass to expand the medium naturally. You'll see a lot of rolling and pounding and shaping, but not very much glass blowing, which is what most people expect. Sorry.

If you're in southern Indiana, it's worth the trip. Take Interstate 64 to State Road 135 to Corydon. Show the Zimmerman brothers your cell phone. They'd love to know what one looks like. They have a regular phone: (812) 738–2206. And they are generally open to the public Tuesday through Saturday from 9:00 A.M. until 4:00 P.M.

Police Power
Elizabeth

Craig Pumphrey of Elizabeth (Floyd County) is one police officer you don't want to tangle with. He's in the *Guinness Book of World Records* because he can take a frying pan in his bare (bear?) hands and roll it into a cylinder with a circumference of 9½ inches.

His brother Paul wouldn't be caught dead doing something so silly. He's in the same record book for blowing up a hot water bottle in 59.3 seconds. Their cousin, Scott, can tear thirteen decks of playing cards in half in thirty seconds. He's in the *Guinness Book of World Records*, too.

Craig started doing feats of strength as a kid, but later when he and his friends got involved in music, he realized that muscle demonstrations might give their band some needed publicity. Now their band, Lucent, plays all over the country. Their grunge heavy-rock music is punctuated by demonstrations, which also include concrete breaking, bar bending, and phone-book tearing.

The Pumphreys are always on the lookout for new feats of strength. In fact, skillet rolling and card tearing were both new categories that Craig and his colleagues suggested to *Guinness*. *Guinness* liked them both and incorporated them into their book.

Many have tried to break the boys' records, but as of press time, they remain the champs. "I think this has really intrigued people," claims Craig, who travels the world defending his title, "because we're not all that big. We're just everyday common people."

Yeah, right.

You can reach these hunks and find out about their band by calling Ivan at (812) 248–0797 or via their Web site: www.lucent rocks.com.

Setting records, brick by brick.

HOW TO FIND AN INDIANA CURIOSITY

Sorry to interrupt you here in Fortville, but this seemed like an opportune place to make a personal request.

Books like this are a bear to write. It would be so much easier if a few of you out there helped me find weird stuff for the next collection of offbeat people and places. I can't pay you anything, gas prices are through the roof, and I'm very, very difficult to work with. Have I got your interest?

Now that you have accepted my offer, how do you find an Indiana curiosity?

Many unusual things are visible along the back roads, but for the more obscure stuff, you can't simply knock on a door and say, "Hey, is there anything really weird going on in your house?"

Instead, wander into places where people congregate: barbershops, pubs, cafes, country stores. Explain to people that you're looking for fascinating oddities that dot the Hoosier landscape. The first response will often be: "This entire place is odd." Or, they'll point to some guy in a red baseball cap and say, "There's the oddest thing in town."

Next, give them a better idea of exactly what you're looking for. I often mention other offbeat finds to get people thinking—like the guy in Muncie with the collection of 6,000 fruit jars, or the square-dancing llamas of Kokomo.

So here's the bottom line. Keep your ears open. I learned about many of my favorite curiosities, like the sign man in Bedford, just from casual conversation. And keep your eyes open. That's how I found the rock church in Thorntown.

Come up with something really good that I can use for my next book, and I'll mention you in the introduction.

Now, let's get back to Fortville. How about that bespectacled, martini-drinking pink elephant on SR-67? Would you have considered him an Indiana curiosity? See, this isn't so tough, after all.

Good luck!

Church Lady

Fortville

Phyllis Baskerville of Fortville spends most of her days and nights in a church. But she's not praying; she's playing. Playing with toys, in fact. That's thousands and thousands of toys that this close to eighty-year-old woman has amassed over the past ten years. So many toys, in fact, that she purchased and moved into an abandoned Pentecostal church where she now lives and stores her collection.

Preserving past presents for the future.

The obsession with toy collecting began after her husband of thirty years took ill with Alzheimer's. The stress and frustration led her to a hobby that has created joy in her life and for all her visitors. Baskerville, who bills herself as the "Dolly Mama," secures her playthings at antiques shows, flea markets, and garage sales, but she is adamant that every toy be in perfect working order. "If it doesn't work, it doesn't go home with me," boasts Baskerville, whose first collectible was a doll named Jess.

After Jess has come a barrage of board games, lunch boxes, mechanical dolls, banks, thermoses, cookie tins, Disney memorabilia, promotional toys, posters, and children's books. They fill every nook and cranny of every room in the church. More than a few of her toys and dolls are truly priceless. And she knows which ones are. But Baskerville will not sell any of her toys. No exceptions. No way. Don't even ask. Yet she knows that she needs to find someone, someday, to take over her collection. "All this preserves the past," says Baskerville, "and I need someone who understands that to watch over my toys."

If you want to see them, check into the Ivy House right there in Fortville. Overnight guests get a special invitation to see Baskerville and her collection. Generally, her home is not open to the public, but give her a call and ask (317–485–5339). Who knows? You'll love Baskerville. She's a doll.

Training Grounds

Fortville

John Kitterman has a one-track mind. He is one of the premier model train layout creators in the country. And he does it all in his 3,500-square-foot workshop in Fortville, Indiana. Santa would be envious.

Kitterman's passion began with a Lionel train, a gift from his dad in 1957. That train that still chugs along today on his mega-layouts. John creates designs for people like Neil Young, whose layout is 10,000 square feet and features actual remnants of the redwood trees that surround the musician's house in California. Another client, talk show legend Tom Snyder, calls Kitterman at all hours, asking for advice.

But Kitterman doesn't just toot for the stars. He also creates train prototypes that have been adapted by Lionel for the average hobbyist and might well be in your basement right now. John also realized there was a need for easy-to-assemble track layout systems that could be broken down quickly when not in use. Yes, that could be in your basement, too. Or tucked neatly in the closet.

There was a hiatus between that first Lionel train and the passion that was later fueled, but sometimes you have to feel good about being an adult before you go full steam ahead back into your childhood.

Kitterman is a trainaholic. "I'm here first thing in the morning. I can't wait to get up and see what comes from my tools and out of my head." Recently, his head came up with a 200-square-foot layout designed for a mall in Annapolis, Maryland. The layout will serve as a magnet for kids—dragging their parents—to come and see. Truth is, many parents will have to drag the kids, John says, as the passion for model trains is grinding to a halt.

Next time you're in Fortville, first visit the pink elephant, then go to Dolly Mama's Toy Museum. Last stop: Kittworks. Ya gotta call first (317–485–5563). John is not always running on schedule.

Trunk Space
Fortville

Elephants may never forget, but there are some elephants that can't be forgotten. Like the one on State Road 67 just outside of Fortville. The pink pachyderm was purchased almost thirty years ago by Paul Dyer, who first rented the goliath for $200 a month. Dyer saw the elephant as a good promotional tool for the front of his package store. "Everybody loved the big guy," says Dyer, "so I bought him for $6,600. And it was worth every penny."

The elephant sits on a trailer so it can be moved when necessary or dragged in a parade. "Our biggest problem was people ramming into it," says Dyer. Apparently all the customers at the liquor store are not sober. Go figure.

The elephant is still there today, but he has had a few facelifts and paint jobs. His glasses were stolen once, and the martini glass held by his trunk could use a new olive. The new owner, Don Hunt, wouldn't part with the elephant for the world. "That's part of who we are. When you start seeing a pink elephant, it's time to stop at Wagon Wheel Liquor."

If you're in Fortville, ask about Paul Dyer's Calliope Museum, one of the few in the country. Dyer makes 'em, fixes 'em, and displays 'em. Lots going on in Fortville. It's worth a stop. Call Dyer first at (317) 485–5524.

The town trunk, standing outside of Wagon Wheel Liquors.

No Loafers Permitted

Friendship

There are no loafers at Robin Dyer's business in Friendship. But there are lots of moccasins—maybe the best-made moccasins in the world.

The company was started in the 1920s by Dyer's late father-in-law, Walter Dyer, who learned the trade as an apprentice and later taught the craft to Carl, Robin's late husband. Walter Dyer's work was so well thought of that in 1933 he crafted a pair of moccasins worn by Charles Lindbergh on his historic flight.

The company's reputation for quality workmanship has never waned. Dyer's has made moccasins for Rupert Murdoch, Johnny Depp, and Billy Golden of the Oakridge Boys, as well as Lars Lindbergh, the aviator's great-grandson. Dyer's moccasins are revered by hunters and hikers, but they are also purchased by people who just like to wear them around the house, at the mall, or when they're in their jammies.

The cowhide for the moccasins comes from Switzerland and is then tanned in England. Swiss hides are superior because dairy herds are government protected from slaughter until they can no longer give milk. Dyer's also makes moccasins from native buffalo and lines the shoe with elk fur.

Robin Dyer begins the process by cutting the basic outline of the shoe, then her small staff of artisans craft the final product. Most shoes require three to five hours to complete and cost between $150 and $400, depending on which of eight styles you choose.

By the way, don't look for Dyer's Moccasins in shoe stores. You can buy them directly from Dyer's small showroom in Friendship or by mail order. And if you'd like to see Dyer's craftsmen—and women—making moccasins, call in advance (812–667–5442) and you might be lucky enough to see just how hard it is to make soft shoes. "Hours vary," warns Robin Dyer, "by when I'm in the mood and how much work we have to do."

Dyer's is located at 5961 State Road 62 in Friendship. Or put your tired feet up and see the moccasins from the comfort of your home via www.carldyers.com.

Muzzle Up
Friendship

To the men and women of the world who love their muzzle loading rifles, it's a perfect friendship. That's because Friendship is the home of the National Muzzle Loading Rifle Association, an organization started in the 1930s that seeks to keep the history of muzzle loading rifles alive through research and competitions.

Muzzle loading rifles, which require a reload after each shot, were used from the founding of this country through the Civil War. According to Terry Trowbridge, executive vice president, the group has more than 20,000 members, many of whom find their way to Friendship twice a year for national contests in the spring and fall.

The pistols and rifles are authentic remakes of the originals (the originals would be much too costly), and the black powder used is identical to the original. While some contestants dress the part, shooting the part is what the competitions are really about. According to Trowbridge, accomplished shooters who load and discharge from a standing position can rival today's modern shooter, who depends on scopes and eyepieces. Shooters stand between 25 and 500 yards away from paper targets as well as silhouettes of men and animals. There is no competition for speed of reloading, which would jeopardize the safety of the participants.

The competitions are twice yearly, the second Saturdays of June and September. For more information call (812) 667–5131 or take a look at www.nmlra.org. Friendship is on State Road 62, just east of State Road 129, southeast of Versailles.

SUGAR HABIT

Now this is sweet. Phil Miller of Greenfield is a sucrologist—a grown man who collects sugar packets. And he's not alone, although we couldn't find one other person in Indiana who does this. But Miller knows that the art of sugar-packet collecting is healthy in England and France, where annual meetings draw hundreds of people. Of course they also eat calf's brains.

Miller stole (how else can you get one?) his first sugar packet some thirteen years ago in Ohio. Intrigued by a series of packets printed with images of the U.S. presidents, he was immediately on a sugar high. Now, 7,000 packets later, he won't claim he has the most packets in the world, just the most in Indiana. The person with the second most has about seventy-five.

Miller gets his packets from restaurants, friends, and from visitors to his Web site who want to feed his habit. Sugar packets are fun to collect, but they're not in the same ballpark as stamps and baseball cards. "There are no Honus Wagners in sugar packets," says Miller.

By the way, Miller is diabetic. I'm not making that up.

Want more info? Go to the sugar collector's Web site: members.iquest.net/~phillip. Miller doesn't want us to give out his number because he's afraid he'll be deluged with calls. Besides, if you want to start your own collection, you know what to do. Just don't get caught.

Pack Rat
Greensburg

Some people collect mousetraps, some collect sugar packets, others collect business cards, but John Pratt of Greensburg collects collections.

He was hooked at age three on baseball cards, then addicted to beer . . . cans (in middle school). At age twenty-two, he fell in love with a *Hogan's Heroes* lunch box. Soon he had 150 lunch boxes. But he had no keychains, no flags, no *TV Guide* covers. It was downright embarrassing. So since the early 1970s, Pratt has collected everything. Which means he throws away nothing. The trash collectors love him.

John Pratt is Goodwill's biggest competitor.

Here's what Pratt collects: scripts, flags, fossils, artifacts, keychains, globes, beer cans, games, props, stubs, lunch boxes, newspapers, magazines, records, phone books, yearbooks, masks, books, *TV Guides*, dime novels, photos, comic books, basketballs, animation cels, index cards, View-Masters, old cameras, license plates, FBI wanted posters, Big Little Books, rosaries, prayer cards, bibles, buckeyes, tin signs, coffee mugs, old scrapbooks, patriotic stuff, tennis racquets, pins, Burger Chef advertising, All-American Girls, Professional Baseball League memorabilia, movie banners, movie snack boxes, baseball bats, postcards, float pens, matchbooks, Taylor Hotel items, TV books, Hoosier-author books, costume jewelry, sleds, bikes, plastic cups, bumper stickers, sports cards, Chinese fortunes, coloring books, programs, cardboard cutouts, old coins, buttons, collector plates, marbles, hats, seashells, videos, 8 and 16 mm films, coupons, toys, and baseballs. Whew!

Pratt moved back to his native Greensburg from Franklin in 1999. His massive collection needed a home so Pratt renovated a hundred-year-old barn. The last Monday of each month, he invites the public into the barn to wander through the displays. You should stop by. If you can't make it on the last Monday, just call him at his bookstore (Pratt Books and Other Fun Stuff at 225 North Broadway) and he might give you a tour. Here's the number: (812) 662–7896. Don't call collect.

The Wright Stuff

Hagerstown

The birth home of aviator Wilbur Wright has had more ups and downs than he and his brother had takeoffs and landings. The aviation pioneer was born just outside of Millville in Henry County. The house suffered two fires, one in 1884 and another in the 1940s. In 1955 the state of Indiana tore it down after recurrent vandalism had taken its toll. Then in 1973 the house was reconstructed. Why? Who knows? Hey, this is the government.

The Wilbur Wright home. For awhile, its future was up in the air.

The state still was not happy with tourist response to the historic site, blaming attendance on its very rural location. But that's where the guy was born. Some thought the place would fly if they moved the house up to Summit Lake, some 6 miles away. Locals were unhappy with this idea and convinced the state to give them three years to get the tourist attraction off the ground, and so the state of Indiana handed over the deed in 1995 to a group known affectionately as the "Birthplace Groupies."

Apparently, the state made the Wright decision. The Wilbur Wright Birth Home and Museum is finally taking off. Visitors can begin with the welcome center, then proceed to the birth home, a two-story house that has been reconstructed and furnished in a style reminiscent of America after the Civil War. Then it's on to the museum, where a replica of the Wright Flyer has been constructed, true to size and exact in all the details. Inside, a functioning wind tunnel shows the dynamics of flight. There is even a replica of the bicycle shop that the brothers ran in Ohio. Also on the drawing board is a timeline with sketches showing events that shaped the lives of the brothers.

Outside the museum is a jet fighter. No one really knows why. Probably a government idea again. By the way, some purists complain that the house is kind of a fraud because it is pretty much just a reconstruction. We don't think that's wrong. But it's not all Wright, either.

The museum, at 1525 North County Road 750 East, in Hagerstown, is open March 15 through November 15 from 10:00 A.M. to 5:00 P.M., Tuesday through Saturday. In the winter you can call for an appointment: (765) 332–2495.

Delivering Hope

Hope

Albert Hitchcock was Indiana's first rural mail carrier and the man who invented the mail buggy on display in the Indiana Rural Letter Carriers Museum. The museum is in Hope because, in 1896, Indiana's first successful Rural Free Delivery began here—the second RFD in the country. And that accomplishment is celebrated in Hope's storefront mail museum. In addition to Hitchcock's buggy, such items as early mailboxes, old-fashioned sorting cases, and hot-water foot warmers are on display. "The carriers would use them to keep their feet warm while they drove their buggies," says Damon Jones, museum curator and retired rural carrier. "When the water got cold, they'd refill them with hot water at a farmer's house."

The museum is located on the town square in a small building where the public can visit, free of charge, any time they'd like. That's because the museum's entire collection can be viewed through the large display window, and it's illuminated twenty-four hours a day. They may as well proclaim, "See Indiana's only 24/7/365 museum!" With slogans like that, those tourists are signed, sealed, and delivered.

To find Hope—something we are all looking for—take I–74 south from Indy to State Road 9, then 9 south to Hope.

SHOE BUSINESS

His grave marker is in the shape of an anvil, testimony to a man named by the 1892 Chicago World's Fair as the World's Greatest Horseshoer. That's where William Jennings Wedekind displayed 350 horseshoes, 250 of which represented the newest and most improved methods of making horseshoes and shoeing the horse. His awards during the exposition were for workmanship, quantity of items displayed, the tools, and the tightness of his tongs. We don't know what the last one means, but no one was tighter. He also invented rubber horseshoes, which created a lot of talk among the horses.

Wedekind is also credited with developing improved swedges for racehorses. We don't know what that means either. But we do know that his technique was groundbreaking because the shoes helped balance the horse. There is nothing worse than an unbalanced horse.

Wedekind was offered $100,000 for his collection. He turned it down, and now you can see the collection at both the Wayne County Historical Museum in Richmond and the Nettle Creek Valley Museum, at 96 East Main Street (765–489–4005), right in the heart of Hagerstown. While inside the latter, check out the incredible murals painted by Charles Newcomb at the turn of the twentieth century, which entirely surround the museum. Here, too, you'll see the first cruise control device, invented by Hagerstown's own Ralph Tettor in

William Wedekind's kids had big shoes to fill.

1950. To visit Wedekind's anvil grave, ride over to the West Lawn Cemetery, just down the block. In fact, there are several offbeat gravestones in this tiny graveyard, including a rocket ship. Have fun!

Timing Is Everything
Jeffersonville

There is no excuse for being late in Jeffersonville. You can see the time day or night from more than 2½ miles away, and the clock is accurate to within fifteen seconds a month. Okay, it's not the biggest clock in the world, but it's the second biggest. On the face of it, that's plenty big enough. Located atop the Colgate-Palmolive plant in Jeffersonville, this huge timepiece is 40 feet in diameter. The hour hand alone weighs 500 pounds and is 16 feet long. The minute hand is 600 pounds. A tiny motor, not much bigger than a sewing machine, drives the clock. At night, the clock is aglow with neon lights, so parents in Jeffersonville don't even bother to say "Do you know what time it is?" when the kids are late.

Jeffersonville is across the river from Louisville on State Road 62. If you can't find the Colgate clock, you are in the wrong city.

The ticking is bad enough. But that alarm!

Steamy Museum

Jeffersonville

It may be the coolest museum in southern Indiana. And the hottest. The Howard Steamboat Museum in Jeffersonville is an eyeful before you even step inside. The stately Victorian architecture with its leaded glass windows is a wonderful introduction to the world of the 1890s, when it was built by Edmonds J. Howard, son of the world's great steamboat magnate, James Howard, founder of Howard Ship Yards.

The twenty-two-room mansion cost nearly $100,000 to build in 1890 and is replete with original furnishings, intricate carvings, exquisite chandeliers, arches, and a grand staircase. Because master artisans at the turn of the twentieth century crafted the decor, visitors do feel they've stepped back into history.

While there are no full-size steamboats on the premises, models, photographs, paintings, and artifacts abound. Some thirty-eight steamboat models are displayed, including a large collection of hulls (known as half-breadths), particularly important because the Howards distinguished themselves in this aspect of shipbuilding.

If you do want to see a working steamboat from this era—there are only seven in existence—you need to cross the river and visit the *Belle of Louisville*, not a Howard steamer, but similar in style. Sadly, none of the 3,000 ships built by the Howard family remain in working order.

Tours take a full hour and have the personal touch. Interested? Then full steam ahead to 1101 East Market Street in Jeffersonville. For details call Yvonne Knight at (812) 283–3728.

Bullish on Books
Jeffersonville

The Carnegie Library in Jeffersonville may be the most unusual "library" in the country.

Suppose you want to borrow a copy of *Common Sense* by Thomas Paine. No problem, plus:

1. No library card needed
2. No late fees
3. No annoying bun-haired librarian

Oh yeah. That edition of *Common Sense* is the original.

Okay, you can't *borrow* the book—but Brian Bex, the founder of a unique public educational foundation known as the Remnant Trust, is committed to getting great works of literature and science into the hands of the average person. And he does it by loaning his treasures to educational entities that will appropriately display the works so people like *you* can actually pick them up and thumb through them. They do ask that you wash your thumb first.

Bex was first motivated to do this when his mother (a Phi Beta Kappa in math and physics from the University of Chicago back in the 1930s) made the point one day that "all professors were really interested in was old books." That motivated Bex, and now his son, Kris, to find a way to make those books more accessible and more exciting to students and the public.

"Great ideas belong to everybody," says Bex.

With the help of some well-heeled bibliophiles who shared Bex's passion, the group sought original and first edition copies of such classics as the Emancipation Proclamation, *The Republic* by Plato, *On Liberty* by John Stuart Mill, and *The Federalist Papers* and *Das Kapital* by Karl Marx. There are works by Rousseau, Sir Isaac Newton, and a first edition of the Gettysburg Address. There are now hundreds of documents in the collection.

Bex won't talk about the monetary worth of his collection. He wants people to know that the value is not in cash, but in the history that his documents represent. He does admit that in more than a few cases, he found his gems at a relative bargain. In some cases he found the manuscripts at old book sales or buried in private collections. Even at junk sales. "Nobody even knew they were there," claims Bex, who is constantly searching to enhance the Wisdom of the Ages Athenaeum.

So if you have an original *Huck Finn* or a first edition of *Walden*, and they've just been collecting dust on your bookshelf, contact Brian or Kris (765–489–5566). They're very busy, but trust me, they'll take your call.

Back in the Saddle Again

Madison

When Joe Schroeder closed up his family's little factory in Madison in January 1972, he left behind a hundred-year-old history in saddletree making. A saddletree is the inner structure of a saddle, the internal wooden works supporting the saddle that help the saddle sit on the horse, which in turn helps you sit on the horse. There are saddletree makers today, of course, but the hand methods used by two generations of the Schroeder family are gone forever.

Well, almost gone. The folks at Historic Madison Incorporated were dedicated to restoring the one-of-a-kind Schroeder factory, which sat suspended in time for twenty-five years. In the spring of 2002, the Ben Schroeder Saddletree Factory reopened as an industrial museum, a place where people can walk into an operable, old-time woodworking shop and learn how saddletrees were made in an era before cars replaced the horse—a time when Schroeder saddletrees were being shipped to all fifty states and around the world. Tours and demonstrations in the factory and exhibits in the family home will tell the story of Ben Schroeder, his family, and his business.

Joe Schroeder left behind all of his family's equipment (hand tools, belt-powered woodworking machines, steam engines, a sawmill, a blacksmith shop, patterns) used to make the wooden frames of saddles. Visitors also can discover other Schroeder products like clothespins, gloves, stirrups, and even lawn furniture.

Back in the saddle again—a lost art rediscovered.

Visitors see exactly how the saddletree was made, but no instruction manuals were left. "We are reverse-engineering the process," says John Staicer, a local history buff. "We study the tool marks in the finished product and match them up with the machines and hand tools in the factory to figure out how the Schroeders made each of the five or so parts of the saddletree. Perhaps along the way we'll learn some of the family's secrets and preserve a craft tradition that helped settle our country."

To visit the Saddletree Factory Museum, take U.S. Highway 421 to Milton Street, and head a half block west to number 106, in downtown Madison's National Register Historic District. For more information call (812) 265–2967.

Barber in Training

McCordsville

Gary Wiley has a great caboose. That's about the raunchiest thing you'll read in this book.

It's true. Wiley, who had been a barber in Indianapolis for twenty years, had always dreamed of having a shop inside a train car. The wish actually first surfaced in barber school in the 1960s, but his instructors were unsympathetic to his fantasy, considering he didn't even have his license yet.

Then in 1985 Wiley had a rare opportunity to buy a caboose for a song (imagine any train song in the background to make this sentence funny). In fact, he bought two cabooses. One for himself and one to sell—to pay for the one he bought for himself. Then he took the 37-foot caboose and literally attached it to his traditional shop on State Road 67 in McCordsville. It fit. Whew! How lucky was that?

Ever since, Wiley's shop has been a virtual magnet for people looking for a hair-lowering experience. Half his customers are regulars, but many tourists passing by are drawn to the caboose and stop in with the kids for a little tour. Then those same children want to come back for a haircut. That's why Gary has happy young customers from Fort Wayne, Lafayette, and Vincennes. He also has unhappy parents from Fort Wayne, Lafayette, and Vincennes.

Enter the McCordsville Barber Shop and you're in the waiting room. Then climb the stairs to the caboose. Kids can sit where the conductor

"That will be $10." Gary Wiley's parting words.

would have sat, or they can play with one of several sets of model loco-motives. There are train DVDs to watch and a candy machine full of free bubblegum. (So don't stick your hand under the barber chair.)

There are other touches of nostalgia. Haircuts, for example, are only ten bucks; however Wiley requires payment *before* he begins cutting. He does not take appointments. Oh, and no credit cards.

If you don't like those arrangements, you can get a $22 haircut a few miles away in Indy. To get to Gary just take State Road 67 north to McCordsville from Indy. You can't miss it. Okay, maybe by a hair.

Making the Rounds

McCordsville

The one-hundred-year-old Round Barn Inn Bed and Breakfast in McCordsville, Indiana, is sometimes known as the Ice House. Not because of faulty heating—but because the owners are Dean and Dana Ice. Everything else about the 7,000 square feet of roundness is warm and fuzzy.

There are fewer than one hundred round barns left in Indiana. This one is unique because it is not being used as a working barn—or a the-ater or a restaurant, as a few are. It's a bed-and-breakfast. And it's also the home of the Ices. Nothing else like it in Indiana. Fact is, I can't find a place like this anywhere. And I know how to Google.

While so many of these structures have fallen into disrepair, this one is candy to the eye. Ironically, just 2 miles north of this barn is the biggest circular barn in Indiana, the Kingen Barn. You can visit that, too, but it's simply run-of-the-mill (if you'll excuse the expression) compared to this one. For example, you can't stay overnight at the larger one—unless you want to sleep with pigs.

The Ices bought the barn in 1996 from a man who had already made the barn into his living quarters. That inspired the Ices to go a step further and open it to the public. With some major internal renovation, the Ices created four upstairs bedrooms and a huge recreational downstairs, now decorated with antiques and period pieces collected from all over the country.

The third floor is the loft area. A visit up there, which everyone is treated to, is quite stunning. The roof is a virtual web of hundreds and hundreds of pieces of wood, each magically bent to create a lattice-work supporting the domed roof.

The barn attracts bed-and-breakfast fans from all over, especially those who lived on a farm as kids. Visitors are only thirty minutes from Indy, so they can enjoy the big city as well as do some antiquing right in McCordsville. Easy to find. Take State Road 67 north of Indy to Mt Comfort Road. Look for the signs. For more info call (317) 335–7023 or visit www.roundbarn-inn.com.

Dana cooks a great country breakfast for her guests. What better way to start the day than a well-rounded meal?

The Round Barn Inn. Great rooms, great food. And they only had to cut a few corners.

BURNSIDE'S SIDEBURNS

This is not a hair-raising story; it's a hair-lowering story. Major General Ambrose Burnside was not a particularly great general. Word is, he wasn't a particularly great tailor either, but he didn't stay long in that profession in the tiny town of Liberty just prior to the Civil War.

When the Civil War broke out, Burnside accepted a command and found moderate success as a military leader, but he seemed dogged by insecurities. When he was offered even higher commands—once by President Lincoln himself—he declined. Ultimately, he did take over the Army of the Potomac.

We'll leave the particulars of his military successes for historians to debate, but some of Burnside's mishaps are legendary. He once approved a plan to place explosives 500 feet below a Confederate stronghold. The huge explosion that followed effectively took out most of the Confederates. But story has it that Burnside's men charged into the giant crater and then couldn't get out, finding themselves at the mercy of the remaining Southern troops.

But here's the important part. Major General Ambrose Burnside let the sides of his hair (known then as his "whiskers") grow down and over the front of his ears. While he was certainly not the first ever to do this, his celebrity status resulted in what most etymologists agree was the beginning of the term "sideburns," a simple reversal of his two-syllable name. And that's why we remember the general today. And very few, except those in Liberty, where there is a plaque on the courthouse lawn in his honor, even remember that.

By the way, this little piece is called a sidebar. The general's hair had nothing to do with it.

Hoop-De-Do

Milan

It may be the greatest Indiana sports story of all time. So it deserves its own museum, right? Of course. That's a slam dunk.

Presently, the Milan Museum, which commemorates the 1954 Milan High School state basketball championship, is inside an antiques store owned by super-fan Roselyn McKittrick. But there are plans to move the collection to a new location. Local benefactors have donated a number of town buildings to Milan 54 Inc., a group of movers and dribblers who want to preserve the story of this hallowed team. One relocation possibility: the historic Krick Hardware Store.

Ever since that celebrated game, Roselyn has been the premier collector of artifacts from that memorable season. Fans from all over the country have visited her antiques store, peering at original varsity jackets, a pair of trunks, video segments, posters, tapes, basketballs, newspaper clippings, and photos. "These same fans," says Roselyn, "have also donated 1954 news articles, ticket stubs, and other memorabilia, along with their stories, which we have recorded."

Wrinkled shorts of old, getting full press coverage.

Most impressive is the re-creation of the twelve team members' individual lockers, each chock-full of authentic memorabilia. Atop the lockers you can read the final score: Milan 32, Muncie 30.

As interest in that unforgettable game grew, fueled in part by books and the Hollywood movie *Hoosiers*, McKittrick found herself with more and more great stuff and less and less space. That's why there's a full court press to find a new home for this gem of a museum.

You can visit Roselyn McKittrick's antiques store, Milan Station Antiques & Collectibles, now at 113 West Carr Street in Milan. The museum is right inside, at least for now, but call ahead (812–654–2772). You may have to walk a few blocks if it finds a new home. No penalty for traveling.

Courtly Museum
New Castle

The only freestanding high school basketball museum in the country is in Indiana. How weird is that? Not the "Indiana" part—the "only" part. You'd think that some other state would have wanted to immortalize their men and women of the hardwood. Nope. Just us.

That's why Roger Dickinson, who oversees the Indiana Basketball Hall of Fame, thinks "it's the greatest museum in the state." He used to say, "It's the greatest high school basketball museum in the *country*," but people aren't stupid.

Although it's been around since 1989, a surprising number of Hoosiers, even diehard basketball fans, have never dribbled their way to New Castle to see the place. You really need to go more than once to see it all. That's right, double dribbling.

The idea for the museum originated with the legendary Tom Carnegie and Ray Johnson, whose initial inclinations were to have the

Hall of Fame in downtown Indy. When that idea failed, other cities made proposals and New Castle ultimately was awarded the plum.

When the building was completed in 1990, Vice President Dan Quayle presided at the opening ceremonies, where he ran smack-dab into his old basketball coach, Bob Straight, who had cut him from the Huntington squad back in the 1960s. Quipped Straight in response to Quayle's allegation that the coach ruined his NBA chances, "If I had known you were going to be vice president, I'd have kept you on the team." You can interpret that remark any way you want.

Memorabilia was collected throughout the 1980s, spearheaded by *Hoosier Hysteria* author Herb Schwomeyer, with the help of scores of people dedicated to the search. A coordinator was appointed from each of the ninety-two counties to direct the project, ensuring the museum would represent all of Indiana. Volunteers and board members gave speeches, visited high schools, and sought out garage sales and antiques shows looking for pieces of basketball history. Man, did they find some neat stuff.

You can see one of the first electronic scoreboards, circa 1928. Peer through the glass at a 1910 basketball, with laces so thick you wonder how they bounced it. They didn't. There was no dribbling in the original game.

The museum is filled with photos of great players of yesteryear, like 1914 Wingate star Homer Stonebreaker, a 6-foot-4-inch equivalent of Shaq who in those years towered over everybody. His team was the first to score one hundred points in a game.

The museum is interactive, providing young people with not only a fun experience, but an educational one. You can listen to Coach John Wooden giving a short speech about success; attempt—in five seconds—to make a shot to win the state championship; or humiliate yourself trying to block a jump shot by Oscar Robertson. Everything is simulated, but everything is super.

The museum has two levels. You walk in on the upper level, over-looking the first floor, not unlike many old gymnasiums. There's a ramp to the bottom floor, a feature reminiscent of Hinkle Fieldhouse at Butler University that hosted the state championships for years.

The outside bricks—each signifying a donation—create a huge fac-simile of a basketball, but within the sphere is the outline of the state of Indiana. Many of the bricks represent donations from people who wanted to commemorate their former high schools, some of which no longer exist.

New Castle is only about an hour from Indianapolis. Take I–70 east from Indy, then State Road 3 north. If someone doesn't know where it is, you must be in Kentucky. The Indiana Basketball Hall of Fame is located at 408 Trojan Lane (765–529–1891; www.hoopshall.com).

Go see it: No penalty for traveling. And it's a slam dunk.

Game Boy
New Castle

He's hooked, he's hooked—his brain is cooked.

Tom Duncan has been called the Ty Cobb of video games, but that's giving too much credit to Cobb. Duncan holds even more records than the Georgia Peach. Duncan earned his reputation by setting a mark that will be "envied and challenged by all players to come," according to the Web site www.twingalaxies.com. According to the site, Duncan owns 1,082 video game records. As you read this, the number is likely rising.

The humble gamer's perseverance is the stuff of legend. He blew past the former video game world-record holder (Matt Leto, with 742) and kept on playing. He once played a game for twenty-one hours straight to set a new high score (*Missile Command* on GameBoy).

Another time, he stayed up all night studying a newly released game

(*Zelda*). "When I looked out the window, the sun was coming up," he laughs. "And I had to go to work that day." Don't worry, he's not a doctor. Or a pilot.

Working twelve-hour shifts and driving an hour each way to his factory job would seem like it would limit his playing time. But not surprisingly, the master of gaming systems has a system for gaming. "I set speed records during the week when I get home after work, and I go for the marathon records on my days off."

The quest to be the best hasn't come without sacrifice. Duncan once strained his trigger finger during a marathon session and had to quit. (He had already scored seventy-eight million!) "My finger just quit working," he says. "If I hadn't played another game for five hours before playing that game, I would've scored a hundred million."

Of course he already had the world record in the bag. But like a true champion, he proved that the person he really needed to beat was himself. Game on!

Safe and Sound
New Palestine

Here's a safe bet. Billy Jay Espich may be the only person in Indiana who collects and restores old safes. With a background in sign making and refurbishing race cars, Espich found the right combination when he sandblasted and repainted his first safe about twenty years ago. Now the Hancock County resident has an entire studio filled with safes and vaults, many rescued from old garages or landfills.

His safes usually are more than a hundred years old and weigh as much as two or three tons. "The old ones are out there," says Espich, "because it's really hard to throw one away." For him, the technique involves finding the old intricate designs that lie beneath the surface and creating a piece of art that looks the way it did a century before, when safes were not only functional but somewhat of a status symbol.

Typically, Espich buys an old safe for a couple hundred bucks, though often a person is just happy to get rid of the thing. Solid research is required to see what the vault looked like years earlier. Espich must be especially careful to preserve the original design and intent of the safe maker. "They don't make safes the way they used to," says Espich, who marvels at the detailed designs frequently found inside the safes as well, made for when they were displayed open during the day.

Some safes come to him locked. So how does he get into a 150-year-old safe without the combination? "I have someone who is very good at that," smirks Espich, "and that's all I'll say." Need a safe restored or cracked? Call him at (317) 861–6017.

Better safe than . . . well, just a better safe.

Turtle Scoop
New Palestine

Marty La Prees is not a con artist, but her life is a shell game. And it has been for the past twenty years, ever since one of her Kentucky relatives gave her a couple of wild turtles as a gift. This gift rekindled her child-hood interest in the leathery reptiles, but she soon realized her new pets would have been better off left in their original environment.

Now, two decades later, Marty is considered the Turtle Lady of New Palestine, although Department of Natural Resources officials say she may be the premier turtle rehabilitator and sanctuary in the entire Hoosier State, what with eighty or so of her hard-backed buddies taking up resi-dence behind her house.

Marty and her old pals, in New Pal.

Her backyard has several small ponds, a variety of plants and grasses, and a few natural and woman-made enclosures, all to simulate the native habitat for the variety of species that spend their days doing whatever turtles and tortoises do, which as far as I could tell when I went there, is pretty much nothing. Take your handy pocket turtle guide and you'll identify box turtles, painted turtles, sliders, and snappers, to mention just a few. Marty has one turtle that came all the way from Russia, which, as you can imagine, must have taken an awfully long time.

Marty is convinced that while her charges are slow moving, they are not without distinct personalities. Several respond to the sound of her voice, popping their heads above the water when they hear her whistle or call. If I hadn't seen it, I wouldn't have believed it.

Many of the turtles are brought to Marty after a brief encounter with an SUV on a county road. A couple spent a few unpleasant seconds under a lawn mower; still others were relinquished by owners who realized they didn't have a clue how to care for a turtle.

With the help of a local vet, Marty can repair shells, clear up ear infections, do tube feedings, and administer medications. Marty says you know a turtle is sick when it becomes lethargic. (I thought that's how you knew it was a turtle.)

Since Marty began her work, only a few turtles have run away. I felt dumb just writing that sentence.

Check out Indiana Turtle Care at www.pogospals.com. You can visit Marty's turtles, but you'll have to contact her first. Use her e-mail address: zooperior@insightbb.com. You know how long snail-mail takes.

TWO ROOMS, NO BATH

Things are looking up at Micah Corsiatto's house in Richmond. In fact if you don't look up, you can't even see the house. Corsiatto built a two-level, 110-square-foot tree house, one of the biggest you'll ever see. It's 25 feet off the ground. Real estate in Richmond is high, but this is ridiculous. Corsiatto made the local paper and several national papers; there was even a national TV story about the house.

Corsiatto never thought of himself as much of a carpenter, but he once built a sandbox. Why not go for the stars? Influenced by a scene in the movie *Stand by Me* and convinced he had the perfect tree in his backyard, Corsiatto set to work. Six weeks later, his tree palace with four real windows, two ladders, and a couple of bunk beds was finished. But it was too small, so Corsiatto, to the delight of his neighbors, put on a second story. His two kids loved it, too. "Another story, Daddy, PLEASE. One more story." You can see the tree house from your car. Take Thirteenth Street in Richmond to 1305 Wernle Road and look up.

Go out on a limb—build a tree house suite.

Please Harp on It

Rising Sun

When folks find out that William Rees is a luthier, some people look up to him. Others just look it up. A *luthier* is any person who builds a stringed instrument. Ain't learnin' fun?

William and his wife, Pamela, moved from Yosemite National Park in California to Rising Sun in 1999—possibly the first couple in American history to make that move. They have no regrets. Rees Harps remain the best-selling custom lever harps in the world.

Rees Harps are specially made for the harpist, unique in the industry. Artists choose the wood, ornamentation, and type of levers. A harp takes about two months, and you can pay as much as $6,000—and that's without personal ornamentation. But now, thanks to an innovative technique honed by William, you can also buy a harpsicle for $295. That's right, a harpsicle. These harps come in different colors that remind you of candy flavors. "And they really sound good," says Pamela, who claims that cheap harps traditionally have been pretty poor musical instruments. "We've sold these all over the world, to professionals and beginners."

Not sure what you want? Enter their quaint two-story building in Rising Sun, and spend time in the harp gallery, replete with harps, gifts, and Irish music. In two other rooms, tourists can see the harp-making process, including the crafting and stringing of the instrument by Rees's seven artisans.

Rising Sun is on State Road 56, about as far east as you can go in Indiana and not be in Kentucky. Rees Instruments also makes psalteries. Look, I told you what a luthier is. You need to look this one up yourself. But you can call (812) 438–3032, or check out the 150-page Web site, www.Reesharps.com.

SPEED DEMON

Rising Sun's J. W. Whitlock was an Indiana man quite proud of his *Hoosier Boy*. The doting father admired his boy's speed, good looks, and sleek design, and bragged about how easily his boy sped across the Ohio River. Whitlock brought *Hoosier Boy* into this world, but it was, of course, not his son. It was his world-class speedboat.

When Whitlock began tinkering with boats in 1907, top speeds hovered around 12 mph—bicycles could outrace them. Less than twenty years later, Whitlock christened crafts that pushed the envelope up to 60 mph and helped earn Rising Sun the moniker of "home of the fastest boats in the world."

In 1909 *Hoosier Boy* won every hydroplane race from Peoria to Buffalo. In the following years, Whitlock built a series of *Hoosier Boys* and continued his winning ways on America's rivers. His most famous race, however, took place on the familiar Ohio on October 9, 1924, when he made a record round-trip run from Cincinnati to Louisville. Dodging boat-sinking flotsam and rolling waves from a dozen barges, Whitlock clocked 267 miles in 267 minutes, 49 seconds, an average speed of just under 60 mph. While today's unlimited hydroplanes can go more than twice that speed, this record may never be broken, as the Markland Dam separates the two towns, preventing boats from making a high-speed, nonstop run.

Even though no one is allowed to drive *Hoosier Boy* or *Hoosier Girl* (also on display), visitors are welcome to see the boat—and many of its trophies—at the Ohio County Historical Society Museum at 212 South Walnut Street in Rising Sun. For more information call (812) 438–4915.

Red Wolf Sanctuary

Rising Sun

Paul Strasser never met a wild animal he didn't like or that he couldn't lodge. That's why his Red Wolf Sanctuary is a haven for wild animals that need a home.

Strasser started his nonprofit organization in 1979, after purchasing twenty-three acres of land just outside of Dillsboro. Strasser, who has a degree in fish and wildlife management, was originally intent on saving the red wolf, an endangered species that ranged throughout Indiana, Kentucky, and Illinois.

But soon he expanded his mission to include all North American predators requiring some kind of medical or behavioral assistance and who are not ready to be released back into the wild. The twenty-one-acre facility included raptors, bears, bobcats, eagles, coyotes, owls, buffalo, and two red wolves. In 2006 Strasser moved his entire facility (lock, stock, and more stock) to Ohio County to a 450-acre sanctuary in Rising Sun, Indiana. And you thought moving your family was tough.

Most of the animals are rescued from people who have illegally harbored them or who have taken them in as pets and now can't handle them. In some cases they were seized by the state and given to Strasser because the animals could no longer fend for themselves in the wild.

Strasser and his wife, Jane (who both donate their time), along with just a couple of employees and several volunteers, care for the animals, which are all enclosed in huge pens, maintained to be as close to natural habitat as possible. The predators are fed a steady diet of road kill supplied by the state. "I've spent a fair amount of time butchering deer," says Strasser. Once animals are judged ready for return to the wild, they are released.

Education is a top priority for Strasser, and he conducts tours for interested tourists and provides programs for local schoolchildren (reservations required).

Visit them online at www.redwolf.org, or call (812) 667–5303.

TALL STORY

Sandy Allen is a tall woman, the tallest in the world at just a hair above 7'7", according to the *Guinness Book of World Records*. In fact, she is taller than any NBA player in history. And her sense of humor is big, too. Ask her what she had for breakfast and she'll tell you "short people." This Shelby County native will also tell you that she was a normal-sized newborn, but by the time she was eleven, she was as tall as Michael Jordan. In fact, if an operation on her malfunctioning pituitary had not been performed when she was nineteen (she was already 7 feet tall), Allen might have rivaled Illinois native Robert Wadlow, who lived in Alton, Illinois, and is the tallest human on record at 8'11".

Unlike most giants, Sandy's life was not part of any fairy tale. She was essentially abandoned by her mother when she was just six weeks old and raised by her grandmother. And despite years of teasing and ridicule, Allen grew—girl, did she grow—into a warm, caring woman with a deep compassion for everyone.

Allen has traveled the world, been on dozens of network talk shows, and even made two movies. She wears a size 22 shoe, which necessitates specially made footwear. In fact, most of her wardrobe must be custom-tailored. The Indiana Pacers gave her a pair of Rik Smitts's size 22 shoes (Smitts was the Pacers' 7'4" center in the late 1990s); otherwise, finding sneakers would have been almost impossible and out of reach financially. Little else is out of reach.

Allen is pretty much confined to a wheelchair now, living in a rehab center in Shelbyville. Her height and weight (400 pounds) make walking difficult. But she does have a custom-made van, driven by her companion. In order to appear on the *Sally Jessy Raphael Show* to promote her book, *Cast a Giant Shadow*, several years ago, Allen had to make the 600-mile trip by ambulance.

The world's tallest woman and me. (That's me on the left.)

2% SOLUTION

How old is 2% milk? Well, several weeks old, in my fridge. But the concept of 2% milk goes back to 1948. And the man who invented what is now the best-selling type of milk in America still lives in Indiana.

Roy Robertson started work for the Salem Creamery in 1936. In the late 1940s, Aura Qualkinbush, one of the owners of the creamery—and a home economics teacher—complained about the chubbiness of some of her students. Robertson was asked by his boss to perfect a new product that had less butterfat. Skim milk had already been invented, but consumers had no choice between the 3.5% milk and the virtually tasteless skim, nicknamed "Blue John" by many country folks.

Robertson worked for more than a year tinkering with how to remove the fat and then replace it with other milk solids so that the taste would still please milk lovers. Robertson and his creamery never really got the credit, and Robertson never profited from his invention. Because he never got a patent for his discovery, other dairies were soon producing his 2% milk.

Robertson lives in Salem, where the Stevens Museum (307 East Main Street; 812–883–6495) chronicles this little-known story.

By the way, 1% milk was invented by Robertson's half brother. Just kidding.

Tree-Mendous
Starlight

Let's just call it a would-be wooded area.

We're talking about an indoor forest—the only one in the United States. The Forest Discovery Center is filled with a variety of actual tree trunks and man-made trees and even has a flowing stream. The leaves are glued on one at a time and there's an ambient sound system that captures the sounds of the forest. There's a real forest down the street, but it's outdoors. Yuck.

A hike along the winding, wooded trail while listening to crickets, birds, and the gurgling stream sure gives the illusion of walking through an actual forest. And while computers obviously don't grow on trees, a handful of interactive screens are scattered about the path. While one informs of Indiana's native trees, another asks the question, "Are we running out of trees?"

The FDC's answer: "No."

The center, sponsored by Koetter Woodworking, believes in utilizing forests wisely and promotes the idea that forests are healthier if we all practice responsible management. To bolster that point, the FDC leads tours along its glass-enclosed skyway to the mill, where guests see molding cut from trees and the resulting sawdust recycled and burned in the company's kilns, a testimony to its zero-waste policy.

The center's director, John Blair, hopes the hike through the indoor forest and the mill will leave children better informed about forest management. "Some kids come here believing that trees have souls and that it's painful for them to be cut down," says Blair. "We hope the kids leave with a better perspective." We sure hope so, too.

The center is located at 533 Louis Smith Road in Starlight and is open 9:00 A.M. to 2:00 P.M. Monday through Friday and 1:00 to 5:00 P.M. on Sunday. For information call (812) 923–1590.

Bridge Enthusiast!

Trevlac

Sonny Rodgers first became a bridge enthusiast as a senior citizen.

Not so strange really, except that he wasn't playing bridge, he was building one.

And not just any bridge, but a twenty-ton full-size covered bridge that is so authentic-looking that people want to drive over it in their car. Which they could, but they probably wouldn't—because the bridge doesn't go over anything worth going over. There's a dry creek bed a couple of feet below, and after a real downpour there's water in it.

Sonny days in Trevlac. A bridge over troubled dry beds.

186

Sonny built the bridge on his property in Trevlac, Indiana, using local timber, including poplar, beech, and walnut. Included are what he calls "planned mistakes," to add authenticity to the product. (That is what I did in high school when I plagiarized my term papers from the *World Book Encyclopedia*.)

His original plan was to sell it to the Nashville (Indiana) Fairgrounds, which apparently needed a new bridge, but Sonny claims that there's too much red tape and politics when you want to sell a bridge. (You mean someone has done this before?)

From the time Sonny cut his first timber until he drove his two-ton pickup across the structure took five years. Sonny admits he stunned even himself, considering he had never built anything like this before. "I'm just so darn happy it worked," which means it didn't collapse when he drove over it.

Sonny's next project is to build a log cabin on the west half of his land. "That will be a lot of work," he admits, "but I'll finally have a reason to cross the bridge."

Ode to a Geode
Vallonia

Paul Wheeler doesn't have rocks for brains; he has brains for rocks. The octogenarian retired logger jokes that he has more than two million cerebral-textured stones, known as geodes, in the bins around his yard. Gazing upon the oodles of rocks, nearly ten to twelve truckloads of them, few would argue with his estimate.

Wheeler loves to talk about his rocks. In a single breath, and with the flair of Ross Perot, he'll tell you that he has . . . (inhale) "pink ones, yellow ones, orange ones, reddish ones, and white ones. I have some shaped like footballs and others shaped like bears. I have rocks resembling hoot owls and one that looks like a teddy bear with a bowtie. I have geodes as small as dimes and others as large as bathtubs. One geologist told me that I had one that was a hundred million years old." Wheeler exhales.

People come from all over to buy his rocks, many of which were harvested from his creek. "I just got to picking them up and people started wanting 'em," explains Wheeler. Large geodes—the biggest tops the scales at 275 pounds—are used for landscaping. Smaller, novelty geodes adorn many Hoosier desktops and mantels. Still others are carved into rings and other jewelry.

Some customers like whole geodes. Others like them split open, revealing the stones' mystical crystals. In all his collection, though, no two geodes are quite the same. "If you find two that are exactly alike," says Wheeler, "I'll give them to you."

Oh boy!

Paul Wheeler lives 15 miles southwest of Seymour, just south of U.S. Highway 50 and State Road 135. Call before stopping by to see his collection: (812) 358–2573.

The Grapest Festival Ever

Vevay

The good folks of Switzerland County have a lot to cheer about. And they stomp their feet, too. But first a little history: In the early years of our nation, this part of the country was a premier wine-producing area. But by the late 1800s, the wine production had, well, fizzled, and today there is only one winery in the area. But who cares! Not the people of Switzerland County, who have deemed the week before Labor Day "The Swiss Wine Festival" to celebrate the Swiss who emigrated to America with the express purpose of developing a wine industry. When bad weather and plant disease ruined their crop in Kentucky, they moved to the Indiana Territory about 1802 and founded Switzerland County—the only Switzerland County in America.

The four-day-long celebration includes the obligatory music and food, but also features stine tossing. Stines are "rocks" of different sizes that are heaved by competitors in Olympic-shotput fashion. There is no record in Switzerland County of anyone ever training for this event.

The highlight of the festival is a four-day grape-stomping marathon. Competition is fierce, often pitting (this would be funnier if we were talking about olives) young against old, Democrats against Republicans, or rival corporations against each other. Those producing the most juice go on to defend their title the next year. Only top-seeded teams (now, *that's* funny) get prizes, but everyone can enter and share in the toe-to-toe competition. What happens to all that juice? The liquid has to be tossed. Did you think someone would drink it?

The event is the week before Labor Day. Call the tourism folks at (800) 435–5688 for more information.

Hurry! We're thirsty. Step on it!

Bigger Than Life

Vevay

Josiah Leatherbury called himself an itinerant barroom muralist, not that it's a job there's a lot of call for. It all started when Indiana-born Leatherbury, estranged from his wife, decided to take his four horses and drift through Montana in search of . . . he didn't know what.

But one night in 1987, while Leatherbury was perched on a barstool in Roberts, Montana, the innkeeper asked if anyone could paint a scene on the back wall. Leatherbury, who could draw as a kid but had never painted a lick, volunteered. To his surprise, he was "pretty darn good."

Other bar owners heard about what he had done. Soon he was the West's only barroom muralist. Go figure. In 1989, when Leatherbury returned to his home in Vevay, in Switzerland County, he was commissioned by the county to paint a historic mural. Not just any mural, but a HUGE mural. "There may be bigger ones," says Leatherbury of his 140-by-60-foot painting, "but I have never heard of one."

The mural depicts the county at the turn of the twentieth century, featuring horse-drawn wagons hauling hay down to the steamboats. Because Leatherbury grew up in the area and had heard old-timers talk so much about that era, he had a great feel for the image he wanted. His biggest problem was the necessity to step back—way back—to get some perspective on his work. After painting a minute or so on his electric lift, he'd have to get down and walk back an entire block to see his work. "And then people would want to talk to me, which kind of messed me up. I got real evil-tempered," admits the artist.

If you want to see the mural, just get yourself to Vevay, which is at the end of State Road 56. Trust me, you'll see it.

Mural, mural on the wall. Getting the big picture in Vevay.

Very Sharp Basement

Waldron

Don Miller of Waldron is in this book because he has old tools in his basement. So how come you're not in this book, you might ask? You have old tools in your basement, too. Big difference—Miller's tools are as much as 50,000 years old. And he didn't borrow them from the guy next door.

Miller's basement is actually a museum filled with what might be one of the biggest private collections of Stone Age tools in the Midwest, certainly the biggest in Indiana. And most of the antique relics were found by Miller himself, a world traveler who, by his own admission, spends most of his vacations looking down, not up. The result is a prize grouping of arrowheads, spearheads, axes, malls (bludgeoning rocks), and fossils.

He also has an extensive collection of pottery, most of which was also literally uncovered by Miller and then carefully repaired. "It is rare," says Miller, "to find these pots whole, but all the pieces are usually nearby."

After visiting scores and scores of foreign countries, Miller can spin a story about virtually every one of the thousands of artifacts, recounting where he found it and what it represents in the evolution of toolmaking. His passion is contagious, especially when he places the tool in your hands, and you realize it was crafted by humans—well, sorta humans— tens of thousands of years ago.

And Miller has other stories, too. During one of his adventures in New Guinea, he and his party ran into a tribe of cannibals and were served for dinner. Let me rephrase that: They ran into some friendly cannibals and the cannibals cooked a hog and served them dinner. Yes, there are friendly cannibals.

He also has stories about meeting pygmies. Those stories are shorter.

Miller's museum is not open to the public, but here's his e-mail address: Wyman@svs.net. If you have a real interest in stuff like this, he would be happy to give you the caveman's tour. Drag your wife along.

Miller, by the way, has a Ph.D. in electrical engineering and worked on the first testing of the atomic bomb back in the early 1940s. We wanted you to know that in case you get tired of talking about tools.

A case in point. Actually, points in cases.

Split Decision
West College Corner

The border between two states has to go through something. Maybe a forest, a field, even a parking lot. In rare cases, it may split a city. But a school gymnasium?

Half in Ohio, half in Indiana. No penalty for traveling.

SOUTHEAST

The town of West College Corner was platted by tavern keeper Gideon Howe in 1827. It lies on U.S. Highway 27 in eastern Union County and is geographically split by the Indiana-Ohio state line. Today there are two distinct city governments, although these two tiny towns share some services. But in what has to be one of the most bizarre examples of multistate commerce, the trustees of West College Corner, Indiana, and College Corner, Ohio, decided more than fifty years ago to build a high school overlapping the border.

And it gets weirder. Not only was the high school split in half, but the school gymnasium is half in one state, half in the other. Which means that when you go down the basketball court, you are running from one state to another and, during daylight savings time, the time changes by an hour after every score because Indiana does not recognize daylight savings time. In recent years the high school was transformed into an elementary school, ending the traditional basketball rivalries, but the gymnasium remains a curiosity and attracts visitors from all over.

People in the area will tell you there used to be a tavern that was also split by the state line, creating a pub with two different drinking ages. We can't find any evidence of this, but it's a great story, no matter what state you're from.

SOUTHWEST

Brick Chapel
Bainbridge
Cloverdale
Brownsburg
Indianapolis
Trafalgar

Eugene
Newport
74
231
136
Clinton Falls
Danville
Greencastle
Mooresville
Center Point
Martinsville
Terre Haute
Morgantown
Edinburg
Franklin
Gosport
Yellowwood State Forest
Ellettsville
Nashville
Dugger
Solsberry
Story
Linton
Bloomfield
Heltonville
Oolitic
Bedford
Bruceville
Vincennes
Shoals
Pumpkin Center
Lucky Point
West Baden Springs
French Lick
Milltown
Lincoln City
Dale
Bristow
Santa Claus
Evansville
Newburgh

Champaign

Embarras River

Illinois

Kentucky

Monroe L.

Ohio River

Wabash R.

Rough River Res.

0   50 Miles
0   50 KM

SOUTHWEST

Everyone agrees that southwest Indiana is the most beautiful part of the state, except the people who live in the northeast, southeast, and northwest parts. There's no argument that autumn is exceptionally breathtaking in the rolling hills (Not mountains. Who are we kidding?), and there's no argument that some of the strangest new additions to this book come from that part of Indiana. How about the world's only hair museum? The biggest jack in the world? Or a machine that can launch a pumpkin more than a mile? Would you like to spend the night in a yurt? You'll even read about a guy who drove a lawn mower across the United States. Twice.

Shingles Club
Bainbridge

Don Wilson of Bainbridge is a big fan of the American flag. He wants to shout his love of country from the rooftop. And he's found the perfect way to do it.

Stars and stripes forever. Well, for 60 feet, anyway.

SOUTHWEST

While building a new garage for his car restoration business, Wilson decided he wanted to show his patriotism. Instead of flying the flag from his roof, he made the entire *roof* into a flag, a 60-by-40-foot replica of our nation's emblem.

But this is not some fly-by-night paint job that will wash off after the next rain; it's 2,000 red, white, and blue shingles, perfectly aligned, making Old Glory visible to all who pass by—and to all who fly over.

Wilson and his builder began with a 60-inch flag and used that to scale the design. Once the colored shingles were in place, the stars were cut out of rolled roofing, thus completing the tapestry.

According to Wilson people honk, gape, and slam on their brakes as they pass his facility on U.S. Highway 36. "I've had veterans come by just to see the roof, and our sheriff got out of his car just to salute the flag," claims Wilson.

Wilson knows the flag doesn't wave, but in his heart it is always flapping in the wind, a symbol to all that we live in a great country and that if you search long and hard enough, it is possible to find red shingles. Only in America.

The roof can be seen right on US 36, just west of Danville. Be careful when you look up. There are cars behind you.

Sign of the Times
Bedford

Sam Shaw is Bedford's town curmudgeon. But no one has ever called him that before, as far as Sam knows. "Heck, they've got better words than that to describe me," says Sam. "Too bad you can't print them."

Shaw is known affectionately as the sign man, but that's about as far as the affection goes. For the past ten years, Shaw has posted dozens of signs in his front lawn reflecting his personal views about everything from religion to education to waste management.

The mayor and town board are not happy with some of the signs but admit they are somewhat powerless to force their removal. Instead, claims Shaw, the city has gotten him on a slew of petty violations and misdemeanors that have cost him a pretty penny.

Say it again, Sam. It's a lawn story.

What's not so pretty is that things have also gotten petty. According to Shaw, he is banned from schools and lodges and has been labeled the town crazy. "All because I want to exercise my First Amendment rights," says Shaw. The signs are not professionally made, just drawn by Shaw in his living room. "Sometimes, I spell words wrong, to get people's attention." (Yeah, in high school I used that method on my English teacher all the time.)

This all started in 1995 when Shaw wanted to post a sign in his tree plat and was told that city ordinance prevented it. Shaw capitulated, but then noticed that local church members had similarly placed signs publicizing meetings. "It's not where the sign is, it's what it says that makes a difference," says the sixty-five-year-old bachelor. "And that's against our Constitution."

Shaw has even written a song to show his commitment to this cause. Here's one of the verses to the tune of Ray Price's *Heartache by the Number*.

> *I've got headaches by the number*
> *Headaches by the score*
> *Since the day the mayor sent law officers to my door*
> *They say that I can't win*
> *But the day that I stop fighting*
> *That's the day my world will end*

Shaw claims that people come from all over to gawk at his signs, and that he'll happily debate anyone about his position on any issue, anywhere, any time of day. Here's his number: (812) 275–6102. Good luck. Remember, he doesn't have a Web site. He has a lawn.

SPACE CADETS

There have only been 200 astronauts trained by NASA in the last fifty years. There are over 3,000 counties in the United States. So what are the chances that three of those astronauts would hail from the same rural county in Indiana of only 45,000 people, in a nation of almost 300 million people? Seriously, what are the chances?

Well, astronomical, really.

But it's true. Virgil Grissom, Kenneth Bowersox, and Charles Walker are all from Lawrence County. No, they didn't all walk on the moon, but they all had distinguished careers in space, which there is plenty of in Lawrence County.

The county is so proud of this that there is a huge sign commemorating this fact as you enter Bedford. I'd like to make fun of this bravado, but I can't. Actually, I think it's really cool.

Okay, you're not overwhelmed. Listen to this: Twenty-two of our astronauts went to Purdue University. Still not impressed? I give up.

High Hopes
Bloomfield

Do you sometimes feel you don't know jack? You'll feel much more informed after you read this chapter.

You'll know, for example, that the biggest jack in the world is in Bloomfield, Indiana. Not only can't it really lift anything, nothing can lift it. It weighs two and a half tons.

The jack, which is over 20 feet tall, sits on a concrete slab and is visible from the road, just a stone's throw from the county courthouse. Steve Dowden, CEO of Bloomfield Manufacturing, explains that his plant has been making the 48-inch version of the jack for decades. When the company celebrated its 110th anniversary in 2005, their suppliers created the cast iron monster as a thank you. Gee, thanks a lot.

Dowden said the jack has lifted spirits and boosted morale. Then he ran out of jack jokes.

You can see the jack from just about anywhere in Bloomfield. Just don't get a flat tire. They can't help you. And I can't help you get there. It's easier if you look at a map.

Sticky Business!
Brick Chapel

Arthur Harris likes to talk about maple syrup. He's kind of a slow talker, so you'll hang on every word—and that's the way it should be when you learn about maple syrup.

Arthur likes to tell you that maple syrup production is an age-old art and that it figures importantly in the founding of this country where for the American Indian and the pioneers this food was a staple. Actually, Arthur can talk for hours about maple syrup and is happy to do that, so we're warning you now, in case you plan to visit.

Drive up to his Harris Sugar Bush farm, just outside of Greencastle, and the area will at first look like a giant crime scene. Fifteen miles of white rubber tubing connect the thousands of maple trees on his one-hundred-acre property, making it appear as though the police got there before you did and didn't want you to touch the evidence.

The sap is actually being sucked out of the trees by giant vacuums, collected in tanks, then trucked to the sugar house for processing. The neat thing about Sugar Bush farm is that the production method is really a unique blend of old fashioned and state-of-the-art techniques. You'll see all kinds of high-tech monitors and gauges surrounding a huge 500-gallon vat of bubbling syrup, filling the room with smoke and an aroma to die for. Kinda like Einstein meets Frankenstein.

The system is actually somewhat complicated and precision is paramount. At one point in the procedure, the syrup must hit exactly 221 degrees or a lot of pancake lovers are going to be unhappy with the product.

It's not just your eyes that will feast at the facility. You can taste the maple syrup, maple cookies, maple butter, pure maple sugar, maple cream, and even maple tea.

Syrup is only produced from the end of January to the beginning of March, because evening temps must be consistently low for the cells of the maple tree to contract to form a vacuum. I don't understand that, either. That's why you have to visit Arthur.

Trust me; he'll explain it to you. But you do need an appointment.

From Greencastle drive north on State Road 231, then east on 200 N, then north on 50 E, then east on 325 N. Then you'll see a sign. Finally! Call (765) 653–5108 or visit www.harrissugarbush.com for more info.

You Always Yurt the Ones You Love!

Bristow

Am I the only person who didn't know what a *yurt* is? My wife knew. My editor knew. Heck, my son knew.

In the unlikely event *you* don't know: It's an ancient Mongolian hut used by nomadic tribes centuries ago when they were nomadicking around Mongolia. Rumor has it that Genghis Kahn slept in one, which is pretty good testimony because he basically could have slept anywhere he wanted.

Now *you* can sleep in a yurt. But you have to go to Bristow, Indiana, and visit the Mary Rose Herb Farm and Retreat. Mary Rose and her husband, Dick, were "chasing rats" in Seattle, two fast-paced executives who battled stress and health problems until one day—after Mary's heart attack—they decided it was time to make a major life change.

No TV, no phone, no toilet. Call early for reservations.

Dick took off on a major road trip, looking for land to build a place where people could relax and reconnect with what's important. Dick found heaven in southern Indiana, and they opened their therapeutic retreat in 2000.

For less money than it takes fill up your SUV, Mary and Dick will rent you a yurt and cook you a breakfast of baked herbal eggs and chocolate chip sour cream coffee cake. Then Mary Rose will advise you on Chinese herbal medicine.

Of course you can enjoy all the privacy you want. Swim in the lake ("Skinny dip if you want," says Dick. "It's very secluded."), walk the trails, build a campfire, or soak in the Japanese hot tubs.

The retreat lacks some traditional amenities. Mary Rose describes it as a "step up from luxury camping." No phone. No TV. No Starbucks. But there is electricity, hot water, and "very, very, very clean Porta-Potties." Mary Rose was adamant I include all three of those *very*s.

At night, retreat to your 16-foot-diameter yurt, which is kind of a cross among a teepee, a tent, and a house. Climb into bed and gaze through the dome skylight at the stars. Relax; forget about everything.

The next morning, get in your car, go back to your rotten job, and tell your boss that he's a big jerk and that the stress is killing you.

Tell him Mary Rose told you to say all that.

Well, maybe not. But do make a reservation for next year.

Finding this is not easy. It's in Bristow, Indiana, on Cattail Road. Call (812) 357–2699. Their Web site can help: www.maryroseherbfarm.com.

Hooked on Traps
Brownsburg

Tim Evans of Brownsburg is hooked on traps. Mousetraps, that is. The obsession began more than thirty years ago when he and his father found an old mousetrap, circa 1915, while restoring an old home. "It looked more like a prison than a trap," says Evans, "and that got us interested. I mean, how many ways were there to kill a mouse?"

The mousetrap, a metaphor for the inventive spirit of America, has come in all shapes and sizes. So do mice, by the way. But more interestingly, the minds behind these traps, those steel-trap minds, have come up with dozens of ways to effectively dispense with our rodent friends.

After his dad passed away in 1993, Evans inherited over a thousand mousetraps (going back a hundred years) and the collection has continued to grow. Now his private museum is packed with contraptions whose makers were all in search of the better mousetrap. Evans cares little about the effectiveness of the trap, attracted instead to those traps that reflect a kind of Rube Goldberg approach to mice murder. He has traps that crush, electrocute, spank, decapitate, and strangle. One of his favorites has a mouse literally walk a plank into a little tub of water. The mouse is not blindfolded.

All the trappings of a snappy collection.

There's one trap where the mouse ends up in a kind of hamster wheel, then runs itself to death, unlike a hamster who knows when its little heart can't take it anymore and stops. "I don't know if that's true," laughs Evans, "but it's a great story."

Many of the traps were collected for their advertising and promotional themes. Even Bing Crosby had a mousetrap named after him. And Crosby's face is on the box. This drove Sinatra crazy. By the way, the bait of choice over the years, according to Evans's research, is cheese or peanut butter. Don't ever say you didn't learn anything from this book.

Evans's museum is in his house. But if you love mousetraps and have absolutely nothing else to do one Saturday afternoon, you can reach him at JTEvans@netdirect.net. Hope you catch him at home. He deserves to be caught.

Wayne's World
Brownsburg

Jim Duncan only made one concession to his wife regarding his obsession with John Wayne: He agreed not to name his second-born son Rooster, after Wayne's character in *True Grit*. But other than that, Duncan has had pretty much free rein to pursue his love for the cowboy star. In fact, when his private collection of some 4,000 items got too big for his house, he erected a small building in his backyard, creating what can only be called the John Wayne Museum. What else would you call it?

Although the 500-square-foot structure is too small for the 5,000 items displayed, Duncan is always expanding his collection, looking for unique items in catalogs, on the Internet, and at garage sales. He has been lucky, often finding old photos and statues at real bargains, but the enthusiast is not opposed to spending a few bucks, like on the $650 comic book featuring John Wayne. "The only thing I ever turned down was $5,000 for the shirt the Duke wore in *Donovan's Reef*, but I'll pretty much buy anything that's connected to the Duke."

Duncan has most of Wayne's movies on video, all the bios, magazines that sport the Duke's visage, Franklin Mint items, original posters, comic books, cutouts, and novelty items.

Duncan loves to show his collection. Just be sure to call for an appointment at (317) 852–8437 or e-mail him at JDunk1956@earthlink.com. And don't try to do a John Wayne imitation on the phone. Even Duncan is getting tired of that.

Only one john in Jim Duncan's museum.

High Roller

Bruceville

John Ivers loves roller coasters, but living in rural Indiana creates a problem. Every time he has a desire to take a thrilling ride, he has to travel a good 200 . . . feet. Ivers, you see, built a roller coaster in his backyard. Not some dinky Erector Set contraption, but a coaster 188 feet long and 20 feet high. It gets up to 25 miles per hour with a 360-degree corkscrew turn that still thrills the bejeebies out of the creator. He calls it Blue Flash.

Ivers, who had some background in mechanics, was still a little unsure whether he could match his plan with his vision. He worked without a blueprint, using parts he collected from around town or bought at the hardware store. He worked when he had free time and completed the project in just over a year. The coaster is a near work of art, attracting not only the neighbors, but newspapers and national TV shows as well. His kids and grandkids ride it; so do the neighborhood kids. Is it safe? "Darn tootin' it's safe," says Ivers. "And I ride it first every day just to be sure."

John Ivers having fun around (and around and around) his yard.

Is it the only backyard, self-built coaster in the world? Probably not, say the experts, but it's probably the only one with a 360-degree corkscrew where the car travels upside down.

But John Ivers doesn't spin his wheels. The next project is on the drawing board—assuming he has a drawing board. How will it differ, other than being bigger, faster, and better? "I'll be able to take this apart and travel with it," says Ivers. You can call him at (812) 324–9030. Or stop by Bruceville. He's usually somewhere around . . . and around.

The Cat's Meow
Center Point

The Exotic Feline Rescue Center in Center Point, Indiana, is an exotic feline rescue center. This explains its creative name, but it doesn't begin to explain the passion of its founder, Joe Taft, a bachelor who lives on the premises with three leopards right in his home. Imagine that: a bachelor.

The center was founded in 1991, and since that time Joe has had to claw and scratch to raise funds to house as many as 200 large cats (tigers, lions, bobcats, leopards) on his 110-acre facility. Taft claims that his felines wolf down 3,000 pounds of meat a day, making it the premier low-carb facility in Indiana. Joe buys some meat, and he also serves up road kill or dead farm animals donated by local farmers.

Joe is not a big talker, but if you can corner him (generally not a recommended maneuver in a facility like this), he'll tell you some heartbreaking stories of large cats he has rescued from deplorable conditions. Some had spent a dismal life in a circus and were then literally abandoned. Other suffered at the hands of people who thought a little 700-pound kitty would be a nice pet and then discovered that cleaning the litter box was the least of their problems. Joe's original rescues were two tigers that were being kept in the back of a Volkswagen Beetle.

All the cats are kept in huge outdoor cages that include shelter for the animal during inclement weather. The animals all seem to know Joe, but even he is cautious of getting too chummy with an exotic. "They are still wild animals, and I need to be an example to other people who are visiting the facility."

During my visit there, I witnessed the neutering of a Siberian tiger.

I think the thing that impressed me most . . . well, never mind.

The Exotic Feline Rescue Center is open to the public every day but Monday, from 10:00 A.M. to 5:00 P.M. Joe says his center is a no-kill facility. That's good news for the animals, but I think it's even better news for visitors.

Call (812) 835–1130, or check out their Web site at www.exotic felinerescuecenter.org.

Wild Experience
Clinton Falls

Since 1978 Larry Battson of Putnam County has roamed the halls of elementary schools throughout Indiana, herded kids into gymnasiums, and paraded wild animals in front of them. "I figure I've reached three million kids since 1978," says Battson, whose home in Clinton Falls is a preserve for more than sixty exotic species. "Now I'm starting to run into principals who remember me from when they were in elementary school." Battson feeds and cleans up after lions, tigers, and bears (oh my!), as well as badgers, snakes, baboons, macaws, tarantulas, alligators, pythons, tigers, and coyotes, to mention just a few. Sorry to be such a game dropper.

Battson is unique in Indiana. Others will champion a certain type of animal, like raptors or snakes, and do a specialized show. But only Battson brings a virtual zoo to kids across the state and lets them get up close, sometimes closer than they ever thought, or hoped, they'd get.

Battson transports the animals in his van to each location—quite a job considering he visits more than 220 schools a year with only his wife, Cheryl, to assist him. Once in the school, Battson entertains the kids with a combination of snappy banter and important information about each animal, letting kids, when appropriate, interact with the creatures. "They laugh and learn," says Battson. "That makes it all worth it."

Food runs almost two grand a month and requires daily trips to the supermarket for huge quantities of meat, grain, and vegetables. "It's not a job," says Battson, who can never really take a vacation. "It is my life."

Despite the fact that Battson takes wild animals into schools, no youngster has even been scratched. Not so for Battson, who claims the real danger is in feeding and transporting the animals. "I've been bitten by just about every animal you can name," he admits. He spent a week in the hospital at the hands (if it had hands) of a pesky rattlesnake.

If you want to book Larry Battson for your school, call Wildlife Educational Services at (765) 739–6719, or e-mail Lbattson@peoplepc .com.

Larry Battson with three kids and a snake. Menagerie à trois!

Pool Party

Cloverdale

Meet Dr. Cue. He has a wife, Miss Cue. ("Mrs." Cue just doesn't sound as funny.) In real life (assuming he has one) Dr. Cue is Tom Rossman, quite possibly the most entertaining artistic pool player in the country. That means he does trick shots.

Notice I didn't say "*best* artistic pool player." Oh, he's good. He's real good. But it's not his pool—it's his patter that makes him your best shot if you're looking for a demonstration to wow a crowd.

Dr. Cue never misses a shot. Yeah, right. Fact is, he not only misses, he sometimes misses on purpose. That gives Rossman a way to relate to the audience and an opportunity to pocket one of his perfectly timed "excuses," which he practices more often than his bank shots. If a ball seems to be going astray, he attempts to save face by following the sphere with his finger slightly ahead of the ball and saying, "And I want this one to land right *there*." When the ball comes to a stop, Rossman looks pleased and the audience laughs and applauds. Is that a great scam, or what?

Rossman's repertoire is endless, more shots than he can shake a pool stick at. Some of his favorites are:

- Snap, crackle, jump, nip, draw
- Yo-Yo Masse
- Chattanooga-switchyard version
- Starburst (all fifteen balls are pocketed)

He can play for two hours and never repeat a trick, encircling the table like a panther, setting up the next configuration of balls to ensure each one will collide in the proper sequence. He never stops moving, never stops talking, never stops embracing the fans.

Rossman brings with him a spiritual message as well, hoping his skill at the table will spread his belief that we must to use the talent God has given us to make the world a better place.

By the way, Rossman has won a bunch of trick pool competitions over the years. But again, it's the talk, not the technique that makes Tom a real Indiana curiosity. Check out Tom's schedule on his Web site (www.drcuepromotions.com) or call (765) 795–4968. Yes, Tom may miss an occasional shot, but don't miss Tom if he's in your area. Not on purpose, anyway.

Bellman
Cloverdale

The late Francis Kennedy always heard ringing in his ears. And it certainly didn't take a doctor to figure out why. The source? More than 230 bells on display in his front yard.

It appears that Kennedy never met a bell he didn't like. For strewn about his farm, located just outside of Cloverdale, are church bells, school bells, steamboat bells, and dinner bells. There are plain ones and elaborate ones. Some are cast from iron and others formed from bronze. On one chain alone, twenty-five bells dangle in the wind, ringing during strong gusts. Aside from the bells, there are windmills, bear traps, and a replica of Paul Bunyan's axe.

Locals know the place simply as the Bell Farm. (Apparently, the original name, Evergreen Farm, just didn't ring true anymore.) Two of the largest collectibles are next to the mailbox, anchored in concrete. "When the tires roll over a lever in front of the mailbox, the bells ring," says Kennedy's nephew, Paul Slaven. "My uncle did that so he'd know when the mail was here."

Kennedy died in 1988, and since then the paint has peeled off many of the bells and their wooden stands look badly weathered. Adding to the air of disrepair, the current mailman has taken a dislike to the ringing mail alarm. "The years have taken their toll on the place," says Slaven. We think he has used that joke before.

Cloverdale's house of bells can be found just east of town, off State Road 42.

Music to Our Ears

Dale

It's hard to leave Dr. Ted Waflart's place without feeling much better. And we're not even talking about his medical practice. We're talking about his museum: Dr. Ted's Musical Marvels.

While practicing medicine in the Appalachian Mountains, Waflart found a broken pump organ in an antiques store. Researching how to reconstruct it, he became intrigued with some of the older, mechanical musical instruments that he read about and started a collection in his home in the 1970s. He always dreamed of opening a museum, and his idea got a jump-start when he found a DeCap Belgian Dance Organ while traveling in Belgium. This incredible instrument is a veritable symphony with its accordions, saxophones, cymbals, and bass drum, to name a few. At 4,000 pounds with 535 pipes, it's an eyeful and an earful.

With the DeCap organ as its base, his collection expanded to include a turn-of-the-twentieth-century Wurlitzer organ, calliopes, music boxes, player pianos, street organs, and dance organs—a total of sixteen mechanical musical instruments that play all by themselves. There's also a gift shop that sells moderately priced collectibles. Music boxes are the hot item.

His right-hand gal, Millie, runs the museum and give tours, whether to one person or a large group. "I once gave a tour to a double-decker bus, so I've decided that ninety-seven is my limit." Visit Dr. Ted's daily from Memorial Day to Labor Day, then weekends through September. They open up again for weekends in May. To find Dr. Ted's, take Interstate 64 to exit 57, and go a half mile north. You can also call at (812) 937–4250 for information. But it's hard to hear on the phone.

Paper Trail
Danville

Poor Betty Weesner. At the same job since 1962 and never a single promotion. Not one. She'd complain to the boss, but she is the boss. She's both the editor and the publisher of *The Republican,* the oldest newspaper in Hendricks County, 160 years to be almost exact. Unless this book has been in your basement for five years.

Betty started her journalism career at *The Republican* in the 1930s, writing school news at about age ten. The editor was a crusty old journalist who also happened to be her father. The publisher was a crusty old journalist, too. Same guy.

After attending the Indian University School of Journalism, Betty took over for her dad in the mid-1960s. The tiny storefront on Main Street in Danville has housed the newspaper for more than one hundred years. During Betty's seventy-five-year career, there hasn't been a single missed issue. "People love their local paper," says Weesner. "If we messed up, we'd hear about it."

The building is chock-full of everything. Old news may not be worth much, but an old linotype machine and wood type from the Civil War must be worth something. Betty has computers to print copy, but the paper is laid out the old-fashioned way—by cutting and pasting stories onto huge boards, then sending the proofs off to the printer.

Betty echoes the philosophy of her father, who was once asked why Lindbergh's crossing of the Atlantic was not reported in *The Republican*. "Lindbergh was not from Hendricks County," said the late Edward J. Weesner. And he meant it. "If you want to get in *The Republican* you have to be born in Hendricks County, or live in Hendricks County, or get in trouble in Hendricks County," says Betty. And she means it.

When the Danville High School established a hall of fame two years ago, Betty was the first woman inductee. She's been an influential force in the community for decades and still covers city council news. Betty believes in local newspapers. "They confirm the gossip you've heard all week."

Would you like to meet Betty in person? Sorry, she's too busy. If you do call (317–745–2777), just be sure you have some good dirt.

Betty Weesner, a special edition to Hendricks County.

SOUTHWEST

Miners Allowed
Dugger

Dugger's major celebration is a miner affair. That's because Dugger's weeklong Coal Festival celebrates coal miners, mining, and the company and the man for whom the town was named. Francis Dugger, it seems, was a digger.

Dugger and Henry Neal platted the town in 1879 next to his Dugger Coal Mine. His company was the town's main industry. To honor the town's founding father, the residents changed the city's name from Fairchild to Dugger.

More than one hundred years later, the coal industry is still a major economic force. To mark its centennial, the town held its inaugural coal festival. According to festival organizer John Dobbins, there's something going on most every night of the week during the late September gala. There's the firemen's fish fry, the American Legion's free bean supper, and the Masons' steak night. There are children's games, awards for the oldest and youngest miner, softball, volleyball, soccer, live music, and a parade.

The star of the parade used to be the coal miner's daughter. Since there are no more daughters—or granddaughters for that matter—organizers have begun crowning a coal queen. The bituminous beauty is selected from local high school seniors and awarded a scholarship of around $500.

The really old miners are on display at the Coal Museum. (Just kidding.) There is a museum, though, and it does have many of the tools these miners used. There are mule harnesses (used to pull wagons out of the mine), headlamps, coal jewelry, and statues carved from the black fossil fuel. If you reside in Sullivan County and don't know about this event, you're living in a cave. You're certainly not working in one.

The Dugger Coal Festival is held in Dugger, 37 miles southeast of Terre Haute, east of U.S. Highway 41 on State Road 54. For more information call the museum at (812) 268–6253.

That's Italian
Edinburgh

It's a tiny chapel at Camp Atterbury in Johnson County, no bigger than your average bedroom, but with walls replete with breathtaking Italian frescoes painted with the juice of berries, crushed flower petals, and even human blood to achieve the desired colors. It's quite a story. And one almost forgotten.

Camp Atterbury played a vital role during World War II. Created in 1941 as a training camp for forces on their way to Europe, it later served as an internment camp for prisoners of war. By the middle of the war, more than 3,000 Italian POWs were being held in Atterbury, awaiting their fate.

A strong religious fervor existed amongst the POWs, who asked the American chaplain that they be allowed to construct a small chapel within their recreational area. Permission granted, the captives—many of whom were skilled artisans—built this tiny church from raw materials they scrounged from the immediate area. Inside, the walls were hand-painted with elaborate religious designs, vibrant colors, and religious imagery. They dedicated it to the Blessed Mother and named it "Our Lady's Chapel in the Meadow."

After the war ended, Camp Atterbury was deactivated, prisoners returned home, and the chapel fell into disrepair. Despite occasional halfhearted attempts at restoration, it seemed little more than a nuisance, destined to be destroyed when the first bulldozer was available.

In 1987 Ed and Betty Suding (Betty is legally blind), in search of a place to have a family reunion, came upon the chapel. When Betty felt the broken altar, she knew that something needed to be done. With some local grants and expert artistry, the chapel, on State Road 52 between Franklin and Morgantown, was refurbished and lives again. The Italian Heritage Society of Indiana, in conjunction with the Indiana National Guard, presents an annual rosary mass and picnic at the site each year. Still, far too few know about the chapel. But now you do.

Visitors are welcome at the chapel. Call (812) 526–1112 for information, or just stop by. Take the Taylorsville exit (76) off of Interstate 65, go three lights to Hospital Road, and follow the signs directly to the chapel.

Small chapel, huge history.

Pumped for Pumpkins

Ellettsville

Whattaya make of all this?

> 700-gallon air tank
> 12-inch butterfly valve
> 30 feet of 12-inch black iron pipe
> Ford truck front end
> 40-foot-long house trailer frame
> some serious hydraulics
> a lot of reinforcing steel
> 200 pounds of welding rods
> a gallon of aspirin
> an understanding wife and neighbors
> an unlimited supply of 5-gallon buckets for wading

I'll tell you what you make. You make a pumpkin launcher that can propel a pumpkin over a mile or make it slam through the side of a car and come out the other side.

Aren't you glad you asked?

This particular pumpkin launcher belongs to Jim Bristoe of Ellettsville, a man who frightens people every Halloween without even wearing a mask.

Bristoe's interest in propulsion began when as a kid he made a potato gun, a weapon of mass infraction since it is technically illegal, because the hairspray he used to fire the potato wad is considered an explosive propellant. I was going to leave this whole paragraph out, but I knew some of you guys would be interested.

To make a long (and loud) story short, Bristoe became fascinated with the idea of hurling something out into space through a tube and ultimately made his first pumpkin cannon using a pneumatic valve. He was a little embarrassed about his plaything, *especially* when his wife accused him of "not being all there," a label that had a nice ring to it and is now the name of his Web site. Later Bristoe discovered there were national competitions for this kind of thing. "I felt better when I learned I was not the only one who liked to blow up vegetables."

Bristoe entertains not only himself, but local kids who love to see a frozen pumpkin torpedoed through a car, boat, or barn door. I guess this is better than playing violent video games, but I'm not positive.

If Jim can find an open field long enough, he claims he can launch a pumpkin a mile and a quarter, reaching speeds of 1,300 miles per hour. This is twice as fast as a jet plane.

Jim is not obsessed with shooting pumpkins. He has other interests. In the summer, he shoots watermelons.

You can't visit this monstrosity. You just have to be lucky enough to be somewhere Jim has lugged it. So, good luck.

Pumpkin power: Loading up on veggies.

Talkin' Trash
Eugene

Junky Joe's real name was Joe Gebhart, a man consumed by the love of junk—junk that he learned he could make money on. It all started in 1959 when Gebhart was rinsing off some old pieces of glassware that he had purchased for six bucks. When an antiques dealer offered him $18, Joe was hooked.

Before long, the garage was full of junk. I mean FULL of junk. And Mrs. Gebhart wasn't happy, especially when she couldn't park her '61 Valiant station wagon inside the garage during the dead of winter. And so, in the early 1960s, the extended Gebhart family erected several buildings to give the junk the home it so poorly deserved.

For over twenty-five years, Junky Joe collected every manner of trash imaginable. Another thing he collected every day was his grandson, Steve, whom he picked up at school and took junking. "We'd go all over," says Steve Axtell, who took over the business in 1980. "We'd clean out sheds, barns, blacksmith shops—anywhere there was junk, we'd be there."

When Grandpa Gebhart died in 1986, Steve knew it was his destiny to stalk trash the rest of his life. Axtell now has seven barns filled with junk. That's seven buildings chock-full of every conceivable thing thrown out by man. And the stuff is scattered, with no rhyme or reason to explain why some stuff is in one building and not another. "When I first bought the place I got things really organized," says Axtell, "but people didn't like it. That ruined all the fun. People like to dig, man."

What can you find at Junky Joe's? Let's put it another way. Junky Joe's has everything, the question is whether you can find it. Axtell claims that even in tiny Eugene, he gets visitors from all over the country. Recently several Parisians paid him a visit and brought an interpreter. "Just call me a junque dealer," smiles Axtell, a joke that is funny in print, but made no sense on the phone.

To find Junky Joe's from State Road 63, take State Road 234 west for about 1.4 miles until you see North Elm Tree, turn right at the corner, and go half a mile. You can call first (765–492–3639), but Steve can never find the phone.

Ghost Writers
Evansville

The Willard Library in Evansville, housed in a beautiful Victorian Gothic building, is the oldest public library in the state. Board members often boast about their original charge in 1885: "a library for use of the people of all classes, races and sexes."

Okay fine, but no one said ghosts were welcome.

Yet ever since 1937, when the library's janitor swore he saw the image of a veiled lady dressed in gray from head to toe, sightings of her apparition have persisted. Stories abound: unexplained running water, the inexplicable aroma of perfume, and smoky images caught by cameras throughout several rooms of the library. And the sightings continue to this day.

Whose apparition is it? Most believe (if they do believe) that it is the ghost of Louise Carpenter, daughter of the library's founder, who once sued the board of trustees because she believed her father had been unduly influenced to establish the library. When she lost the suit, she also lost all claims to the library's property. So after her death, Louise came back to haunt the building. Some say she will continue to do so until the property goes back to the living heirs of the Willard Carpenter family.

This may be the only ghost motivated by a bad real estate experience.

You can see some of these unexplained phenomena at a Web site dedicated to detailing all recent "confrontations" with the Lady in Gray. The Web site shows ghost-sleuthing photos of various rooms in the library. Look closely and you may see a hint of something from another world. Whether you think it's a glitch in the photo or a rip in the universe, is up to you.

But the library's "ghost-cam" is worth checking out: www.courier press.com/ghost. And so are the books in the library.

Happy haunting.

The Willard Library is at 21 First Avenue in Evansville (812–425–4309; www.willard.lib.in.us).

Ship Shape
Evansville

"The future of our empires is tied up with some damn thing called the LST [landing ship tank]." Those are words of Winston Churchill, talking about an amphibious vessel of which he, himself, conceived and then urged the United States to build during WWII.

Little did he know, but that "damn thing" would become the best darn tourist attraction in Evansville, Indiana.

The LST was pretty much a flat-bottom ship. How flat was it? Torpedoes shot from German warships passed harmlessly right underneath. And flat enough that the vessel could land on beaches so that tanks and other armored vehicles could be easily off-loaded. Oh, and that baby is long, too. Over 300 feet. That's like a football field, for you Colts fans out there.

This is the only remaining operational WWII LST in existence, the other 1,000 or so having been junked or having fallen into disrepair. Despite its storied past—it supported the Normandy invasion on D-Day—the ship ultimately ended up serving the Greek navy from 1964 to 1999 as a donation from the U.S. government.

Then a group of retired military men decided the ship needed to return to its home in the United States. Although this particular ship was built in Pennsylvania, Evansville did have a riverfront shipyard during the war, so the idea of making Evansville a permanent home to an LST struck many locals as a good idea.

Several other cities, like Jeffersonville (also a shipbuilding port), vied for the honor, but Evansville was chosen. A huge fund-raising effort began and the ship went through some major restoration so that it could remain both seaworthy and also serve as a museum.

Floating history in downtown Evansville—finally in ship-shape condition.

And what a museum it is, afloat on the Ohio River. Groups of ten can get a thirty-minute guided tour from stem to stern (and starboard to port). See where twenty Sherman tanks sat ready for action on Omaha Beach, as well as scores of anti-aircraft and machine guns. You can even read graffiti scrawled on the walls by soldiers lonely for loved ones back home during WWII. Visit the pilothouse and—sorry, they asked I include this—the gift shop (that's new since the war).

The ship originally required a crew of 121, but Mike Whicker, who spearheaded the effort to bring the ship to Evansville, says that they can now sail with a crew of 35. "We don't need gunners anymore," says Mike.

No, the war between Indiana and Illinois never amounted to much.

Evansville is easy to find. From Terre Haute drive forever on US 41. Then ask for the Ohio River. Here's the Web site for the USS LST Ship Memorial: www.lstmemorial.org. Or call (812) 435–8678.

Batting a Thousand
Franklin

Jon Rogers lives in a beautiful home in Franklin, Indiana. Four bedrooms, a living room, a den, and four *batrooms*.

Batroom? What else would you call what might be the Midwest's biggest collection of Batman memorabilia? And how big is it? Scores of movie posters, original art work, storyboards, toys, figures, and movie props. Jon's favorite: an original Bat-a-rang from the Batman movie *Batman Forever*.

Rogers first had his radar up as a kid, attracted to the superhero because, well, he wasn't super. "He was just a regular guy without superpowers, who wanted to do good."

While his fascination goes way back, the collection only began in the early 1990s when Jon's work as a mortgage banker took him on the road throughout the Midwest and up and down the East Coast. After he purchased an original storyboard signed by comic artist Bob Kane, Rogers knew he had been bitten by the Bat bug. When Warner Brothers started opening retail stores around the country, Rogers realized his passion might be getting out of hand. "When those stores started sending me stuff in the mail to look at, I knew I was in trouble."

Rogers has a Bat garage, painted to look like the Bat Cave, including the skyline of Gotham City, and the accompanying Bat Cave tunnel. And what would a Bat Cave be without the Batmobile, a black 1996 Dodge Viper? Throw in a pricey costume, and it's pretty eerie when you see Rogers sitting behind the wheel. "I was thinking of buying a real Batmobile (whatever that means) but that would be about a quarter of a million, so I decided not to." Good Bat decision, Jon.

At Halloween, Jon dons his costume and gives out candy at the local fire station, where he entertains the kids and scares up a few new fans.

Jon knows that people love to see his collection, but he does question what they really think about his obsession with the caped crusader. "Maybe they think I'm batty," says Jon. Good. I was hoping he'd say that before I did.

Want to see the collection? No Bat phone, but he does have an e-mail address: JRR7373@yahoo.com.

DEAD CENTER

Residents of Johnson County have taken the phrase "dead center of the road" a bit too literally. The proof can be found south of Franklin on County Road 400 South, a road intended to be a straight shot. In 1905, however, the builders were "encouraged" to alter their original plans. That's because Nancy Kerlin Barnett was buried where the road was platted and Daniel Doty, Nancy's grandson, protected the grave with a shotgun and suggested the road crew construct an alternate route. He threatened that anyone attempting to move her grave would join her.

The road crew presumably had heard of shotgun weddings, but this was probably the first time they thought of a shotgun bypass. But they heeded Doty's warning and split the road accordingly.

Over the years, cement markers stood as tribute to the standoff. Great-great-great-great grandson Don Hardin even recalls Boy Scouts tending the site by trimming weeds and planting flowers. "The cement marker was stolen twice by vandals," Hardin says. Since Nancy's relatives couldn't guard her grave with shotguns on a daily basis, they gently persuaded state officials to erect a sturdy, theft-proof historical marker. Officials took the family's suggestion and dedicated the marker in 1982. You can see the grave site, approximately 5 miles south of Franklin's city limits on U.S. Highway 31. Turn east on County Road 400 South and go about 1½ miles. But please don't bring a crowd. You know what they say: RIP.

SOUTHWEST

Parting Words
French Lick

According to cosmetologist Tony Kendall of French Lick, hair is on everybody's mind. I think he meant everybody's head. But that's close enough.

Kendall has run the Hair Museum in French Lick, Indiana, since 2000, a project that began with a 1920s blow dryer that weighed five pounds and has grown (excuse the expression) into the nation's only hair museum.

When customers at his traditional salon, Body Reflections, were intrigued with a few of Tony's artifacts, he began combing the Internet for other hair pieces. The museum, which is housed inside his salon building, showcases hundreds and hundreds of items that reflect the human obsession with hair over the ages: scissors, blow dryers, hair tonics, wigs, permanent wave machines, and curling irons. And snake oil.

Part of his collection is a lock of Elvis Presley's hair that Tony bought on eBay, so he knows it's legit. (That's where I got my baseball signed by William Shakespeare.) He also has a priceless wreath of hair that represents human strands from one extended family. These wreaths are rare today, but Tony says they were once real *hair*looms. Okay, maybe he said heirlooms, but I like hairlooms better.

The museum is in French Lick, one hour south of Bloomington on State Road 37 to Paoli, then State Road 56 west to French Lick. The museum is across from the French Lick Springs Hotel. The Web site: www.hairshow.biz/museum.htm.

You can call for an appointment at (812) 936–4064. If Tony admires your hair, be careful.

Sports Racquet
Gosport

John Baker is a singing evangelist, but that hasn't stopped him from being one of the top dealers of sports memorabilia in the country. While traveling from place to place to sing the Word in the 1980s, Baker often shopped at flea markets and antiques sales, feeding his passion for baseball cards and old ball gloves. Before long he was known on the circuit as the singing collector, a man who had both a great voice and a perfect pitch. Then it was on to trade shows and national conventions.

When Baker's hobby became a business, he moved it out of the corner of his son's room and into a 2,000-square-foot warehouse adjacent to his Gosport home. Inside he has more than a thousand old

John Baker: Looking for glove in all the right places.

baseball gloves, each an endorsed model with names like Preacher Roe and Babe Ruth. "The Babe's," says Baker, "looks like a pot holder—no lacing, nothing, flat as a pancake." He also has leather football helmets, antique baseball bats, pitching machines, lockers, scoreboards, shoulder pads, javelins, vintage photos of high school sports, even Dick the Bruiser's shorts. "Not junk," cautions Baker, "but vintage stuff for collectors or theme restaurants."

People from all over the country come to shop at Baker's warehouse, but he's hit it big on eBay as well, where the memorabilia mogul spends hours each day buying and selling. His most expensive buy was a vintage Rose Bowl ring from the fifties, which he bought for big bucks and sold for bigger ones.

Baker's best buy? An eighty-year-old baseball glove with Ty Cobb's name on it.

"I paid a dollar for it at a flea market," he laughs. "Sometimes you strike out and sometimes you hit a home run."

There are a lot of ways to reach Baker: phone (812) 876–8580, e-mail jjsportscards@hotmail.com, or drop by his Gosport warehouse Monday through Friday from 10:00 A.M. to 4:00 P.M.

Taking the Plunge
Gosport

Residents of Gosport apparently took the phrase "take the plunge" literally. At least when it came to holy matrimony. From the late 1800s to 1945, townsfolk would whisk away young couples after they exchanged nuptials and ceremoniously dunk them in a spring-fed trough. Over the years, historians have mislabeled the watering hole the "Chivalry Trough." The real word is "Shivaree," a mistake that's easy to make. But there's a big difference.

"Chivalry is how men should act toward women," admonishes Sue Trotman, Gosport History Museum curator. "Shivaree is an old tradition of treating newlyweds to a trick. It's a lot like a fraternity prank because it's their closest friends who dunk them."

The Shivaree Trough itself is not much of an attraction. The 8-by-4-foot concrete receptacle is hardly glamorous. It resides near the abandoned Brewer Flour Mill and is shrouded by weeds. Its legend, though, is certainly worth preserving. Trotman is unsure if the trough holds water anymore. She is sure, however, of the last couple who was plunged. "John and June Burns were one of the last ones to be shivareed in 1945," she recalls. "John was a great practical joker, so his friends were really looking forward to getting him."

The trough is located in Gosport, 21 miles northwest of Bloomington, east of State Road 231 on State Road 67. The Gosport History Museum (812–879–4873) can you get you there.

Why does a great wedding tradition like this fade while the "Chicken Dance" grows in popularity? We just ask 'em, we don't 'splain 'em.

The Buzz in Greencastle

Greencastle

Have you ever wondered why in the last edition of *Indiana Curiosities* I didn't include the tree in the courthouse roof in Greencastle? That's because it's in Greensburg.

I'm just trying to keep you on your toes.

The truth is, I didn't have anything from Greencastle. Let's change that right now. How about the Buzz Bomb Memorial? It's a plane that sits right smack in the southwest corner of the Putnam County Courthouse Square. It is the only buzz bomb on public display in the U.S.

SOUTHWEST

The buzz bomb, built by the Germans during WWII and also known as the V-1, was the precursor to the cruise missile, a pilotless aircraft that was essentially a flying bomb. It was used by the Nazis to bring the British to their knees, but many of the 8,000 aircrafts never reached their destination due to mechanical failure and because of their susceptibility to anti-aircraft fire. Nevertheless, the bomber took its toll of human life and was feared by the citizens of London.

How it got to Greencastle is a story in itself, but it all began in 1946. Captured German armaments had been shipped to the U.S. but were taking up a lot of room. Many items, like the buzz bomb, were about to be "recycled." Junked!

Frank Durham, a Greencastle reservist serving in Maryland, had a better idea. He wanted to bring the bomber back to Greencastle and make it into a memorial. Durham, with the help of members of a local VFW, managed to acquire the aircraft, but it literally took an act of Congress to accomplish this goal.

The limestone V that the bomber sits atop was designed by Art Perry of DePauw University, and the limestone was donated by a state senator Hoadley whose son was killed in the war. The memorial beneath the bomber lists the name of every Putnam County resident who lost his life in World War II—sixty-seven in all.

Durham, at age ninety, still practices law in Greencastle.

It is really a very moving experience to see this. More so than that tree in Greensburg.

To see the bomber, take Interstate 70 west from Indy to U.S. Highway 231 north, which runs right into Greencastle. Just keep going and you'll hit the town square. You'll see the bomber, unless they're repairing it, which they were last time I was there. Good luck.

HAZZARDOUS DUTY

The only *Dukes of Hazzard* prop more in demand than the original General Lee car are the cutoff jeans worn by Daisy Duke. Since there are only four known pairs of shorts—with one of them in the Smithsonian—Travis Bell of Greenwood settled on the car that started it all.

The flashy orange Dodge Charger, emblazoned with a rooftop rebel flag and "01" on the doors, flew over Roscoe's police car to open every show. Unfortunately, that was the first and last jump the car ever made. "Anytime the car was in the air, it was destroyed," says Bell. And those who remember the show know that those cars were launched more than the space shuttle.

Bell estimates there are more than 300 General Lee replicas. As co-president of the *Dukes of Hazzard* fan club, he should know. He owns one of the replicas and two of the squad cars. (He also owns the truck from *B.J. and the Bear* and the car from the *Blues Brothers*, but that's another story.)

His pride and joy—"the mecca of all things holy in the *Dukes of Hazzard*"—is branded with the I.D. plate of Lee1.

Bell found the car haphazardly during a Dukes-paraphernalia-gathering trip to Georgia. He met a man who not only was on the set when Lee1 made its fateful jump, but knew of the junkyard where the car was abandoned. Some fifty cars were wrecked while filming the first five episodes. Most of them were smashed and sold as scrap metal. So when Bell laid eyes on Lee1, his heart raced faster than when he dreamed of Daisy.

Hazzardous road conditions in Greenwood.

It was in rough shape. In fact, its trademark paint job was veiled by a coat of green from when the car was patched up and reused in a later episode. "The rebel flag was still visible, barely burning through the paint," Bell says.

When the first edition of the book was written, Bell had no plans to restore it, saying he'd have to cut the whole thing apart and replace everything. In the last two years, though, he's changed his tune. During his coast-to-coast travels to help promote the release of the *Dukes of Hazzard* movie, he had a change of heart.

Lee1 now rides again—in its full rebel glory. "Seeing it all battered was like allowing somebody to throw paint on the *Mona Lisa*—I just had to restore it."

For more information visit www.generalleefanclub.com.

Hello, Dolly
Heltonville

Virginia Turner has been helping Santa bring smiles to the faces of kids and adults alike for twenty-five years. Virginia and her husband, Boyce, own the Turner Doll Factory, just outside of Heltonville in Lawrence County.

Believe it or not, a doll factory in America is a real rarity. In fact, Virginia and Boyce may be the only manufacturers around today who construct virtually the entire doll right on the premises. A few parts, like hair and shoes, come from overseas, but the important parts, like the head, eyes, and clothing, are made at their factory.

Virginia sculpts the heads in clay, then makes a plaster of Paris mold. This allows the Turners to make a porcelain prototype. Virginia takes the resulting doll to different toy shows to see if buyers are intrigued with her creation. When Virginia feels she has a green light, she has a permanent metal mold created. From one mold can come many different dolls, a result achieved by varying accessories like hair and dress.

And what's even better is that you can visit the factory and observe the entire procedure, which includes the molding, assembly, and painting of the doll. The clothing, much of which is designed and patterned by an on-site seamstress, caps the process for all who are watching.

Making a doll is art, but selling it has a touch of science. Or at least marketing. "The outfits we make need to reflect the trendy colors of the day," says Virginia, who recognizes that many of her creations are not only played with but also displayed.

Turner Dolls are known worldwide and are often featured in *Doll Reader* magazine. Some of their creations, like the limited Wizard of Oz series, are worth several thousand dollars. But Virginia suggests you do not buy a doll as an investment. "The market has its ups and downs. Don't ever forget Beanie Babies." We'll try, but it's hard.

By the way, the Dorothy doll has silver-colored shoes, not ruby. (Lawyers, don'tcha know.)

Heltonville is south of Bloomington on State Road 446. Call for more specific directions at (800) 887–6372 or go to www.turnerdolls.com.

Roaming Charges

Lincoln City

They call it the Buffalo Run Farm, Grill & Gifts—not exactly a name that national franchises are made from, but catchy nonetheless. And you can catch some great food here, especially if you're willing to try their famous ostrich and buffalo burgers. Of course as you munch on this exotic fare, you can observe the buffalo and ostriches grazing in the field behind the restaurant, all watching and wondering if they will be your next meal.

For more information, please call their head buyer.

Ice cream flavors reflect the ambience: Pioneer Pecan, Wild Frontier Strawberry, Choctaw Cookie Dough, Ostrich Orange Sherbet, and Chocolate Covered Wagon. There is also Mint Buffalo Chip. It's not what you think (we hope).

But the food is just half the fun. A visit to the gift shop is an absolute must for bison and ostrich fans looking for a buffalo-leg lamp, some poopaper (paper made from buffalo dung), ostrich feathers, or painted ostrich eggs. Frozen buffalo and ostrich meat are also available. You can even buy a buffalo-penis walking stick. I wish I were making this up.

The restaurant is just a mile from Lincoln's boyhood home, but as the eatery is only a few years old, "Lincoln never ate here," says Kathleen Crews, the owner. "But he would have loved our ostrich burgers." Yes, but would he buy a walking stick?

You can drive your Lincoln, or Pinto if you're feeling lucky, to the Buffalo Run Farm, Grill & Gifts by taking I–64 to the Dale exit, then go south on US 231. Then left on State Road 162 for about 3 miles. Buffalo Run is open every day, but hours differ by season. Call (812) 937–2799 for more information.

Middle America
Linton

Question: When can the center of everything be in the middle of nowhere?

Answer: When the U.S. Census Bureau decides that the center of the United States population is located in a rural Indiana county.

From 1930 to 1940, the center of the American people was near a reclaimed strip mine, off a dirt road, just outside of Linton, in Greene County. And they have the stone historical marker to prove it.

Only God can comprehend the complicated computations, logarithms, and elaborate geographical matrices the Census Bureau used to pinpoint this spot. One thing we're certain of: The formula could not be as complicated as the directions needed to visit the marker.

Getting to Linton is relatively easy: Just take State Road 67 south, then State Road 54 west. Finding the road that leads to the Linton Conservation Club, the park that hosts the marker, is a bit trickier—especially since County Road 1100 is not well marked. Once in the park, grab a compass and put on your hiking boots. As the authors of *Indiana: A New Historical Guide* describe it, the terrain is "geared more to the outdoorsman than to the sightseer."

A half mile of hiking over the wooded, undulating, sporadically marked trails of the reclaimed strip mine brings weary tourists to the weathered marker. (That's if you've been lucky enough to follow the map correctly.) After taking a couple of snapshots of virtually nothing, all you have to do is find your way back to your vehicle.

If you want an even more useless journey, visit Indiana's highest point (but that's another story).

Lucky Charms
Lucky Point

For many years the area of White River floodplain was a hotbed of UFO sightings. So many sightings, in fact, that in the late 1980s the town marshal from nearby Monroe often came down to Lucky Point to direct traffic. Needless to say, he was trying to control the extra tourists, not the extraterrestrials.

Lucky Point has a rich history of UFOs, as well as grizzly ghost stories and unspeakable murders. The stories go back to the first white settlers in the 1760s, although even before then Native American oral histories reflected the belief that this area of the country was, well, different.

More recently, sightings have included black triangles in the grass, Bigfoot sightings, quaking power pole lines, cattle mutilation, orange balls of light, and dead calves with their brains "surgically" removed.

A sheriff's deputy once reported seeing small slender beings with huge eyes peering from the windows of a spaceship. In another case, after a series of hundreds of nocturnal lights punctuated a pinkish orange glow over the area, the local weatherman checked his radar and saw nothing but squiggly lines. Apparently that means something.

In recent years Jerry Sievers, executive director of MUFON (Mutual UFO Network), claims that "men in black" have been seen in the area, questioning people who claim to have made these sightings. According to Sievers, the men claimed they were from the local power and light company, investigating improper photographing of their equipment, and wanted some snapshots that were allegedly taken of UFOs.

By the way, Lucky Point got its name because hunters in the eighteenth century found game plentiful in this area of southern Knox County. The Point has also become a favorite spot for boys to take their dates for a little romance. Lucky can mean lots of things.

Take State Road 61 out of Vincennes to Monroe City. Lucky Point is just a couple of miles east of Monroe. Ask directions from Monroe, but most people will tell you there's not much to see. Of course, you could get lucky.

If you want more information, you can go to www.Indianamufon.homestead.com. The site has everything you ever wanted to know about this stuff. Actually, it has more.

SOUTHWEST

Star Power
Martinsville

The Goethe Link Observatory in Martinsville remains a secret even to nearby residents. Although it sits atop a mountain (okay, a steep hill), it is nestled behind a grove of trees and, thus, is nearly impossible to see from the road, a few miles below. That's probably the way Dr. Goethe Link wanted it.

The observatory was conceived and constructed by Dr. Link, a noted surgeon in the 1920s and '30s who made his name by performing scarless goiter surgeries. A renaissance man with myriad interests ranging from hummingbirds to copperhead snakes, he had a fascination with ballooning but was discouraged by his wife, who felt that moonshiners, thinking he was a federal agent looking for illegal stills, would shoot him down.

That's the rumor, at least. One thing is sure: Link had a love of astronomy and was intrigued with the idea of a private donation to fund such a project. The telescope he commissioned and later donated to Indiana University was constructed entirely in Indianapolis and, at the time, was one of the eight largest in the United States. The observatory dome, which rotates like a fancy penthouse restaurant, weighs 34 tons and is 34 feet in diameter. The telescope, with a 36-inch mirror, weighs more than 5,000 pounds.

The observatory is now utilized by the Indiana Astronomical Society for its own members and to educate the public. More specific scientific research has been curtailed in past years because of increasing light pollution from nearby Indianapolis. But from mid-spring through mid-fall, the society meets on the second and fourth Saturdays of each month and the observatory gate is opened by 6:00 P.M. Visitors are welcome to come, ask questions, and bring their own telescopes.

The observatory is at 1656 Observatory Road in Martinsville. Call first, (317) 297–1405, or e-mail Schoppy@mw.net for more information. You can also check out the Web site at www.iasindy.org.

FAST BACKWARDS

They call him Mr. Backwards. And why not? Roger Riddell is the Ginger Rogers of stunt cycling. He can do what Evel Knievel can do, but he can do it backwards. But no high heels.

In 2001 Riddell drove his Harley Davidson 50 mph up a ramp and flew 62.5 feet backwards over five cars and another motorcycle. It broke his old record by 2 feet and it almost broke everything else in his body. It did get him in the *Guinness Book of World Records*. Riddell, who lives in Martinsville, has been doing this backwards thing for more than twenty-five years, and except for the fifty times he's broken one of his bones, he's loved every minute of it.

Riddell used to jump the normal way back in the 1970s, but Evel Knievel was such a big name at that time that Riddell knew he needed a little twist on his act to make it fly. The first time he jumped backwards was Mother's Day 1975. He did it in front of a crowd. He had never practiced it, never trained for it, and never really planned it. He just did it. "I still don't practice," says Riddle. "If I'm gonna miss, I'm gonna miss."

Riddell was hurt in Boise, Idaho, in 2003, when he attempted to jump over six cars backwards on his Harley. He broke his arm, three ribs, his hand, and his pelvis, as well as dislocating his hip. Other than that, it was a successful jump.

Riddell has appeared on *Monster Nation* and on *Ripley's Believe It or Not!* and was in the *Guinness Book of World Records* for several years.

At press time Riddell was recovering from injuries. Riddell is always recovering from injuries. Check out Riddell's latest plans at www.mrbackwards.com.

Shoe Tree

Milltown

If you've ever wondered how that single shoe ends up on the side of the highway, you'll really be perplexed when you see the Shoe Tree in Milltown. Since the early 1960s, folks have been coming from all over Indiana, Kentucky, and the rest of the Midwest just to toss a pair of old loafers, sneakers, or wing tips up in the tree.

There's some disagreement about how the tradition started, but Maxine Archibald, who for twenty years has owned and operated Maxine's Market just 6 miles from the tree, claims her father has the real story.

"He believes it was the Boy Scouts walking from Marengo Cave to Wyandotte Cave in the 1960s who often carried an extra pair of shoes. I guess they just started pitching them up in the tree," she explains. "And then the neighborhood boys followed suit. Next thing you knew, we had a Shoe Tree."

A better selection than Shoe Carnival.

Now you know how to start your own.

The shoes are usually tied together and flung to the overhanging limbs of the mighty oak. "It's not easy to do," claims Maxine, "but the tree is sure loaded." No one has counted the shoes, but locals say it's easily several hundred pairs. Some of the shoes blow off in storms and find their way to the nearby creek, but for the most part, the shoe population is growing.

In 2003 lightning hit the Shoe Tree. "Some of the footwear melted," says Maxine, "but I think the tree is going to make it."

The Shoe Tree, which sits on Maxine's brother's property, has had its share of TV, radio, and newspaper coverage. We hate to say it, but there's no business like shoe business. Old State Road 64 goes right into Milltown. And you can't miss Maxine's place. Ask her where the tree is, and she'll point you in the right direction.

Religious Convictions
Mooresville

The Assembly of God Church, at the corner of Harrison and Jefferson in Mooresville, was where John Dillinger baptized himself in a life of crime. On the night of September 6, 1924, Dillinger, age twenty, and Edgar Singleton were drunk on moonshine. The pair had wobbled their way through town and sat clumsily on the church's back steps. Unfortunately for grocer Frank Morgan, the church lay between his store and his home.

Dillinger and Singleton pummeled Morgan as he passed by and relieved him of his weekend's receipts ($150). Singleton escaped by car, Dillinger on foot. Not yet possessing the criminal prowess that made him a legend, Dillinger staggered back into town to inquire how Morgan was doing. Suspicious townsfolk alerted the police, who later arrested him.

A heavy-handed judge gave Dillinger the maximum sentence. It was during his incarceration, note many historians, that he honed the skills that would transform him from greenhorn thug into public enemy number one, from bumbling bandit to bank-robbing, prison-escaping legend. And they say prison can't rehabilitate.

Some Dillinger buffs like to go to Chicago's Biograph Theatre, where he was betrayed by the "Lady in Red," or visit the "escape-proof" jail from which he sprang himself. Still others like to pay homage at the Dillinger Museum at the Lake County Welcome Center in Hammond. We suggest you go to the church.

"We can't all be saints."—John Herbert Dillinger

The original church remains, although several different sects have occupied the building over the years and added numerous additions to the structure. Presently the Heritage Christian Church makes its home there, at the very same location in downtown Moorseville.

John Dillinger had more hits than your favorite radio station.

Uphill All the Way

Mooresville

Seeing apples roll up Kellar's Hill would have driven Sir Isaac Newton to discover hard cider instead of gravity. Gravity Hill, also known as Magnetic Hill, can be found off State Road 42, just southwest of Mooresville. People have been perplexed by this anomaly since the road was gravel and passengers rode in rumble seats.

Here people park their cars at the bottom of the hill, put them in neutral, and coast backward 50 to 100 feet. At the top of the hill, they get out and try to push the cars back to the bottom. To their (and our) amazement, the cars won't budge. Curiosity-seekers also make the trek with buckets of water to watch rivulets run uphill.

Folklore suggests an apparitional force from an Indian witch doctor buried at the hill's base pushes the cars uphill. A surveyor pooh-poohed such tall tales by proving the hill's "crest" was actually 18 inches lower than its apparent "bottom." An Indiana University physics professor also helped dispel the myth by noting that land contour, rock formations, and the tilt of fences and utility poles add to the optical illusion.

The influx of traffic-stopping, bucket-toting tourists prompted law officials to ask people not to stop in the middle of this now-paved and busy byway. An article in *Outdoor Indiana* summed it up best: "Heavy traffic coming at you may result in a different sort of gravity."

But if you want to try it, take State Road 42 for 1 mile southwest of Mooresville, turning right on Kellars Hill Road, which is usually unmarked (unless they marked it, but you'd better ask someone anyway because we hear they sometimes move the mark). Gravity Hill is 1 mile past this intersection.

Marriage on the Rocks

Morgantown

James "Smith" Knight had twenty children. Some say twenty-two. Some say twenty-six. But who's counting? Apparently no one. This was considered excessive even in 1894. But Knight built more than a big family; he built one of the most curious houses in Indiana.

The Rock House, as it is now called, was unusual for being constructed from cement blocks, a practice that would not be in general use for another twenty years. What makes the house truly unique is that before the concrete on each block set, Knight embedded stones, usually geodes, of varying sizes into the wet cement.

People in stone houses shouldn't throw glass.

There's more. When he tired of stones in the cement, he starting throwing in personal items like coins, jewelry, dishes, bike chains, and pottery. Even a ceramic doll's head sticks out of the cement. Oh yeah, and a wild boar's jaw. Doug Strain, the current owner, is still discovering new things. "I walk around the house and see stuff sticking out that I never saw before."

The ten-room Victorian home has been a bed-and-breakfast for many years, a perfect place for parties, retreats, private dinners, and teas. Well, almost perfect. Doug Strain says that many believe the bed-and-breakfast is haunted by Isabel, Knight's first wife, who loved the house and is just keeping her eye on things. "She's a friendly ghost," says Strain. "At least that's what the clairvoyants tell me."

In 2005 the Rock House closed, but they plan to open again for private parties only. It's worth the trip just to drive by.

The Rock House is in Morgantown on 380 West Washington. Call for reservations: (888) 818–0001. If you don't think this is a neat place, you have rocks in your head.

Don't Be an Idiot
Nashville (Story)

Every locale has a village idiot. But only Story, Indiana, has made it an elected position. We're not sure what the connection is, but ever since the election of Bill Clinton, the good folks in this tiny hamlet—too tiny, in fact, for a mayor or town council—have searched for the person most deserving of this hallowed (and hollow) title.

Inside the city's historic Story Inn is the Story Still, a pub that's become the stuff of legend. The Story Still serves as a kind of "election central." Tavern regulars submit written nominations to the bartender, who keeps track of the voting. The process is not perfect, but it's better than Florida's.

SOUTHWEST

In the application, Richard Hofstetter, owner of the Story Inn, cautions those making nominations. "Remember, this country is full of qualified candidates, so be specific."

Here are some nominations from the past couple of years:

- The woman who borrowed her grandfather's pickup and drove over her own foot.
- The guy who mixed chlorine bleach with ammonia to make a cleaning agent, resulting in a mass evacuation from Story's largest office building. Granted, it isn't that big . . .
- The waitress who kicked off her shoes to dance and discovered that one had landed in the deep fryer.
- A tavern regular who bought a yacht online, sight unseen, for $200,000.
- The tavern guest who knocked himself out opening the door of his own car.

And my favorite:

- The man who was learning to hunt with a bow and arrow and brought down his own Chevy Cavalier.

Winners get a $100 credit at the bar and the honor of having their certificate of idiocy hung on the wall.

If you are interested in becoming the village idiot, you don't have to actually live in Story or even do something stupid right in town, but your nomination must come from a regular patron of the tavern. You might not even know you've been nominated, but your stupidity makes for great bar conversations.

Where is Story, Indiana? Who knows? But if you can get to Nashville, someone can get you to Story in five minutes. Unless they're an idiot.

The Story Inn is located at 6404 State Road 135 South (812–988–2273).

Belle of Nashville

Nashville

Okay, we're not 100 percent sure of this, but we think the Joybell Theater and Gift Shop in Nashville, Indiana, is the only handbell theater in the world. Even if we're wrong, we might as well really ring its praises.

Kristine Stout is the bell ringer. And a true musician. Watching Kristine is a bit dizzying. She glides up and down the 8-foot table, grasps one of thirty-seven bells, gives it a shake, returns it to the same position on the table, then dances to a new bell. Sometimes she'll pick up two. Make note of this: The musical arrangements are all hers and they must be completely memorized (she's always moving; she can't look at sheet music). Kristine is a soloist—unique, really. Her only accompaniment is a preprogrammed keyboard.

Kristine first got the bell bug when she heard a handbell concert in the early 1990s. That's when the dream started. She wanted to bring this kind of music to a theater of her own. And Nashville seemed the perfect place.

She took a thirty-minute class. She was awed. "My chin was on the floor," says Kristine, but she admits that is not the most effective way to play the bells.

Kristine gives two concerts a day. Or none. Or five. It depends on the crowds. Some concerts are an hour. Some are fifteen minutes. "I can be very flexible," says Kristine. "I'm the only one in the band." She plays hymns, patriotic, and classical music. "In theory I can play almost anything. But that's just a theory," laughs the bellmeister. (Bellmeistress?)

The gift shop offers novelties with a musical theme, as well as inspirational and handmade items. Both the theater and gift shop are open April through Christmas. Kristine and her husband, Kirt, usually travel in the winter when business slows down in Nashville.

The Joybell Theater is in downtown Nashville at 79 North Van Buren Street (800–462–1241; www.joybelltheater.com). The show is ten bucks. You'll love the ringing in your ears.

Picture Perfect

Nashville

Sometimes a picture is worth a thousand words. Sometimes it's worth about $500. That's true in Nashville, one of only three places in America where you can have a hologram (a true 3D image) made of yourself or a loved one. Or a pet. Or your mother-in-law.

Walk into Forth Dimension Holographics in Brown County and you'll know just how eerie (and realistic) this stuff is. You'll come face to face with Ronald Reagan, who you'll swear is right in the wall looking out at you. You'll see images of children, clowns, and pets, all in a three-dimensional presentation that is so lifelike it will give you the creeps. In some photos the hologram is two channels, meaning that you can see different images that magically change with your viewing angle.

Sitting for a pulsed hologram is like sitting for a regular photo, but what the subject doesn't know is that the laser flash from the holographic camera is twenty billionths of a second. Needless to say, a slight movement won't make too much of a difference. Owner Rob Taylor can "develop" the film and have your photo in about five hours.

There's no danger involved, of course, unless your subject is the white Bengal tiger who took a playful bite out of Taylor's leg. His youngest subject was a nine-day-old baby.

Customers in his studio can buy stock images of animals, model cars, nature scenes, and limited edition fine art, but people with any real perspective on life opt for a personally commissioned hologram.

The studio is at 90 West Washington Street in Nashville, just off the main drag. You can call (812) 988–8212 or go to its Web site: www.forthdimension.net.

Deadly Museum

Newburgh

The Simpson Mortuary Museum in Newburgh isn't a hall of fame for morticians. It is, however, a place that preserves and displays the tools of the trade. Virgil Simpson, museum owner/curator, is a tough man to get in touch with. It's best to try to call him before noon on weekdays. That's because the retired mortician (his name still graces the family funeral home across the street) runs the museum more as a hobby and less as a business. "I'm not over there as much as I'd like," says Simpson. "I'm getting pretty old myself."

Once an appointment is made, Simpson gladly shows off his wares. Housed inside the centuries-old building are items once employed in his funeral home. Long before mobsters spoke of icing their enemies, morticians were chilling their clients with cooling boards. The bodies were placed atop the perforated top, while underneath, pans of ice kept the deceased cool during wakes. The boards proved especially useful during steamy summer days in this Ohio River town.

Other displays include gravity-fed and hand-pumped embalming apparatuses, wicker body baskets (used to pick up bodies in out-of-the way places, like the woods), and some incredibly low mortician bills. "There's one bill that was only $25," notes Simpson. "Like everything else, that price has gone up."

One fee that hasn't been inflated, however, is the museum's admission price: free.

Newburgh is 10 miles east of Evansville. The museum is open by appointment only. For tours call (812) 853–5177.

Over the Hill
Newport

It's been almost a hundred years since the first antique car grinded up the hill in Newport. Come to think of it, there were no antique cars in 1909, but the point is that this hill was a testing ground for automobiles of the early 1900s. Even Henry Ford is said to have used the incline to test his cars. Ditto, the Chevrolet brothers. By 1915 use of the hill had declined due to financial problems and the fact that a new decade of cars could easily navigate the 1,800 feet and 8.5-degree grade.

In 1968 interest in the hill was renewed by the local Lions Club, which sought to reestablish the tradition in the Newport Antique Auto Climb, a race that now attracts more than 80,000 folks every October. Race is the operative word here. This is no beauty contest, but a demonstration of sheer speed by more than 200 car owners who chug into town from all over the country with their Model Ts, Model As, Reos, Packards, and Studebakers. No car can be newer than 1942, and races are divided into twenty-six classes.

They go up the same hill as in 1909. It's still 1,800 feet long. The grade is still 8.5 degrees. "Not only hasn't the hill changed in ninety-five years," says Ed Conrad, one of the event organizers, "but neither has Newport. Not one bit, not an iota."

See or join the race the first Sunday in October. Call the Newport Lions Club for more info at (765) 492–4220 or climb the Web site at www.newporthillclimb.com. If you're driving an antique car, you can drive right into town after taking US 36 about 60 miles west to State Road 63, then going 6 miles north to Newport. If you're driving a 2006 Honda, avoid embarrassment by parking in Fountain County.

255

The B-I-G Palooka

Oolitic

The big joke about the Joe Palooka statue outside of town hall in Oolitic is that even he doesn't know what he's doing there. That's selling the big guy short. You don't want to do that.

Here's the story: Limestone is a big thing in Indiana. (Did you know that NYC's Empire State Building is built with Indiana limestone?) There was even a move in the town of Bedford to build a limestone replica of the great pyramids of Egypt, until Senator Proxmire came along and squashed the idea. But back to Joe. Joe Palooka, a comic-strip hero of the 1940s created by cartoonist Ham Fisher, was a boxer who ultimately enlisted in the United States Army. Fueled by American patriotism, the cartoon figure became a symbol of American might. Joe's nickname: "Defender of Justice."

Stoned in front of Oolitic's Town Hall. Not a good idea, Joe.

SOUTHWEST

In 1948 the limestone industry decided to build a statue of Joe Palooka to commemorate its hundredth anniversary. Two noted limestone carvers, George Hitchcock and Harry Easton, chipped away at the project at the Indiana Limestone Company and completed the work on the square in Bedford.

Joe got shuffled around for the next twenty-five years, and was often the victim of vandalism. In 1984 the Bedford Fraternal Order of Police donated the statue to Oolitic, where it now stands on Main Street between the town hall and the post office. People often arrange to rendezvous in front of the statue. You can't eat at Joe's, but you can meet at Joe's. And many do. Oolitic is thirty minutes south of Bloomington on State Road 37.

All Sorts of Stuff
Punkin Center

In Orange County, in Punkin Center, on Tater Road, you'll find Add's Museum of All Sorts of Stuff, where, not surprisingly, you'll find a collection of, well, all sorts of stuff.

The museum is as muddled as that opening sentence. For Add's and the adjoining Punkin Center General Store are not really open for business anymore. Why write about a place that's closed? Because it's an interesting place, and it's not really closed, per se. Does that mean it's open to the public? Yes and no. Is there a tour guide? Sometimes there is, other times there's not.

Here's the scoop: Add Gray and his wife, Mabel, opened the store in 1922. Years later as the couple accumulated antiques, knick-knacks, and assorted relics, they decided to open a museum. In its heyday a sample of the collection included saddles, swords, sleighs, scarecrows, chandeliers, and an old-fashioned soda fountain.

257

Add died some time back, leaving Mabel the sole curator and tour guide. If she's home, the museum's open. If she's not, you'll just have to come back some other time. "Nothing special goes on here," she says. "I don't do much. I've just been around here a long time."

Mabel's modesty is exceeded only by her longevity. She has trouble hearing, so it takes her some time to answer the phone or to get to the door. She does like the company, though. And she loves to reminisce and show off her wares. "Why don't you just come down sometime?" she asked me over the phone.

The next time my back-road wanderings lead me down Tater Road, I'll do just that.

Add's Museum can be found in Orange County, in Punkin Center, on Tater Road. Punkin Center is east of Paoli, just off State Road 56. Call Mrs. Gray before visiting, though: (812) 723–2432.

Dear Santa Claus
Santa Claus

Santa Claus, Indiana, is a pretty popular place in the summer, what with its state-of-the art amusement park, considered by many to be the world's first "theme park." But it's wintertime when Santa Claus gets a little crazy. People just go postal.

The tiny town got its name in the 1850s, when local residents discovered that the label they had picked for their fine city—Santa Fe—was already taken. The story goes that on Christmas Eve at the local church (also the town hall and school), when the townspeople were trying to decide on a new name for their hamlet, the church door inexplicably blew open and the children were said to hear sleigh bells. "It's Santa Claus," said one little girl. And there you have it.

Ever since then Santa Claus, Indiana, has been the recipient of more than 10,000 letters each year, letters simply addressed to Santa Claus. The U.S. Postal Service wasn't crazy about this, so it changed the name to Santaclaus back in the late 1800s, thinking that would stem the Christmas tide. Residents protested and got their name back. That's the spirit!

Yes, Virginia, there is a Santa Claus . . . Indiana.

Believe it or not, each letter is answered personally by a contingency of "elves," local volunteers who want each child to feel special. There's also a shopping area called Kringle Place, a tiny strip mall that includes a Santa Claus Museum. They don't even have that at the North Pole.

The original post office is now inside the Holiday World theme park, but a new post office is just a few doors down from the Santa Claus Museum. Each year, right after Halloween, it's time to gear up for the onslaught of mail that has been pouring into this city for more than a hundred years.

Other than the 10,000-plus letters to Santa Claus, the post office accepts boxes of pre-stamped cards and letters from people who want the Santa Claus postmark on their holiday correspondence. Last year, more than a half million letters got this special treatment.

By the way, the official name of Santa Claus Land is now Holiday World & Splashin' Safari. Apparently, Santa's name is hot in the winter, but his appeal cools down in the summer. Go figure.

If you want to write to Santa, send your letters to Santa Claus, P.O. Box 1, Santa Claus, IN 47579. If you're more into riding than writing, then visit the theme and water park and hop on The Voyage, one of the world's neatest wooden roller coasters because it creates multiple pockets of weightlessness throughout the ride—more, it is said, than any other wooden coaster in the country. The Voyage, by the way, is the main course in the Thanksgiving section of the park. There's also Halloween and July 4 sections.

Holiday World & Splashin' Safari are located at the junction of State Roads 162 and 245 in Santa Claus. From I–64, take exit 63 and drive south on SR 162 for 7 miles until the road comes to a T. Turn right and head up the hill; you'll see the parking lot on the right. Call (800) 467–2682 for more information, or visit www.holidayworld.com.

Scissors, Paper, Rox
Shoals

Since the 1800s Jug Rock has been an Indiana roadside attraction—mainly because it is off to the side of a road, U.S. Highway 50. Visitors have parked next to the heralded formation and memorialized it with illustrations, paintings, and photographs. Jug Rock even inspired state officials to dub its surroundings a nature preserve.

The 50-foot sandstone tower outside of Shoals is hailed as Indiana's most famous, most spectacular standing rock. Like most Hoosier rock formations, its appearance—an hourglass shape that must have reminded early pioneers of the earthenware jugs found in their log cabins—inspired its name. The formation is even topped with a sandstone cap resembling a stopper.

Jug Rock. Nature in the balance.

261

The city of Shoals has certainly done its part to honor the rock, and all of Shoals' athletes are known as Jug Rox. The school may have the only teams in America nicknamed after a rock formation. The *Pittsburgh Post-Gazette* thought so much of the moniker that the newspaper included the Jug Rox in its top-ten high school nickname list. The fifth-place honor placed Shoals behind Illinois's Hoopestan Area Cornjerkers, West Virginia's Poca Dots, Indiana's Frankfurt Hot Dogs, and Florida's Lakeland Dreadnaughts.

So when fans say these Shoals teams rock, they mean it. Here are some additional fictional facts about Shoals:

- School's fight song: Bob Seger's "Like a Rock"
- Movie shown before each home game: *Rocky*
- Concession stand favorite: rocky road ice cream
- Music played by marching band: rock 'n' roll (preferably the Rolling Stones)

Hard to Find
Solsberry

Some call it the Greene County Viaduct; some call it the Tulip Bridge; others simply The Trestle. But most just stand there with their mouths wide open as they gaze upon it. It seems very out of place. Stand beneath the massive steel girders and you'll realize how insignificant you really are. Just what we all need.

The trestle is reported to be the second longest in the world (some say the third, but who's measuring?). Spanning 2,295 feet and standing 180 feet high, this steel and concrete structure is supported by eighteen towers. How could something this big be so hard to find?

When the viaduct was completed in December 1906, the Illinois Central tracks on that line extended from Indianapolis to Effingham, Illinois. During the days of steam locomotives, large wooden barrels of water sat on platforms along the viaduct for use in case of fire.

The history of the trestle is full of folklore and mystique. One story contends that more than a few bodies have been buried along the tracks, some of those deaths the result of some serious partying. Old-timers also remember dogs walking the trestle, then panicking when the train came rolling along and jumping to their deaths.

The New York Central line operated on ground-level tracks until 1996 when the line was closed and the tracks were removed. The Indiana Railroad Company, which purchased the Illinois Central Line in 1985, uses the elevated tracks to haul coal from Greene County to Indianapolis.

You can stop at the general store in Solsberry and ask the clerk how to find the viaduct, except he won't call it a viaduct. Anyway, he'll scribble a map for you, but you can plan on asking about six people along the way. Then you'll end up following a guy in his pickup truck. And then when you see it, you'll wonder how you could miss it. IT'S HUGE.

Lawn Man
Terre Haute

Brad Hauter of Terre Haute is in the *Guinness Book of World Records*. He drove a riding lawn mower across the United States in 1999. Then he did it again in 2003. I guess he missed a spot.

Believe it or not, there was no madness to this method. Hauter was selected by Yard Man, a large lawn mower manufacturer, to take one of their vehicles across the U.S. to help promote the Keep America

Beautiful campaign, the idea being that clean, well-kept neighborhoods are less apt to attract and foster crime.

Hauter, a former student at Park Tudor in Indianapolis, was coaching soccer in Minnesota at the time and had done a lot of work with charities. When this opportunity arose, he knew that this was one job worth sitting down for.

Hauter was selected from a group of more than one hundred applicants, all of whom had the drive to maneuver the vehicle over 5,000 miles of sometimes rough terrain from New York to Atlanta to L.A.

Along the way, Hauter and his support crew stopped in hundreds of towns and cities. "Everyone was so friendly," says Hauter, "but I think they thought I was going to mow their lawn."

Truth is that Hauter did not do much lawn cutting at all. Instead he spread the message about a cleaner America. He did, however, spend 600 hours on the lawn mower that first summer, which beat my son by 599 hours.

The mower was retrofitted just a bit, adding cruise control (cruise control?) and a cup holder. Hauter could get the mower up to 30 miles per hour, but admits that while coasting down hills in neutral he often shot up to 50 or 60 mph. "The cops would sometimes pull me over and search my vehicle for grass," laughs Hauter. Ain't cops funny?

By the way, lawn mowers get 30 miles to a gallon. I didn't want you to be up all night wondering about that.

CANDLES Museum

Terre Haute

When this book was first published in 2003, people asked me, "If you had to pick one place I shouldn't miss, what it be?" I had trouble responding to that question. But in this edition, the answer is clear: the CANDLES Holocaust Museum in Terre Haute, Indiana.

The museum was founded by Eva Kor, whose story of survival during the Holocaust is gut-wrenching. Eva and her sister, Miriam, were subjects of Dr. Josef Mengele's notorious experiments on identical twins during WWII. Thus the name of the museum: **C**hildren of **A**uschwitz **N**azi **D**eadly **L**ab **E**xperiment **S**urvivors, or CANDLES.

When Eva began lecturing about her Holocaust experiences in 1977, she realized how little she knew about the history and scope of the experiments she was subjected to. For seven years she searched for other twin survivors. Ultimately, Kor located 122 individual survivors of the experiments from ten countries around the world. The founding of the museum was the byproduct of this search for survivors—an attempt by Kor to educate people about the horrors of Hitler's Final Solution and to eliminate prejudice. There are other Holocaust museums, but this is the only one founded by a Mengele twin and specifically dedicated to children of the Holocaust.

First opened in 1995, the museum was burned almost to the ground by an arsonist in 2003. It has since been rebuilt and is now considered one of the finest of its kind in the country.

The main entrance has six windows symbolizing the six million Jews killed in the Holocaust, but Kor is adamant that the museum tell the whole story of this ghastly period in history. That's why there are three sets of eleven windows, representing the total number of people murdered, eleven million, during Hitler's reign. Inside the new 3,800-square-foot building are photos, artifacts, documents, art, and books.

Kor's message is not without some controversy. The museum displays no photos of the dead, a common site in most Holocaust museums. "What purpose does that serve?" asks Kor. "I want this museum to be about survival."

Eva Kor has forgiveness in her heart after all these years. One thing is certain: You will not forgive yourself if you do not spend a few hours in this museum.

The museum is at 1532 South Third Street and is open Tuesday through Saturday from 1:00 to 4:00 P.M. The phone number is (812) 234–7881. Visit the Web site at www.candlesholocaustmuseum.org.

Terre Water
Terre Haute

It's the largest living coral reef display in America and one of the country's largest saltwater fish and coral propagation facilities—and a mere 800 miles from the nearest ocean. Inland Aquatics in Terre Haute seems like a fish out of water, but it's worth the swim.

Inland Aquatics holds 40,000 gallons of saltwater, hundreds of varieties of fish, and a total population that exceeds several million, if you count the really, really tiny critters. Many of the species occupy their own tanks to avoid infighting. They should try this at the Indiana State House.

Inland Aquatics can sell you guppies for a dollar, a blue spot jawfish for $200, or a black tang for $400. Hey, how about a pair of blue-striped clown fish for a thousand bucks? You can also find invertebrates, "live" rock and sand, hard and soft coral, and ornamental algae. Also, ecojars, cultured banggai cardinals, and deep oolitic sand beds. Not that you asked.

They can even offer you a tiny octopus. Tanks, but no tanks.

Most of the fish sold by Inland have been imported from warmer climes. While breeding tropical fish here would be nice, Mike Ames, manager of Inland, explains how that is virtually impossible because baby saltwater fish require live food, almost microscopic sustenance that cannot be successfully bred in large enough quantities.

Visitors to Inland can look at the fish storage area and filtration devices from observation decks. Except for an occasional guided tour, the public watches from the sidelines, although there is a retail area out front for people looking for an exotic addition to their aquarium.

To find Inland, drive your Stingray or Barracuda west on I–70 from Indianapolis and take US 41 North. When you hit the courthouse, go around back and there's Inland. Way inland. The retail area is open Tuesday through Saturday, noon to 6:00 P.M.; Sunday noon to 7:00 P.M. Phone: (812) 232–9000; Web site: www.inlandaquatics.com.

Barking up the Right Tree

Trafalgar

It's not easy to give up a thriving shiitake mushroom business. At least we don't think it's easy. But that's exactly what Sherrie Yarling and Gordon Jones did in 1991. After supplying this gourmet fungus to Indianapolis's top restaurants from their Brown County farm, they shifted a few gears and are now—so far as we can tell—the only commercial producer of shagbark hickory syrup in the United States.

It all started in the late 1980s, when Gordon was tending to some of the mushrooms that he cultivated from the felled branches on his sixty-four-acre farm. A passing farmer offered to buy some of the logs for firewood and noticed a few hickory trees on the grounds. The farmer stripped off the outside of the trunk and spun a story about how his great-great-grandmother made a dynamite syrup using the bark of the tree.

The farmer was a little shaky on the details, but he ultimately did find the original recipe. Through some rather sticky trial and errors, Sherrie and Gordon produced what many believe is the best-tasting syrup you can buy. They were about to embark (sorry, I had to use this somewhere) on a new career.

Shagbark syrup goes back a long way. Research told Gordon and Sherrie that American Indians—probably the Shawnee—produced the syrup generations before the arrival of the pioneers. The shagbark hickory is indigenous to the Ohio Valley, including Tennessee, Indiana, and Illinois.

And how's business? Well, it would be great if we could say "slow as molasses," but that wouldn't be true. Gordon and Sherrie work 24/7 producing their tasty product for the finest chefs in Indianapolis and have recently branched out to Chicago, Washington, D.C., New York, and California. When they sent a sample to Julia Child, she delighted them with a handwritten thank-you, which included how she enjoyed basting her ribs with the syrup. Other customers use it on desserts, waffles, corn cakes, Cornish game hen, and pork tenderloin. "There are a million ways to enjoy shagbark syrup," says Sherry, who encourages you to call (317) 878–5648 or check out her Web site (www.Hickory works.com), where you can order syrup and download recipes.

Bridge Party
Vincennes

Half this entry should be in *Illinois Curiosities,* because half of this odd-ity is on the other side of the Wabash River.

It's the St. Francisville Bridge, a one-hundred-year-old structure that connects St. Francisville, Illinois, to Vincennes, Indiana. It looks like a hunk of rusted metal, but locals swear by it—and pray when they go over it.

The Cannon Ball Railroad used to cross the bridge, but that stopped running in 1970, at which point a local farmer purchased the structure and used it to carry produce across the river. He allowed others to use it, and charged a few pennies per trip.

Then in 1996 the movers and shakers of St. Francisville realized that if they turned it into a commercial bridge, it would save people time going between Illinois and Indiana, a boon for folks who worked at the Good Samaritan Hospital in St. Francisville and lived in Indiana.

The tracks were then removed and replaced by wood planks. You can even peer through the slats and see the Wabash River. But you have to pay for such scenic splendor. Fifty cents to be exact. And you have to be exact, because part of the time there's no one manning the toll booth. You're on your honor.

During peak times you can chat with the friendly—sometimes too friendly—toll takers like Debbie Harrington, who has lived in the area her whole life and says she knows pretty much everyone who crosses the bridge, which results in a lot of chatter.

"That's my big problem," admits Debbie, who sits in a tiny wooden hut. "Sometimes I'm the cause of the backup." About 700 cars a day pass over the bridge.

The bridge is only one lane, so it's "first come, first served," and while an occasional standoff does occur, most people are pretty friendly and willing to yield. Drivers often put on their lights to alert cars waiting on the other side before they are about to proceed.

I asked Debbie who was more courteous, Indiana or Illinois drivers?

"No comment," said Debbie. But I think we all know.

Hotel Heaven
West Baden Springs

There is a very good reason why I did not put the West Baden Hotel in the first edition of this book. Come to think of it, there wasn't a good reason. What a dunce I am.

This is probably the single most awesome man-made site in Indiana. People who see it for the first time fall to their knees. Then they are encouraged to lie on their backs and take a photo of the ceiling of one of the most beautiful atriums ever designed. Some call it the Eighth Wonder of the World. A lot of those are the people who work for the Indiana Tourism Department, of course, but they do have a point.

With a freespan central dome, the largest in the world before the Houston Astrodome was built, this structure was a testimony to the elegance (some would say opulence) of the 1920s. More than a dozen trains each day rolled into French Lick and West Baden, carrying big-wigs from places like Chicago and St. Louis. Some were attracted to "the waters" (Pluto Water, the springs' health tonic), the golf, and hob-nobbing with the wealthy elite. Others came for the booze and gambling. Not that there's anything wrong with that.

After the stock market crash in 1929, the high rollers rolled over and the property was purchased by the Jesuits for one dollar. They used it as a seminary until 1964, which kind of messed things up because the Jesuits didn't like all that lavishness. They hauled some of the neat stuff away, like the elegant furniture and the larger-than-life-size statue of Sprudel, the hotel's mascot. Northwood, a private college, followed the Jesuits, occupying the place until 1983.

A historical renovation firm then bought the hotel, but the company went bankrupt. After that, the building pretty much fell into disrepair. In 1987 the property was designated a National Historic Landmark and modest amounts of money were dedicated to structural stabilization by the Historic Landmarks Foundation of Indiana, even though they did not own the building at the time.

The West Baden Springs Hotel: Indiana's largest unsupported roomer.

In 1994 another company purchased the hotel, in the hope that proposed riverboat gambling would spark business. When the legislation fell through, the new owners backed out. In 1996 Historic Landmarks officially bought the building for $250,000.

But big money was needed to restore this priceless gem. To the rescue came William and Gayle Cook, Bloomington-based manufacturers and preservationists who contributed over $35 million to the restoration project.

With Lauth Group, an Indianapolis partner, the Cooks plan to re-open the luxury resort in 2007, with 240 guest rooms and a Pete Dye–designed golf course. Right now, you can see the grand atrium as it may have looked in 1920.

Take a tour and see the lush sunken gardens and the spring pavilions. On special days, you can enjoy afternoon tea. After you look up, look down and see the mosaic tile floor that once contained twelve million 1-inch square tiles.

There's just so much history to this place. So get off your butt, go lie down on your back, and take a photo. It's worth it.

By the way, it costs $7,000 a month to heat the place even in its unfinished state, so quit griping about your gas bill.

From Bloomington take State Road 37 south about 45 miles to the roundabout and take first exit onto U.S. Highway 150/State Road 56. Keep going. Can't miss it. Enjoy your stay. Unless you're just looking.

Note: By the time you are reading this, the rooms may be available. But please check in *before* you get into bed. For the latest information go to www.historiclandmarks.org or call (317) 639–4534.

Rockin' Tree

Yellowwood State Forest

How did a quarter-ton rock end up in an oak tree, nearly 30 feet off the ground? Yellowwood State Forest officials don't know. But they certainly don't have any plans to remove the boulder anytime soon.

The refrigerator-sized boulder—christened Gobbler's Rock by an area turkey hunter—has resided in the tree's bough for as long as John Winne, Yellowwood's assistant property manager, can remember. And the anomaly has drawn as many visitors as it has sparked tall tales about how the boulder rose to such lofty heights. "The weirdest stories involve UFOs or black helicopters," says Winne. "My theory is that a logging operation used a skidder [a large bulldozer] and hauled the rock up there."

Another property manager believes that a local climbing club used a block and tackle to hoist the boulder into place. Once in position, the rock was used for rappelling. Another tale credits a tornado for ripping the rock from the ground and depositing it in the tree. "What we do know is that the tree did not grow under the rock and push it skyward," says Winne. "That's the only impossible theory. Anything else is entirely possible."

Yellowwood State Forest (317–232–4105; www.browncountystate park.com) is just west of Nashville in Brown County. Hard to miss, unless you can't see the forest for the trees. Property managers can direct visitors to Gobbler's Rock, as well as to a smaller rock in another tree on the property. The best time to view them is in the spring, before the leaves block the view. Winne points out that it's safe to get as close as you'd like to the tree: "That oak is solid as a rock."

NORTHWEST

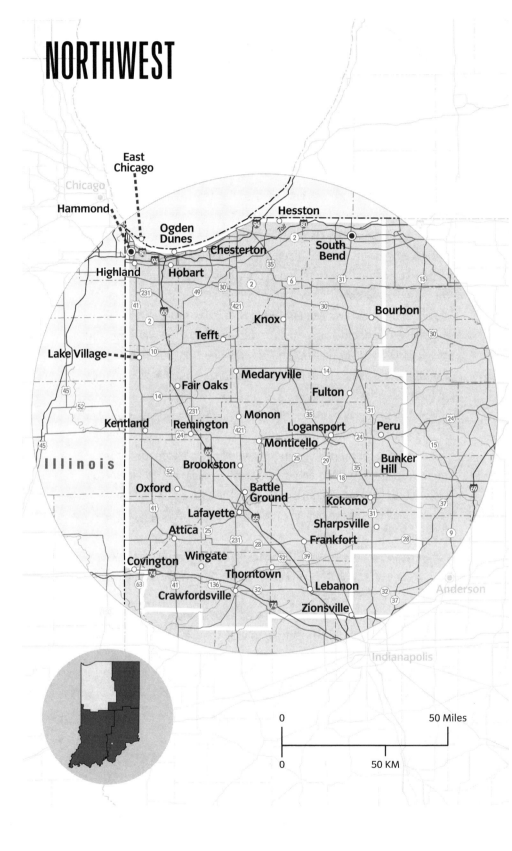

East
Chicago

Chicago

Hammond

Hesston

Ogden
Dunes

Chesterton

South
Bend

Highland

Hobart

Toll

Bourbon

Knox

Tefft

Lake Village

Medaryville

Fair Oaks

Fulton

Kentland

Monon

Remington

Logansport

Peru

Monticello

Illinois

Brookston

Bunker
Hill

Oxford

Battle
Ground

Kokomo

Lafayette

Sharpsville

Attica

Frankfort

Covington

Wingate

Thorntown

Crawfordsville

Lebanon

Zionsville

Anderson

Indianapolis

0   50 Miles

0   50 KM

NORTHWEST

The people in northwest Indiana need to buy this book. And read this chapter. A man living a block from the Wizard of Oz Museum in Chesterton said he'd never heard of it. The local paper in Hammond didn't know exorcisms were being performed in a local church. Some people in Thorntown had never heard of the Walnut Grove Church, a roadside sanctuary built from rocks. And it's right on the highway!

Actually, that's not such a rare occurrence. Many people aren't aware of what's in their own front yard, although one nice lady in Knox, Indiana, *did* know her front lawn was decorated with a rosary—made out of bowling balls.

So for you wonderful people who live in this area, or those on their way to Chicago, you might want to visit the lady with pet skunks in Frankfort. Not interested? How about a gummi bear factory? Wow, you people are hard to please. This is my last shot: Monon, Indiana, now has the best private railroad museum in the country. They're not just tootin' their own horn. Everybody agrees.

Muddied Waters

Attica

As a general rule, we're not big on visiting a place that isn't there anymore. But here's an exception: Kramer, Indiana, which is near Carbondale, which is near Attica. None of which are on most maps. When you get to Kramer, a tiny burg, you'll find a couple of burned-out buildings and a large smokestack. Exciting, huh?

Believe it or not, almost a hundred years ago, this was the site of one of the world's most famous health spas: Mudlavia. Let's go back to 1884 and Samuel Story, a man who suffered from severe rheumatism. Story discovered the curative powers of the local water and mud quite accidentally while cultivating his land. He drank the water while he trudged around in the mud for several weeks on his new farm, only to discover that the affliction in his legs had all but disappeared. Word spread and ultimately H. L. Kramer, who was in the springwater business, developed Mudlavia. The hotel he built became legend: marble and onyx partitions, German silver curtain rods, Tiffany windows. It was the grandest hotel of its day in Indiana—some say the finest east of the Mississippi.

Famous people like James Whitcomb Riley and John L. Sullivan were lured to Mudlavia more for the lithium-and-magnesium-rich water than for its five-star hotel. In fact, Kramer instituted a rather sophisticated advertising campaign nationwide to spread the word of this magical water. The mud from the area was even packaged and sold. How much was hype, how much was true? Who knows?

In its time Mudlavia was every bit as commercially successful as French Lick, maybe more so. Trains pulled in from all over the nation and were met by horse-drawn coaches to take guests to their palatial rooms. Once registered, guests were enrolled in complete health programs, involving diet, exercise, and emotional well-being.

So what's left? After several fires (and assorted hauntings), all that remains are a couple of charred buildings and an original smokestack. The spring still runs and, until recently, the water was bottled under the name Cameron Springs, then Perrier. The present owner, Dean Breymeyer, sells the water to bottlers who market it under different names. Breymeyer really believes the water is special, but you can't say that on the bottle.

To find Kramer, go to Williamsport, the largest city in Warren County, and ask how to get to Attica, and then ask a state trooper who's been on the force for twenty years. He might know someone who knows how to get there. While on your trip, stop in Williamsport to visit Indiana's highest waterfall. It's a beauty and right in the center of town. Or you can try Dean Breymeyer's number (765–762–6559). He loves to talk about water.

Mudlavia. It's like nothing you've ever seen.

Wolf Park
Battle Ground

Wolf Park, in Battle Ground, has been the home of wolves, coyotes, foxes, and bison since 1972, ever since the concept of building a wildlife sanctuary where the public could do their own amateur research was founded by Dr. Erich Klinghammer. But Wolf Park is much more than a wildlife preserve. In many ways, it is the ultimate educational and research park in the Midwest, maybe the country, where you can watch these beautiful predators at work and play.

Although the wolves—more than a dozen of them—have been raised in captivity, they still exhibit all their natural behaviors and are a potential danger. In fact, Wolf Park may be the only known facility where wolves are permitted to "test" the herd. In twenty years, no wolf has taken down a one-ton bison, but the "audience" can witness the technique and posturing displayed by wolves when they are exposed to live game.

Another treat for visitors—and a treat for the wolves, as well—is the presentation of dozens of watermelons that are partially hollowed-out and filled with biscuits, pig ears, rawhides, and liver treats. Observing how the wolves eat the melons and yield to the other members of the pack is an interesting alternative to a day at the mall.

The serious student has several additional educational opportunities, including a five-day wolf behavior seminar that involves not just observation but real interaction with the wolves. Or you can adopt a wolf, pay for its upkeep, and receive regular updates on its life in the park. And on Wolf Howl Night, you can listen with other tourists to the intriguing and still somewhat mysterious chorus of wolves and coyotes as they "talk" the night away.

Take Interstate 65 to State Road 43 (north); go north a mile to State Road 225; then turn right and proceed for 2.5 miles into the park. There are no picnic areas or campgrounds. This is the real thing. Times vary, so call (765) 567–2265 or go to www.wolfpark.org.

Rye Wit
Bourbon

Bourbon, Indiana, *is not* the home of the world's only Alco-Hall of Fame. But that was the staggering suggestion of Keith Bratton.

Bratton is a former advertising man who couldn't get rich creating ads, so he decided to not get rich by creating off-the-wall ideas, inventions, and schemes. He's been very successful. He hasn't made a dime.

It all started in the 1960s when he built a golf ball activator kit. The ball was placed in a box that sported a tiny antenna (to imprint accuracy), at which point the ball jiggled around, accompanied by the glittering of lights and a few sound effects. "I only made two," admits Bratton. "But I bet I could have sold twice as many."

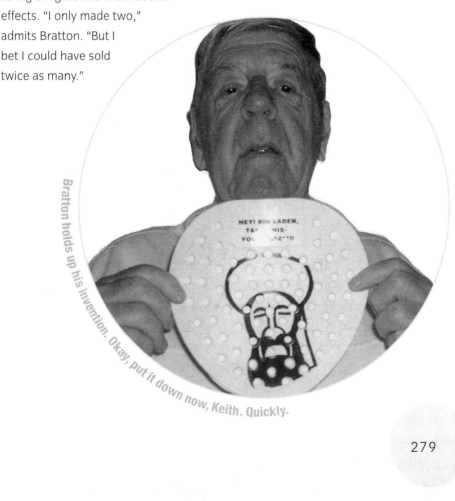

Bratton holds up his invention. Okay, put it down now, Keith. Quickly.

This was just the beginning of a parade of inventions that defy even the wildest imagination. There were Santa-bolic steroids, for people who need energy during the Christmas season. Pick-Up Sticks to play with in bars to attract women, including a black-and-blue version, called Sick Schticks, if wanting to meet a nurse. (The sticks were actually featured years ago on the *Steve Allen Show*.)

Bratton once opened a dental floss stand at the Indiana State Fair, between the Pork Chop Pavilion and the corn on the cob concession. He also had a non-cotton candy booth (40 percent cotton and 60 percent polyester). Bratton claimed it was reusable. "Wash it, fluff it dry."

How about a stain remover called Absorba the Greece? He didn't sell any of that, either.

And for those who wanted the memory of the fair to linger, Bratton made "Bags of Air of the Smells of the Fair." It came in many varieties: Cow Barn, Swine Barn, and Poultry. Oh, and there was a clear window in the bag, so you could see what you had bought. A higher-priced version was vacuum-packed.

By far his most popular invention was a urinal screen with Osama bin Laden's picture on it. He did sell quite a few of those, especially to local taverns. But he ran into an unexpected problem. "People kept stealing them," says Bratton. "It kind of gives you the creeps just to think about."

Back to the Alco-Hall of Fame. Like we said, it hasn't come to fruition yet, but Bratton is still hopeful. "We want to enshrine the legendary drinkers, but we also want to honor people who have made lasting contributions to the world of imbibement, like the inventor of the swizzle stick or the bar stool." Bratton also considered Champaign, Illinois, for his hall of fame, but it was too expensive. Rye, New York, was too far away.

If you're interested in any of Keith's inventions, you may be out of luck. If you already have his urinal screen, you may be under arrest.

We're not giving you directions. There's nothing there, remember?

Daily Paper
Brookston

While in the tiny town of Brookston, we asked a police officer and a utility worker where Twinrocker was. Neither one knew. Kinda odd, because Twinrocker has been the premier manufacturer of handmade paper in America for the last thirty years. By the way, both guys knew where the German bakery was.

But the founders of Twinrocker, Kathryn and Howard Clark, care little about local notoriety. Their company proudly serves museums and state historical societies all over the country that need special papers to complete or restore historical documents. They have done work for the Lilly Library, the Brooklyn Museum, and the Library of Congress. "There's just no other place to get our product," says Kathryn, who started the business with her husband in San Francisco before coming east to work near the family farm.

Twinrocker also makes paper for watercolor artists with special needs, as well as for those with custom projects, including people who want the very finest wedding invitations. The paper comes in all shapes, sizes, and colors. And I think we need to mention this again: They make the paper by hand, an industry that had been virtually defunct in America for 150 years.

Tours are available and you can watch artisans make paper five days a week, the way they made it in Europe in the 1600s—one sheet at a time. You'll see each sheet formed one at a time as the mold is dipped into a vat of pulp. We won't tell you how the whole process works, but it's worth the trip to Brookston, 12 miles north of Lafayette on I–65. Take the first West Lafayette exit and head north on State Road 43 to town. Don't ask anyone in town where the place is—they won't know, but when you see the railroad on State Road 18, Twinrocker is right beside it. Be careful; it's easy to miss. Trust me. When you are lost, call (765) 563–3119 or (800) 757–TWIN. The Web site is www.twinrocker.com.

Madame Chairlady

Bunker Hill

Linda McCoy has been off her rocker for years. That's okay, because thousands of others have been on it. Twenty-five years ago, McCoy and her family were in the furniture-refinishing business. To attract people to their store, just off of U.S. Highway 31 near Peru, they built a huge wooden rocking chair, 13 feet high, and stuck it in their front yard where motorists would see it.

Today the McCoys are no longer in the furniture business, but the rocker still attracts people every day. "I can hear the screeching of breaks," says McCoy, who watches in delight as people "sneak" into her front yard to take a photo of a friend sitting in the chair. No need to sneak, of course; McCoy still gets a kick out of people's reaction to the mammoth chair. "Last year we had eight prom couples come out to snap pictures. It's been so much fun; we've replaced the chair twice."

You can see the chair right off US 31 near Grissom Air Force Base. Bring a friend and a camera. And a huge cushion.

Rock the night away. And bring the family. There's room in this chair for everyone.

SHARP LADY

Oh, look! This is Dick's book. See Dick's book. Read Dick's book. Oh, if only Zerna Sharp were alive today. She could have written a blurb on this book's back cover.

Miss Sharp was born in Clinton County and began teaching in Hillisburg and later taught in Kirlin. In 1924 she took a job with the Scott Foresman publishing company. While walking the beach one day, she observed young children at play. This, coupled with her teaching experience, created an image in her mind of how she wanted to teach reading.

Miss Sharp presented her ideas to educator William Gray, who asked her to develop the concept. Although she never wrote a story or drew a picture, her vision of the project was responsible for what is arguably the most successful series of children's readers in history. Miss Sharp oversaw each story line, each layout, and all the illustrations. She also conceived the idea of adding a new word on each page and then repeating the words to instill mastery of the vocabulary. I actually did the same thing in this chapter. You just didn't notice.

The Dick and Jane series came under criticism in the 1970s, the victim of changing times. See Zerna get angry. See Zerna curse.

Zerna Sharp died in 1981. Beautiful and intelligent, she never married. Her children, she once said, were truly Dick and Jane.

Blown Away
Chesterton

It seems that everyone at the Wizard of Oz Museum in Chesterton has had personal contact with a real munchkin. Even writing that sentence gives me the creeps, but it's true. Chesterton was the summer home of Frank Baum, author of *The Wizard of Oz* and about one hundred other books. Thus it serves as the perfect location for the annual Wizard of Oz Festival and the Wizard of Oz Fantasy Museum, which opened in 1978 (the festival came two years later in an attempt to revive the sluggish economy of Chesterton—and perk up sales in the gift shop).

The yearly festival attracts more than 100,000 people, including a handful of munchkins (excuse the expression) who make the journey to Porter County from who knows where. But munchkins are just a small part—a really small part—of the festivities. How about a Tin Man or Scarecrow look-alike contest, or a Wicked Witch cackling contest? There's Wizard of Oz food, whatever that means, and, listen to this, a Dorothy-calling contest (*DAAARR-A-THEE* . . .).

When you're tired of all the activities, you can follow the yellow brick road to the gift store and sift through hundreds of collector items like mugs, cookie jars, magnets, charms, glasses, and salt and pepper shakers. The attached museum has a display of artifacts from the film. Most are re-creations but they're still fun to look at, like the mechanical Dorothy and an exhibit depicting the Emerald City.

Most of the stuff is pretty neat and fairly priced, but when I was there I bought a Wizard of Oz mug that I saw the next day for about two dollars less at Wal-Mart. If I only had a brain.

The museum is at 109 East Yellowbrick Road in Chesterton; phone (219) 926–7048. It is open Tuesday through Saturday 10:00 A.M. to 5:00 P.M.; Sunday 11:00 A.M. to 4:00 P.M.; closed Mondays except in the summer.

Everything from O to Z.

Courting Artists

Covington

If you're in good shape, the long walk up the Fountain County Courthouse steps in Covington will not take your breath away, but the murals painted on the walls inside certainly will.

The murals are the work of internationally known artist Eugene Savage, whose paintings can also be seen at Purdue University and the Indiana State House. Savage, along with local artists, began painting them in 1937. Their mission: to depict the history of the United States. The murals begin on the bottom floor and work their way around the courthouse walls, providing a thematic and chronological trip through more than a dozen historical issues or time periods, including the tax issue, conservation, the arrival of the pioneers, the canal period, the Gay Nineties, the Civil War, and World War I. But the most thought-provoking aspect of the murals is their thematic depictions. Savage and his associates portray the just and the unjust; the wise and unwise; use of tax money; honest work; and avarice in government (portrayed by an octopus).

The project was financed by the Works Progress Administration during the New Deal era of the 1930s. When completed in 1940, the murals had an estimated value of $90,000. Today the estimate may be five times that, though many would judge them priceless. Over time, the murals had cracked and peeled and required major retouching by artists, and in 1982 a major renovation took place. While most of the murals had been painted directly on the walls, two canvas paintings by Savage needed special restoration, requiring experts from the Indianapolis Museum of Art.

The courthouse welcomes visitors and offers tours to schoolchildren, who delight in this unique opportunity to learn history from a wall. To make your own appearance, head for Covington in Fountain County on Interstate 74, then take U.S. Highway 136 right into town. It's one court date you don't want to miss.

GONE TO POT

Curt Buethe drives a seven-ton trailer all over the country, but despite the fact that he clowns around at the wheel, he's still welcome everywhere he goes.

That's because the wheel is a potter's wheel, one of several in his display vehicle that he takes to schools, fairs, and art shows around the country. It may be the only completely operational mobile pottery studio in the country. But Curt's not just a potter; he's a performer. And his stage name is Mudslinger.

Buethe used to provide his services free of charge—visiting different venues just because he loved the art form. But several years ago a fellow artist clued him in on a way to make a few pennies while making a few pots. So Curt gave up his regular job and started URIMUSIC, a name that required a ten-minute explanation on the phone, so let's just say that if you say each letter fast, there's a message there. Please don't do it now. You have to finish this entry.

Buethe simultaneously works both the audience and the wobbly piece of clay on the wheel. "My performances are 'candy for the eyes,'" says Buethe, who completes each performance in about twenty minutes, before beginning a new piece of pottery.

The show is interactive. Kids, adults, and seniors all take part in his crackpot style. Music blares, Curt chats, and people learn. He might help a husband make a twenty-fifth wedding anniversary present or a youngster create a gift for mom on Mother's Day.

Buethe has taken his show to most surrounding states and even did a stint at the Kentucky Derby. "I don't think anyone else is crazy enough to bring this much heavy equipment all over the country."

Okay, the entry is over. Now try it: URIMUSIC. Here's Curt's number in case you can't figure it out: (765) 794–3829. And here's a neat Web site: www.indianafestivals.org/entertainers.htm.

It's All Hurs

Crawfordsville

It's called the Lew Wallace Study and Museum. It was once called the Ben-Hur Museum. That wasn't totally accurate, but it sure helped attendance. The new director, Cinnamon Catlin-Leguto, who can juggle a name as well as anyone, thinks the change shows a greater respect for this great American Renaissance man.

General Lew Wallace was an author, inventor, diplomat, and soldier. And he was the author of *Ben-Hur*, the number one nineteenth-century blockbuster novel that outsold even *Uncle Tom's Cabin*. Wallace built the study so he could have "a pleasure-house for my soul, where no one could hear me make speeches to myself, and play the violin at midnight if I chose. A detached room away from the world and its worries. A place for my old age to rest in and grow reminiscent, fighting the battles of youth over again."

Yes, that's the way he talked.

The museum, just one large room, is chock-full of artifacts that belonged to this talented nineteenth-century man. You'll see his paintings, musical instruments, and military garb, as well as the writing table where he wrote much of *Ben-Hur*. There's even a fishing rod with an enclosed reel that he invented. He was the original Popeil Fisherman.

Charleton Heston, the man who played Ben-Hur in the movie, visited this museum in 1993. He apparently asked for time alone with the general and spent almost an hour walking through the room. He loved the rifles.

But if you're looking for something spooky, take a look at the painting over the mantel, a portrait of the Sultan of Turkey's daughter, which was given to Wallace in 1885. Notice how the eyes of the young enchantress follow you around the room—her shoulders even seem to tilt as you change position.

The museum is at the corner of Wallace and East Pike in Crawfordsville. If you hit a brick wall, you've either found the place or you went back to work by mistake. For information call (765) 362–5769. Tell them you want to visit the Lew Wallace Study and Museum. It scores you extra points if you don't say Ben-Hur. It's like hearing the "William Tell Overture" and not thinking about the Lone Ranger.

The museum is open Wednesday through Saturday from 10:00 A.M. to 5:00 P.M. and Sunday from 1:00 to 5:00 P.M.

For a long time it was called the Ben-Hur Museum. Holy Moses! Why did they change it?

Arms Talk
Crawfordsville

As general aviation pilots fly over Fred Ropkey's farm in northwest Indiana, they can't help but notice an unusual assortment of historic yard art. What they are seeing is one of the nation's largest private collections of American armored and tactical fighting vehicles.

Ropkey's forty-four-acre farm 6 miles outside of Crawfordsville is home to scores of tanks, fighter planes, artillery boats, jeeps, combat boats, motorcycles, and cannons—all from World War I and II, Korea, Vietnam, and Desert Storm. There's even a shuttle module from a recent space flight. Everything, yes everything, must be in working order, although Ropkey purposely dismantles all weapons for safety reasons.

Tanks—for the memories.

Ropkey, a Marine tank officer during the Korean War, started his collection with a War of 1812 sword when he was just seven years old. Now seventy years later, his collection is so vast that moviemakers keep his name in their Blackberrys. If you saw the movies *Blues Brothers*, *Tank*, *The Siege*, or *Mars Attacks*, you saw some of Ropkey's little babies. His tanks and planes have been seen on the Learning Channel and the History Channel.

Priding himself as a military historian, Ropkey can spin a true story about every piece of equipment he owns. Virtually everything is saved from oblivion when he and his associates rescue items about to be salvaged. "At one time, the government didn't care about this stuff," he says. "Now they want to acquire the very pieces I own for their own military museums."

One prized possession, a cannon from the battleship *Arizona*, had been removed from the ship just months before its journey to Pearl Harbor. Ropkey discovered the cannon at a junkyard, about to be sold for scrap. "I save these items for posterity; they are part of history," he says. "Some of this stuff would have been lost forever."

The Ropkey Armor Museum is open to the public. But you need to call for directions and to let him know you are coming. Hours change by season, so it's best to call for an appointment (317–295–9295 or 765–794–0238). If you dig army stuff, stuff the family in the car. You won't regret it.

Crook Mobile
Crawfordsville

Law enforcement officials at Crawfordsville's old Rotary Jail were good at taking men and women with criminal records and turning them around. And around and around. To allow the authorities to better monitor their prisoners, rotating jails were built in the 1880s. The jail cells literally revolved on a turntable—not unlike a fancy penthouse restaurant—so that the sheriff or his deputies could have repeated face-to-face contact with each prisoner without moving from their desks.

As the two-story jail rotated, only one cell could open at a time, so jail breaks were virtually nonexistent. And the bad guys got a good deal as well, as every few minutes their cell would pass by the only window to the outside world. The jail was turned by hand, no easy job for the sheriff, who often had as many as thirty-two prisoners in custody. It is reported that many sheriffs made their wives do the turning.

Stories abound, like the one about Peg Leg, a local drunk and frequenter of the jail, who often stuck his wooden leg through the bars in the hopes of jamming up the gears. But Peg Leg broke his peg leg so many times that the deputies confiscated his artificial appendage whenever he checked in for an overnight stay.

The Crawfordsville rotating jail, the first in the nation and the last to still actually operate, accommodated prisoners until 1972, but it stopped rotating "guests" in the late thirties when there was concern that prisoners could not get out in time in a fire. Nowadays visitors can enter the jail and be rotated by museum caretakers. Apparently that's good for the gears, but it's hell on the staff.

This must-see in Montgomery County is located in Crawfordsville at 225 North Washington Street. Walk through the museum. You may see some pictures of old relatives. Call on your cell phone: (765) 362–5222.

Crawfordsville's Old Jail Museum is open March through mid-December, Wednesday through Saturday 10:00 A.M. to 5:00 P.M. and Sunday 1:00 to 5:00 P.M. Here's the Web site: www.oldjailmuseum.net.

Fine for Parking
East Chicago

It was once known as Indiana's "ideal city." And it may well be the state's most unique city, the result of a visionary plan near the turn of the twentieth century to build the community of the future.

Marktown, a neighborhood of East Chicago, is surrounded by factories and an oil refinery. It doesn't look like a city that started out as a quaint little burg, modeled after a Tudor-style English village. It all began in 1917 when industrialist Clayton Allen decided that his workers would be healthier and happier if he could provide them with safe, affordable housing. Allen hired Chicago architect Howard Van Doren Shaw, whose vision of utopia was based on English garden city designs. Van Doren Shaw built Tudor-style homes with distinctive double-gable stucco walls with soft pastel colors. He envisioned narrow lanes (VERY narrow) with open streetside porches, so people could walk along the road and talk to neighbors. No alleys, no private garages. All very strange by today's standards.

This grand idea was interrupted by World War I, when only about 15 percent was completed. Those initial 100 buildings and 200 homes still stand today. And people still live in this historic community of 600, including Paul Myers, whose family has lived there for five generations. "It's the Brigadoon of industrial housing . . . a diamond in the rough awaiting restoration for future generations," he says.

Streetwalking is encouraged in Marktown.

How strange is this little hamlet? *Ripley's* made it an entry several years ago as "the only place in America where people park on the sidewalk and walk in the street."

To get to Marktown, take U.S. Highway 80/94 to Cline Avenue, just north of the Riley exit. Go right on Riley Road about a quarter mile to Marktown. Walk the streets and you'll find someone that would love to tell you all the details. Or visit www.marktown.org.

Having a Cow
Fair Oaks

When I asked Julie Basich, general manager of Fair Oaks Farms in Fair Oaks, Indiana, what makes her place unique, I got about ten seconds of silence. She wasn't stuck for an answer; she just didn't know where to begin. "There is not another destination like this in the United States," she finally says. Hey, that's a great place to begin. Especially for this book.

Fair Oaks: Having a cow almost every day. Okay, a calf.

Opened in 2004, this is one of the largest operating dairy farms in the country, with over 27,000 cows. But we're just grazing the surface here.

Visitors tour the farms on what is called a "bio-secure bus," allowing you to watch the farm in action without interrupting the operation or disturbing the animals.

In the visitor center there are over sixty interactive opportunities, including a 3-D 40 movie (that means the seats move, too) that takes you from grass to glass, showing the entire milk cycle. But why just watch the video when you can see real cows being milked and milk processing, as well as the production of ice cream and award-winning cheese?

There is a dairy-themed game and a play area where kids can climb through a huge piece of Swiss cheese or milk a fiberglass cow. There's an anaerobic digester that turns manure into electricity. Not interested? Well, there is plenty more to see.

A new 22,000-square-foot building was just completed, providing arena seating so that spectators can watch cows calving—which means having a baby, for you city folk. More than one hundred calves are born each day, so you actually have to be a bit unlucky *not* to catch a live birth.

Fair Oaks caters to school groups and families, hoping to bring better understanding about one of Indiana's true noble professions.

The farm is forty minutes from Lafayette, about halfway between Chicago and Indianapolis. Take interchange #220 off of I–65, then west on State Road 14 to 600 E; turn south into Fair Oaks Dairy Adventure. Call for more info at (877) 536–1194 or visit www.fairoaksdairy adventure.com.

Yes, there's more than corn in Indiana; there's a whole bunch—I mean herd—of cows, as well.

Buried Treasure
Frankfort

How would you like to see a wheelchair used by Franklin Roosevelt? What about Jack Benny's Maxwell? Or maybe the Leslie Special from the movie *The Great Race*? Well, here's the neat part. You don't have to go to the Smithsonian Institution in Washington, D.C. You can just go to Frankfort, Indiana. To a funeral home.

Bill Miller and his museum: Lincoln kept here. And lots of other neat stuff.

Bill Miller's incredible collection of antique cars, bikes, toys, gas pumps, baby buggies, and hearses was started by his grandfather, William Goodwin, in the early 1950s. And that William Goodwin was the grandson of George William Goodwin, who opened a mortuary in Frankfort in 1856.

Grandfather Goodwin's first acquisitions were horse-drawn funeral vehicles that were probably manufactured just before the turn of the twentieth century. The collection blossomed to include Deusenbergs, an Auburn Boatail, and a Cord, all luxury automobiles that were manufactured—along with 500 other makes—right here in Indiana. You can even see a unique collection of car licenses from the days when people made their own plates.

Bill Miller's grandfather died at age ninety-two, active till the very end and always keeping a special eye out for Abe Lincoln memorabilia and Wooton furniture. All of the antiques—cars included—were displayed in the funeral home until 1997, when the mortuary expanded.

Miller has moved most of his artifacts to a 3,000-square-foot garage right next door. While the collection is not open to the public, Miller loves to talk to people who have a genuine interest in history and his antiques, so if you call for an appointment, you might get lucky. While there, make sure you take a peek inside the historic funeral home to see the notice from the Hamilton County sheriff indicating his plan to impound John Dillinger's car. Yeah, right.

Frankfort is easy to find. From Indy, take I–65 to State Road 39 North to Frankfort. The Goodwin Funeral Home is at 200 South Main, right in the center of town. Or phone (765) 654–5533. You do need to make an appointment for a visit. Not for a funeral.

Common Scents

Frankfort

Cheryl Royer is the Skunk Lady of Indiana. At first she didn't want to be in this book because she was afraid everyone would want to come to her house. Yeah, right.

She was first drawn to skunks when she saw one on a leash, someone's pet, and she wanted to know what it took to own a skunk. Apparently, it's not that hard, although, incredibly, a lot of people pass up the opportunity.

Wild skunks are frowned upon by the DNR, but there are breeders who can provide one—de-scented, of course. *D*elightful. And *scent*sational.

Cheryl has seven skunks—she had eleven at one time—but what with seven horses, four cats, and two dogs, her husband, Steve, put his foot down. That's a very risky thing in the Royer household.

Skunks are bright, loyal, and well behaved. They even come when you call them, says Cheryl, who allows them to pretty much roam the house, where they interact with the dogs and cats. "One of my cats thinks she's a skunk," says Cheryl. I have no idea what that means. When Cheryl sits on the couch they crawl all over her, showing their love and affection. It's downright *scent*imental.

Her skunks eat chicken, veggies, dry dog food—almost anything, "But skunks won't eat lima beans," says Cheryl. It's this kind of information that made this book a best seller. By the way, skunks can be beige, mahogany, brown, or albino. No need to settle for basic black and white.

Apparently, skunk owners feel a mutual bond, which results in "skunk get-togethers" on a regular basis. It is illegal in Indiana to take a skunk in public, so the meetings are private and only members are allowed, although Cheryl has no recollection of any nonmembers trying to crash their parties. During these events, people dress up their skunks.

"How mean can a skunk in a tutu be?" asks Cheryl.

I don't know why I'm bothering, but if you really, really want more information, here's a Web site only a skunk lover could appreciate: http://web.ics.purdue.edu/~royerc. Cheryl's e-mail is skunkie@ geetel.net.

Getaway Vacation
Hammond

For many years the John Dillinger Museum was located in Nashville, Indiana. Mind you, Dillinger never lived in Nashville, but he did bank there on occasion. But when founder Joe Pinkston, a Dillinger historian (and somewhat of an eccentric), died in 1996, the Indiana Welcome Center near Hammond, in Lake County, purchased the concept and many of the artifacts. And they've added to the collection.

According to Luke Weinman, communications director for the center, Dillinger allegedly did "a decent number of bank robberies in the area," which I guess is a compliment, at least to Dillinger. The 2,000-square-foot museum is interactive. Guests can sit in a replica of the Biograph Theatre (outside of which Dillinger was killed), experience a simulated bank robbery, and see an Essex Teraplane 8, a replica of Dillinger's car. You also can compare crime labs of the past and present or see clips of the very movie that Dillinger was watching just before he was gunned down.

There's also a waxed corpse of Dillinger. If you turn a little knob, the corpse lights up. Isn't that a nice touch?

Although the museum features Dillinger, its theme is that crime doesn't pay. But you do. It's four bucks to get in. It's worth it. In fact, it's a steal. The museum is located at 7770 Corrine Drive (inside the Lake County Convention Bureau and Visitors Center). Call (219) 989–7979 for details and directions.

BEAT IT

For almost fifty years Paul Spotts Emrick of Fulton County was the band director for Purdue University. Unlike fellow Fulton resident Elmo Lincoln, the first Tarzan of the movies, Emrick was not a chest beater, but a drum beater. In fact, he was directly responsible for creating the world's biggest drum, and a whole lot more.

Emrick first got on the bandwagon in 1904, when he entered Purdue as a freshman. His family's musical background served him well, and while still a student in 1905, he was named the band's first official director. In 1907, after watching geese fly over his head, Emrick conceived the idea of marching bands forming letters with their units, an idea that became a mainstay of not just Purdue, but most marching bands in the country today.

Emrick knew that people loved drums and was savvy enough to realize that a huge drum would bring notoriety to the university. So in 1921 he worked with the Leedy Manufacturing Company of Indianapolis to create a drum that stands more than 10 feet tall on its carriage. At $800, the drum was considered a steal at the time and is still considered a bargain that's hard to beat. Actually, it's a bargain that's easy to beat.

You get the point. It is still recognized by many as the largest in the world and serves as a centerpiece for the Purdue "All-American" Marching Band. The drum's head, more than 7 feet in diameter, is made from Argentinean steer hides. Since 1937 the shell, constructed of solid maple, has been painted gold and decorated with glittery "diamonds." The drum weighs 300 pounds, 500 pounds with its carriage.

CONTINUED

Thanks to Emrick and his three successors, Purdue University bands can boast several firsts:

- First to carry all colors of the Big 10 schools

- First to play the opposing team's fight song

- First to play at the Indy 500

- First to play from a completely darkened football field, while being lit with tiny battery-operated lights

- First to play at Radio City Music Hall

- First to break military ranks to make a formation of any kind— the Block "P"

And, finally, Purdue University is the first school to have one of its band members go into outer space. In 1969 Neil Armstrong, who played baritone in Emrick's band, set foot on the moon. One giant step for man, one giant step for a band.

Author's note: There are some (mainly IU grads) who say the Walt Disney drum or the University of Texas drum is bigger. Let's just say there are lots of ways to measure a drum, and I'm not going to beat this to death.

Hesssssssston

Hesston

We know this a book for families, but we'd like to tell about one place that is very steamy. It's the 155-acre Hesston Steam Museum in Hesston. The board of directors is a little edgy about the word *museum*. "It has a bit of a stodgy connotation," says general manager Ted Rita, "and this place is about as far from a typical museum as you can get." Boy, is it!

Visitors can ride any one of the three steam-powered railroads as well as see steam at work in dozens of other pieces of equipment, including a cider press, sawmill, traction engines, a ninety-two-ton crane, a huge marine engine, and the first power plant generator that

Still chugging along after all these years.

provided energy for the courthouse and jail in the city of La Porte. The pride of the museum is the Shay logging locomotive, a turn-of-the-twentieth-century superstar known for its incredible pulling power and distinctive sound. The museum also features railroads of several different scales, including a train for kids to ride.

The Hesston Steam Museum is open weekends Memorial through Labor Day, then Sundays through October, when you can see the fall foliage. Then stop at the gift shop or hang around the train depot with other train enthusiasts and tourists and discuss the merits of really hot water. The museum also runs a Halloween and Christmas train, as well as a Labor Day weekend Steam and Power Show, which has been named one of Indiana's top-ten festivals.

From Interstate 94, take the New Buffalo exit south toward La Porte on State Road 39 and follow the signs. Bring a picnic lunch, walk through the park, and blow off some steam. For details call (219) 872–5055 or see the Web site: www.hesston.org.

Free Delivery
Highland

If you choose to spend your Sunday morning at the Hegewisch Church in Highland, you won't notice anything too unusual. Pastor Michael Thierer's sermon and the format of the service are, in his words, "quiet and conservative." But this church specializes in people who have been misled. Thierer's small congregation has been attracted to this ministry because of its worldwide reputation for delivering, well, deliverance—the result of a successful exorcism. First introduced to Hegewisch by internationally known Pastor Win Worley in the early 1970s, this ministry has served hundreds of believers over the past thirty-odd years, many from thousands of miles away.

Pastor Worley, author of *Battling the Hosts of Hell—Diary of an Exorcist*, died in 1993, but Pastor Thierer has continued the tradition, stressing his desire to help those who have failed to find an answer to problems through the more traditional approaches. Thierer, who once struggled with a $2,000-a-week cocaine habit, believes that the devil is the root cause of most serious personal problems, medical and psychological. He laments the rather unrealistic and graphic depiction of exorcism as seen in the movies, but he admits to witnessing strong physical manifestations as a result of the procedure, including levitations. "Some people have to be held down," says Thierer. He also has little use for psychotherapy. "You can't counsel a demon out. They don't listen to you. They are very stubborn."

The church does not charge for exorcisms. (I wanted to mention that so you'd realize just how funny the title of this story is.) The church is at 8711 Cottage Grove Avenue. Call for deliverance: (219) 838–9410. Or see their Web site, www.hbcdelivers.org.

Yummi Gummi
Hobart

Who makes the best candies in America? It's a sticky issue, but we vote for Scott Albanese and his brother, Larry, from Hobart, Indiana.

It would be hard not to vote that way. The Albanese brothers have the United States military on their side. That's because every month or so, Scott and Larry ship 40,000 pounds of—are you ready for this?—gummi bears to our troops overseas.

Of course, these aren't just ordinary gummi bears; they're Gummi Army Guys, replicas of the toy soldiers you played with as a kid, assuming you're about my age, which I'm not telling you.

The idea for Gummi Army Guys came to Scott and Larry when they were at an international candy convention in Germany several years ago. The German locale inspired some reflection about WWII, and when they returned home they wondered if they could make a mold that could be filled with gummi ooze (that's the only word I could think of) to create gummi soldiers.

Sweet support for the troops abroad.

The mold worked, but finding a mass-production method to achieve the same goal was much more difficult. Typically, the ooze would not creep into the rifle part of the mold, for example, so you'd have a gummi soldier without a weapon. Not a good idea.

But Scott and Larry were convinced it could be done, so convinced that they spent the next four years working on the idea. Obviously, they were successful, or you wouldn't be reading this story; and obviously it's a secret, or there would be Hershey Gummi Army Guys and Nestle Gummi Army Guys. There aren't.

World events in the following months, like the war in Afghanistan and 9/11, helped propel the idea into a marketing phenomenon. That and a story about the company in the local paper, the *Northwest Times*, and before they knew it, the media had gone crazy. "At one point I had Paula Zahn on one phone and Bill O'Reilly on hold on the other," says Scott.

The brothers donated thousands of pounds to the servicemen and servicewomen overseas, and before long the company was receiving hundreds of e-mails a day from soldiers who not only loved the product, but saw it as a reflection of support at home—"They liked sticking them on their rifles and tanks," says Larry.

The Albanese brothers still ship their product to the military, which now packages the product under its own label—because we all know how delicious U.S. government candy is. You can buy Gummi Army Guys in many stores around the country. Someday there may be Gummi Navy Guys, Gummi Marine Guys, and Gummi Air Force Guys.

But don't hold your breath for Gummi Indiana Reserve Guys.

It's hard to talk to Scott and Larry on the phone (they always have something sticky in their mouths), but here's the number anyway: (219) 757–6600. Better yet, here's the Web site for more information: www.albaneseconfectionery.com.

The Hole Truth

Kentland

To the untrained eye, it's just a big, big hole in the ground. Of course, it
is just a big hole in the ground. But it is also considered by many to be
one of Indiana's unique geological features. The Kentland Dome is part
of a functioning limestone quarry, the result of a 1-mile-in-diameter
meteorite that crashed to the earth about a hundred million years ago.
Or so the experts say.

The curiosity is that unlike most craters, this hole has no crest, no outline of a crater. And in a typical meteorite impact, the hardest rock would
be at the bottom of the crater. But the folks at Newton County Quarry
claim that the hardest rock is at the top, suggesting huge forces from
above or below the surface did some serious pushing around. And if you
are interested in this stuff (like, you have rocks in your head), you should

Who made this giant hole? No one is admitting it.

also know that the layers of rock in cases like this should be in a horizontal position, but in Newton they go every which way. I mean, go figure.

Most geology experts think the original meteorite must have pulverized, explaining why they have never found any remains of the huge mass. If you want to try and figure it out for yourself, the Kentland Dome (3 miles east of Kentland) is not officially open to the public, but with a phone call (219–474–5125) and some light pleading you can go out on the observatory platform. Gaping is permitted. After all, it's a gaping hole.

Religion to Spare
Knox

If religion is right up your alley, or you're just praying for a 300 game in bowling, have I got the place for you. Linda and Bill Stage of Knox have a rosary in their front yard. And the "beads" are made of bowling balls. The oversized rosary encircles a gazebo in the couple's side yard, enclosing a shrine of the Blessed Virgin Mary. In case you miss it, the letters BVM are emblazoned on the top of the structure and can be seen from the main road.

The fifty-nine bowling balls, divided into five colors to represent the five races of the world, is appropriately named the World Rosary of Peace. All the balls are connected by a plastic landscaping chain through eyehooks that have been set into the balls, thus giving the appearance of a real—albeit HUGE—rosary.

The idea for a giant rosary came in the late 1970s from Father Emil Bloch, pastor of Saint Thomas Aquinas, in Knox. No one is sure where the late priest got the idea, but some speculate that he was inspired by a somewhat similar work of art in the British Museum in London. Either that or the parish bowling tournament. Bloch engineered the design

Bowling ball rosary beads. Oh, Lord, spare me.

and construction himself, beginning with some donated bowling balls, then asked the Stages, who were friends and parishioners, to display the rosary in their yard.

The original dedication of the rosary was in September of 1989. Father Bloch passed away two years later, and now the Stages continue the September rededication celebration in honor of their friend. To see it for yourself, go to the 4200 block of West County Road 200 North in Knox. You can see it from the street. Although it will look like a lane.

SHORT STORY

It is a small wonder that Che Mah lived in Knox, a small town in Starke County. Che Mah was a small wonder himself, once reported to be the shortest man who ever lived. He towered under Tom Thumb, who reached 32 inches. Born in China in 1838, Che Mah was only 28 inches tall and tipped the scales (he was a very small tipper) at forty pounds. He died in 1928 at the age of ninety.

P. T. Barnum saw him in London in 1880 and realized the marketing potential of the act. Later Che Mah traveled with Annie Oakley, Chief Sitting Bull, and other notables in Buffalo Bill Cody's Wild West Show.

Che Mah married a normal-sized woman and settled in Knox, where he owned property, was highly respected, and was considered a gentleman who never angered anyone. This was a good idea on his part. He did, however, anger his wife, who sued for divorce, complaining that Che Mah was jealous and abusive—just two of his shortcomings. Che Mah claimed his wife had ceased to perform her wifely duties. That's more than we need to know.

Pictures of Che Mah can be seen in the Starke County Historical Museum. For more information call the Starke County Historical Society at (574) 772–4311.

Big Ben

Kokomo

One is tempted to say this next story is no bull. But we're better than that. Anyway, it isn't bull, it's steer. Not just any steer, but the biggest steer in the known world—whatever that means. He's dead, by the way. Stuffed. So he now sits (er, stands) in Highland Park in Kokomo, where people actually come to see him.

When Old Ben was born in Miami County, he weighed 135 pounds (equal to several sacks of White Castles) before he even got started. At age four, he was two tons. By the time he slipped on the ice in 1910 and broke both his legs, Ben weighed close to 5,000 pounds (4,720 pounds to be exact, in case you're looking to break the ninety-six-year-old record).

Where's the beef? In Kokomo. Lots of it.

Old Ben was shipped to Indy for his conversion to frankfurters and then given to a taxidermist for posterity. And he had a huge posterity. Oh, and speaking of posteriors, in 2005 somebody stole Old Ben's tail. He has a new tail now, but it's not his real one. It was replaced by the folks at the parks department, who are now officially in the *re-tail* business. There's probably more to this story, but that's enough—you know what—for one day.

To see Ben, take the Atlantic Ocean to England, head for London . . . wait, that's Big Ben. You want Old Ben. Just take US 31 north to Kokomo and ask for directions to Highland Park. Everyone knows where Old Ben is.

Free Gas . . . Station

Lafayette

The Standard Oil gas station on the corner of Sixth and South Streets in Lafayette no longer sells gas. But it does dispense a healthy dose of nostalgia at a very reasonable price: free.

The station is now a museum, restored to look as it did in the 1930s when Standard Oil was one of thirty-three stations downtown. Clyde "Jonesy" Jones leased the building from Standard and for forty years did a one-man show, filling tanks and fixing cars in his two-bay garage. The building was constructed with glazed brick on both the inside and outside (all four walls), which was unique in the world at the time. Only seven examples of this type of architecture remain today.

Over the years the building fell into disrepair, until local businessman Don Stein mobilized volunteers from his company and engineered a sixty-one-day restoration project. Stein did extensive research into how the building used to look and solicited the help of eighty-year-old Clyde Jones, who remembered each person who had bought a piece of the Standard Oil station when its contents were auctioned off ten years earlier.

Virtually all the original artifacts, including the gravity-fed gasoline pumps, were located. Shingles for the top of the decaying roof were found in a Standard Oil warehouse. Almost all the signage is original. Inside the museum you'll find much of the memorabilia associated with the era, including cash registers, candy, film, and clocks. And classic cars.

Stein encourages people with offbeat collections (usually car or gas station related stuff) to loan their wares to the museum. "I think my favorite was the guy with 1,400 hubcaps," says Stein. The oddities are displayed in the museum, then rotated every sixty days or so.

With restoration completed in 1991, the tiny service station began attracting crowds and now plays host to 10,000 folks a year. The museum is open 24/7, but entry requires a phone call to one of the many volunteer hosts. Without a call, you can enjoy the outside of the museum in all its glory or peep through the windows and still get a good look at the past. With a call (765–742–0280), you can get inside. It's a gas.

The gas is thirty cents a gallon. They just don't have any.

RISING POSTAL RATES

Usually the "first" of anything is a hotly contested claim. But most mail historians (and fe-mail, too) agree that the very first official air mail flight in a balloon took place in August of 1859 between Lafayette and Crawfordsville. Problem is, that was not the intended route.

The "mailman" was airman John Wise, a noted balloonist of his day who had actually tried unsuccessfully earlier in his career to deliver a letter from St. Louis to New York. A crash landing burst his bubble, but Wise didn't give up. Months later he attempted still another flight, this time with 123 stamped letters on board his balloon Jupiter, along with a small cadre of scientific apparatuses. Destination: New York City. Wise headed out from Lafayette where westerly winds would be at his back—he thought. Instead, he encountered a southerly wind and 91 degree temperature, enough to force a landing only 30 miles from Lafayette.

So why is this considered the first airmail delivery? Because Wise stopped a passing train and transferred his postal pack to the railroad, which successfully delivered the mail days later. And so, one leg of the journey was indeed by air. Regular airmail delivery did not occur again for seventy years. Some think a balloon would still be faster. But this first official airmail flight was recognized as such by the United States Post Office with a commemorative stamp on its hundredth anniversary.

Bowl Bound

Lafayette

Boilermaker football coach Joe Tiller envies Purdue's entomology department. Why? Because the entomologists participate in a bowl every year. This just bugs the heck out of Coach Tiller.

Entomologists have been playing in Purdue's Bug Bowl for the last fifteen years. It doesn't garner prime-time coverage or draw a stadium-size crowd. But it was featured on CNN and does attract nearly 30,000 people. Two of the bowl's biggest draws are the cricket-spitting contest and the cockroach racing at "Roach Hill Downs." *Guinness* has even sanctioned cricket spitting as an official sport. The record, 32 feet ½ inch, is held by Dan Capps of Madison, Wisconsin, whose collection of tens of thousands of insects and his bug and butterfly tattoos certainly demonstrate his dedication to the sport.

After a stop at the insect petting zoo and an awkward attempt at the caterpillar canter (a three-person, six-legged race), hungry guests can visit a variety of beetle bistros to ingest a buffet of insects. Entomologist and cricket-connoisseur Tom Turpin likens chocolate-covered crickets to a popular snack. "Insects have a nutty taste to them," he says. "So it's just like eating chocolate-covered peanuts." Another booth invites all comers to a blind taste test. The challenge is to figure out which spice cake is made with . . . gulp . . . mealworms. (Just like Grandma used to make.) One past participant said that the Bug Bowl is a great way for entomologists to interact with people. With recipes like that, it's no wonder they need help honing their social skills.

For more information visit http://spider.entm.purdue.edu/bugbowl /index.html or call the Entomology Department on the West Lafayette campus at (765) 494–4554. If no one answers, just keep calling. If you can't bug them, who can you bug?

Nudeton County

Lake Village

Mark Twain once said, "Clothes make the man. Naked people have little or no influence in society." The nudists at Sun Aura Resort may not be influential, but they don't mind. They're busy having too much fun.

Sun Aura, formerly known as Naked City, is a nudist retreat near Lake Village where "clothing is optional and nudity is encouraged." While strolling the grounds you may see naked hikers, nude couples shooting pool, topless women taking to the dance floor on Saturday nights, skinny-dippers at the resort's heart-shaped lake, and what may be the world's sexiest timepiece, a shapely woman's leg sundial, playfully bent with its toes pointing to the correct time. According to one employee, the sundial really works. For some odd reason, though, it takes men nearly three times longer than women to correctly tell what time it is. ("Clock? What clock?")

This adult playground is open year-round. Nude ice fishing has yet to be embraced by the members, but the Valentine's party and the

Sun Aura Resort has a leg up on the competition.

country hoedown inside the heated clubhouse have become popular winter events. According to one Sun Aura employee, "There are plenty of cowboy hats, lots of boots, and lots of naked bodies." Garth Brooks never had it this good.

In the summer, members work on erasing tan lines or attend the crowning of Miss Sun Aura. Sorry guys. Since the pageant is open to the public, all of the beauty queens must wear clothes. Another popular event is the Sun Aura 500, where competitors exchange racing suits for birthday suits and speed around in golf carts. Racing buffs in the buff. Ya gotta love this.

Lake Village is 10 miles west of Roselawn and I–65. For more information call (219) 345–2000. They don't answer the phone all the time, so keep your shirt on.

Pillar Talk
Lebanon

The people of Lebanon don't take their courthouse completely for granted. Nor do they take it for completely granite. The courthouse is also part Indiana limestone and contains eight huge limestone pillars, said to be the largest one-piece limestone columns in the world— almost 36 feet high and weighing 60,000 pounds each. The limestone was shipped to Lebanon from Bedford by train at the turn of the twentieth century, then transported on log rollers from the depot by some very unhappy horses. The columns were carved on the grounds, then lifted by a combination of steam and donkey power. Completed in 1912, the total cost of the courthouse—which also sports a beautiful marble rotunda and exquisite limestone carvings above the portals— was $325,000, a fraction of what a recent renovation cost.

Look up as you gaze upon the columns and you may see yet another surprise. Living on the roof of the courthouse is a cat. We're not going to tell you his name because the cat changes every now and again. The last cat was named Socks. No relation to the former president's cat, but politically well placed nonetheless.

Cats have lived on the roof for several years, usually one at a time. Their job: ridding the roof of pigeons. Don't worry, each cat is well cared for; he (or she) has his own little cat house (excuse the expression), and is fed a standard diet, occasionally supplemented by a slow squab. The kitty is not confined to the roof but can come and go as he pleases, especially in bad weather. In the dead of winter, volunteers take the cat home, returning him in the spring when the pigeons roost.

When not on patrol, the cat can sun himself on the courthouse rotunda. And in case you're wondering, politically, cats are independent. But you knew that.

To find the courthouse, take I–65 north and get off at the second Lebanon exit. Go about 50 mph heading toward town, and a nice police officer will take you right to the courthouse. I know. That's how I found it.

These are the biggest in the world—and that's not just pillar talk.

Circle City

Logansport

We could go round and round discussing where the most exquisite carousel in America is, but our vote goes to the Cass County Carousel in Riverside Park in Logansport.

The hand-carved, forty-three-animal menagerie arrived in Logansport in 1919 from its original home in Fort Wayne. Its carver, Gustav Dentzel, was a German immigrant who settled in Philadelphia and made a name for himself as one of the world's finest carousel craftsmen. While records of the carousel can be traced back to 1902, there is evidence that some of the carved animals date back even further. One hint is that the horses, reindeer, lion, tiger, and goats have a pleasant visage, and Dentzel's style apparently changed after the turn of the

Is it the most beautiful carousel in the world? See for yourself. Just get in line.

twentieth century, when he began creating a more menacing look. "We have the happy ones," says Bridget Eterhaurt, carousel manager.

The carousel, now designated as a National Historic Landmark, is housed in its own climate-controlled building, removed from the elements that once almost ruined it. A major restoration several years ago brought the animals back to life and even uncovered—literally—the fact that a black panther was really a tiger.

What a ride for 75 cents! And as you revolve around the ship's mast in the center of the carousel, everyone has a chance to grab at silver rings. But only one lucky rider snatches the brass ring. And that gives you a free ride. To try for the ring yourself, travel north on US 31 from Indianapolis to U.S. Highway 24 West to Logansport. The carousel is in Riverside Park, and it's open daily Memorial Day through Labor Day. But times vary, so you might want to call ahead: (574) 753–8725.

Craning Your Neck

Medaryville

Those who would contend that Jasper County is for the birds have obviously enjoyed one of the most majestic sights in the Hoosier State. On a clear day in late October or November, you may not be able to see Chicago, but you can see as many as 16,000 migrating sandhill cranes as they take a respite in Jasper-Pulaski Fish and Wildlife Area, feed in the shallow marsh, and then go on to raid the cornfields.

An adult sandhill crane is 4 to 5 feet tall with a wingspan to 7 feet. The sandhill has grayish plumage and red patches on its head. Often mistaken for a heron, these elegant birds represent one of the oldest bird species, dating back over two million years. How to tell the difference? Cranes fly with their necks stretched out, herons tuck the head back. Cranes have loud trumpet calls, while herons have low hoarse croaks.

This stop along the cranes' migration trail from points north is eons old and was in danger in the 1930s, when their numbers severely decreased, probably due to human encroachment, as well as being shot and sold for food. With government protection in recent years, the number of cranes has risen dramatically. The birds, who know a good bed-and-breakfast when they see one, pass the tradition along to their offspring.

The cranes stick around for a couple of months, then head south for Georgia and Florida. Cranes also stop in Jasper-Pulaski in the spring, but October, November, and December are the prime viewing months and spectators flock from all over to see the birds that have, well, flocked here themselves. Best time to look and listen is at dawn when they spring from the roosting marshes and call out in unison; then again at sunset when they return for the evening. Those who know, like Jim Bergens of the Department of Natural Resources, suggest watching the cranes from the Goose Pasture viewing area.

Jasper-Pulaski Fish and Wildlife Area is 5 miles north of Medaryville on U.S. Highway 421, about 40 miles south of Michigan City. We may be sticking our neck out here, but this is one of Indiana's great natural treasures. For more info call (219) 843–4841.

Staying on Track

Monon

I'm going to lay it on the line. The Monon Connection railroad museum is the best little museum in Indiana. But Monon is not the only line we're laying it on. The museum also contains priceless artifacts from hundreds of other railroad lines going back to the Civil War.

The museum is the dream of Dale and Anne Ward, who sold their successful limestone quarry in 1999 and reinvested in this 8,000-square-foot testimony to the history of the railroad in America.

Dale always loved trains, but in 1993 his passion was fueled when he purchased an old hopper car to use as a sign for his quarry business. Then he bought a railroad bell. How about a lantern?

One thing led to another; then it led to thousands of things. He had a house full of stuff and six storage units filled to capacity. He bought from enthusiasts around the country, each item personally acquired by Dale, who admits he couldn't turn down a true collectible. "Sometimes I got a good deal, sometimes I didn't, but I always got something I wanted." Yes, Dale had everything, but he had no place to put it. So he built a museum.

Real railroad artifacts make a great museum. Get the connection?

And what a museum it is. Probably the largest private railroad collection on public display in America.

Outside the museum sits a huge crane, formerly of the Belt Railway of Chicago. Next to it, an authentic whistle stop depot from the 1850s that was transported from Pennsylvania.

Looking for your station in life? Here's the inside track.

Inside the museum are priceless Civil War lanterns, dinner chimes, Edison phonographs, crystal, original newspaper stories of railroad crashes, brass steam locomotive bells, signs, whistles, fire alarms, dining car china, photographs, train cars . . . train everything.

Also inside the museum is *another* train depot. This building is actually a reconstruction, but you can walk through and witness a perfect re-creation of a typical business day inside a railroad station in the early 1900s. Hundreds of original artifacts, including desks, cabinets, writing instruments, telegraphs, chairs, paper money, typewriters, and phones, all accurately depict a real slice of history. It's kinda eerie.

The museum is truly a mission for Dale. A final stop for him, and an opportunity to leave something of meaning behind. "We're only here for a short time," says Dale, "and to take what we've been loaned and share it with other people, that is the big thing to me."

The Monon Connection Museum runs Tuesday to Thursday from 10:00 A.M. to 7:00 P.M., Friday and Saturday from 10:00 A.M. to 8:00 P.M., and Sunday from noon to 6:00 P.M. Closed Mondays. Take I–65 north from Indianapolis to exit 178, then State Road 43 north, which becomes US 421. The museum is actually a mile north of Monon. Call if you get lost: (219) 253–4100.

Plan to spend the day. Here's a tip: Eat in the Whistle Stop Restaurant, which is connected to the museum. That gets you a discount entrance ticket. All aboard!

Heaven Can Wait

Monticello

Some people are driven by their religious fervor. Others drive themselves. That's true of the congregation at the Monticello United Methodist Church where, every Sunday morning during the summer months, the Reverend Wes Brookshire and his associates hold a service at the local drive-in theater. Worshipers here are equally concerned with a place in heaven as a space in the parking lot.

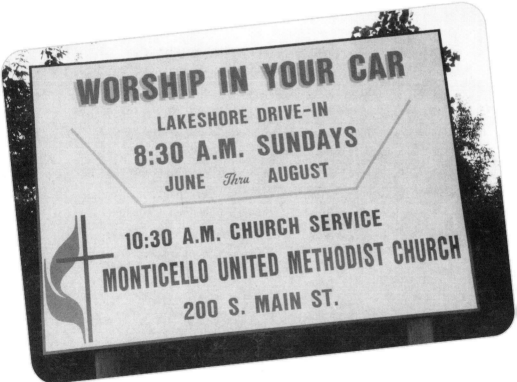

Monticello United Methodist Church:
In Chrysler we pray.

The tradition started in Monticello more than twenty years ago, when the Reverend Ed Helm of the United Methodist Church borrowed the idea from TV evangelist Robert Schuller, who began his own career at a drive-in and then pioneered the concept of outdoor services.

Here's how it works: A pickup truck pulls a wagon equipped with a pulpit and sound equipment. The wagon has a shelter built on it that is affectionately called the "coop," as in chicken coop. The congregation can hear the sermon and music on their car radio via a special frequency in the parking area. Brookshire is not projected on the screen, but most people can see him. "But I can't see them," admits Brookshire. "The windshield is a problem, but you get used to it."

Because Monticello is home to nearby Indiana Beach, the idea of praying to the Son before heading for the sun seemed a natural. On a typical Sunday morning, more than fifty cars drive into the lot, many filled with entire families and their pets. People often pray while munching on breakfast sandwiches and sipping coffee. But the service is interactive. The congregation, for example, is encouraged to toot their horns when it's time to say Amen. I wish we were making this up.

The service is free to the public, but they do pass a Kentucky Fried Chicken bucket for donations. Let's just call it a wing and a prayer. Interested in going to a service? From Lafayette take State Road 43 North to US 24, then go east to Monticello. Or call (574) 583–5545 and see what's praying.

UPLIFTING NEWS

When I decided to write this book, I swore I would not include any historical markers. I mean, ya gotta be nuts to get in your car and drive to see a historical marker. But look at this from Ogden Dunes in Porter County in northwestern Indiana:

> STEEL AND WOOD SKI JUMP WITH ADJUSTABLE HEIGHT AND LENGTH WAS BUILT HERE FOR OGDEN DUNES SKI CLUB, INCORPORATED IN 1927 TO PROMOTE WINTER SPORTS. FIVE ANNUAL EVENTS WITH INTERNATIONAL COMPETITORS WERE HELD 1928-1932, WITH 7,000 TO 20,000 SPECTATORS. REPUTED TO BE THE LARGEST ARTIFICIAL SKI JUMP AT THE TIME. DISMANTLED AFTER 1932 EVENT.

By the way, I didn't drive to see it, either. I'm not *that* crazy. A friend read it to me over the phone.

But ain't that a hoot? Who'd of thought that the tallest ski jump in the world was ever in Indiana?

Well, since we have no mountains, maybe that does make sense.

Going Postal

Peru

Drive on up US 31 one evening, just north of Grissom Air Force Base, and you may be distracted by a cacophony of lights punctuating the evening air. Fighter pilots going on a mission? Nope. Training maneuvers for new cadets? Wrong again. Maybe it's the circus. Everyone knows that Peru is famous for its circus. But that's why it's not in this book. Everyone knows about it.

No, this is the largest collection of ready-to-go lampposts and lamp-poles (we don't know the difference, either) in the Midwest, some say the United States. Paul Knebel of P. K. Distributors has been selling sand-cast aluminum products for more than twenty years. We don't know what that means, but it's apparently a good thing. His shop, just off US 31, has more than 500 lamp-posts, more than an entire town of drunks could hope for.

What a crazy store. Buy polar.

The aluminum castings for the lampposts come from Mexico, but Knebel mixes and matches parts so that, unlike most super-hardware stores, he gives you a hundred different choices instead of four or five. Don't need a lamppost? How about an eagle, a Statue of Liberty, a library lion, or an elephant? Buy that fountain that you've dreamed of. What the heck, get that suit of armor you have always wanted. Oh yeah, he also has giraffes, Clydesdales, dinosaurs, rhinos, pigs, and panthers. Most are full-size, some bigger. He never knows what he's going to get in. And once he gets it, he's not sure if he has it. It's a real adventure. If you can't find what you want at P. K.'s, they probably don't make it.

Knebel says that his roadside location creates a lot of traffic—people intrigued by what they see as they barrel down the highway. The evening hours can get especially crowded. "I think that humans are attracted by the light," says Knebel. This is one of those places that's easy to find and hard to miss. It's just 3 miles north of Grissom Air Force Base on the east side of US 31. The Web site is www.pkdist.com. Or give a call at (765) 472–0369. They'll keep the light on for you.

Fountain of Knowledge
Remington

You won't find Remington in most tourism books. No sun-kissed beaches, no floating casinos, not one Elvis impersonator. But every summer people flock here, to the Fountain Park Chautauqua, the only remaining continuously running chautauqua in Indiana and one of the few left in the United States.

More than a hundred years old, the chautauqua movement is a kind of floating band of educators, entertainers, and ministers who brought the culture of the city to rural America. People would travel from nearby towns and pitch tents to hear such famous guest speakers as William Jennings Bryant, who mesmerized the crowds and then went on to the next location. Although the movement became much less popular as the automobile gained in popularity and the city was only a drive away, a handful of chautauquas still remain today.

The Fountain Park Chautauqua is planned locally and, unlike other chautauquas, there are permanent residences, dozens of cottages built decades ago so folks could enjoy guaranteed access to two weeks of entertainment, educational classes, and fellowship. Those cottages remained in families so each new generation could come and enjoy the festivities, no matter where they lived.

Those without cottages enjoy the Fountain Park Hotel, a grand building with thirty-six rooms and a 136-seat dining room. The hotel, built in 1898, is open only two weeks a year. To re-create the feeling of the past, the ruling committee voted that air-conditioning would not be installed. Oh, and there is no alcohol. And no phones or TV. And it's still impossible to get a room. We hope this concept doesn't catch on.

The Fountain Park Chautauqua has not missed a meeting in more than a century. Start your own streak by visiting the grounds the last week in July and the first week in August. The Remington Chautauqua is a mile north and a half mile west of Remington near the intersection of State Roads 231 and 24. By the way, a few Indiana cities—we won't mention any names—call their annual festivals chautauquas 'cause it sounds cool. That doesn't count. If there ain't no history, there ain't no mystery.

For more info call Linda Emerson at (219) 866–3603. They don't have air-conditioning, but they do have Web site: www.fountain-park.org.

WORLD'S FASTEST

Fly over the tiny town of Oxford and you'll see 1:55 painted atop a tiny structure just on the edge of town. This is Benton County's testimony to Dan Patch, possibly Indiana's greatest athlete. The 1:55 represents Patch's lightning speed in a mile run, a record that stood for thirty-two years. But the story of Dan Patch is more than just numbers.

The story behind this great athlete began here, in little Oxford, where Patch was born with a crooked leg that required him to have assistance just to stand. By the time the little guy was four years old, he was already wowing people with his amazing speed and his desire to compete. He even won his first race. By 1903 many sports enthusiasts considered young Dan Patch the fastest in the world, and he was soon the undisputed world champion.

In the course of Patch's career, he never lost a race and set dozens of records. Those who watched him run said, "He would pass others like they were standing still." He was also probably the first athlete to be marketed worldwide. Way before icons like Babe Ruth, Patch's image was used to sell cigars, watches, sleds, toys, gasoline engines, even cars. Patch's lifetime earnings were in the neighborhood of two million dollars, an unheard of number in the early 1900s.

Like Michael Jordan today, Patch was a giant among athletes. He had his own railway car, and when he went to a new city, throngs of admirers came out to see him. Sportswriters wrote about his intelligence and love of music. But he had his dark side. He never talked to reporters, never signed an autograph. Except for a chosen few, Patch never really warmed up to most people.

DAN PATCH

Standard-bred colt (sire Joe Patchen, dam Zelica) foaled 1896 Oxford, Benton County; raised by Daniel A. Messner, Jr. on this farm. A natural pacer, trained for harness racing, a very popular sport in late 1800s and early 1900s. Dan Patch began his racing career at county fairs in 1900; he became famous in Grand Circuit racing and never lost a race.

(Continued on other side)

ERECTED 1968 INDIANA HISTORICAL BUREAU, DESCENDANTS OF DANIEL A. MESSNER, JR. OXFORD LIONS CLUB, OXFORD CITIZENS AND TOWN BOARD, BENTON COUNTY INDIANA HISTORICAL SOCIETY, INC.

Dan Patch slept here. Standing up.

Dan Patch died in 1916 as a result of heart problems. People mourned the loss of this great athlete. There was even some speculation he would be stuffed and mounted.

Dan Patch, you see, was a harness racehorse. And now you know the rest of the story.

Where is it in Benton County? Just ask. Everyone knows.

HOOSIER APE MEN

I Tarzan.

No. I Tarzan.

No. I Tarzan, and this Jane.

Will the real Tarzan please stand up? If you were asking the Indiana contingent of Ape Men to stand, three Tarzans would rise—and even one Jane.

Elmo Lincoln (Elmo Linkenhelt) holds the honor of being the first Tarzan. The broad-chested bruiser from Rochester was cast as the first vine-swinging, clipped-speaking ape man in the 1918 silent movie *Tarzan of the Apes.* He was discovered while filming a fight scene for an earlier movie. When his shirt was ripped off, the director noticed his rippling chest and later gave Lincoln the role of the scantily clad jungle defender.

Dennis "Denny" Miller (aka Scott Miller) earned the honor of being the first blonde Tarzan. Born in Bloomington, the basketball standout originally went to Hollywood to play for the legendary UCLA coach and fellow Hoosier John Wooden. Upon graduating, he turned down an offer to turn pro, and he went into acting. He starred in *Tarzan the Ape Man* (1959).

Apparently, James "Babe" Pierce took the role of Tarzan to heart. The Freedom native not only costarred with Jane, but he was married to her. His first role as the ape man was in the 1927 movie *Tarzan and the Golden Lion.* Later he married Joan Burroughs (the daughter of Tarzan's creator, Edgar Rice Burroughs), and from 1932 to 1934, he and his wife played Tarzan and Jane on the radio serial that aired in the United States, South America, and Europe.

Pierce and his wife are buried in Shelbyville. Their gravestones are engraved "Tarzan" and "Jane."

Who says Hoosiers aren't swingers?

Back to the Fifties
Sharpsville

Jim Richardson of Sharpsville spent more than a few years of his life driving around the Indiana countryside trying to relive his days as a kid. "Over every crest in the hill, I hoped to look down on a little town just like the one I grew up in back in the fifties."

No such luck, so the Sharpsville resident decided to build his own. Neighbors and friends questioned his sanity, but Richardson lost no time drawing up a series of detailed blueprints for a town complete with gasoline station, firehouse, diner, and barbershop. He called it Summerplace.

With the help of friends and other volunteers, he began collecting artifacts from the 1950s. Inside his gas station, for example, along with vintage cars and bikes, are cans of 1950s motor oil, spark plug boxes, tools, TV sets, and magazines. Outside the building are stoplights, gas pumps, product signs, streetlamps, and a movie marquee, all from the 1950s of his childhood. Some of the memorabilia has been refurbished, but it is all original. No exceptions.

Relive your childhood here. Unless you're under forty.

Summerplace is open by appointment to special groups, and Richardson has a special place in his heart for older folks who want to reconnect with a lost time. "I've had senior citizens sit in this garage and weep. It allowed them to get back in touch with their youth."

Richardson has paid a price for his hard work: several broken bones, cracked ribs, and heat exhaustion. But still, he calls the days of his youth and his re-creation the "fabulous fifties." Sharpsville is just south of State Road 26 and east of US 31. But you can't really see Summerplace from the street, so you'd better call (765) 963–5943.

Bird's Eye View
South Bend

The trees in Bendix Woods just outside of South Bend don't spell trouble. But they do spell S-T-U-D-E-B-A-K-E-R. And they have for almost seventy years. Although you wouldn't know that unless you flew over them.

The idea sprouted in the 1930s, when the Studebaker Corporation was looking for a promotional gimmick that would both advertise their company and capitalize on the nation's love affair with flight. And so, after a Studebaker engineer got out his slide rule and plotted the coordinates, the company planted 8,000 red and white pine seedlings. Today, the trees are 70 to 80 feet tall and were listed in the *1987 Guinness Book of World Records* as the longest living sign in the world. That's a half mile long and 200 feet wide—as the crow flies.

When Studebaker went out of business, the land was purchased by the Bendix Corporation, which deeded some of the property to the St. Joseph County Parks Department. In 1978, when the parks department also acquired St. Patrick's County Park, volunteers just went out of their tree trying to resurrect the Studebaker concept. And so, now you can see both S-T-U-D-E-B-A-K-E-R and S-T. P-A-T-R-I-C-K from your Cessna. C-O-O-L, H-U-H?

McCarthyisms

South Bend

The fans are going wild in the fourth quarter as the Irish of Notre Dame lead the USC Trojans, the top-ranked football team in the nation. The crowd suddenly goes completely silent. Has Brady Quinn asked the masses to quiet down? Has Knute Rockne been resurrected?

Nope. Tim McCarthy is about to make an announcement.

Who?

For more than forty-five years, McCarthy, now an Indiana State Police retiree, has been making his fourth-quarter safety announcements that address drunken driving, being courteous and polite while navigating heavy post-game traffic, and driving in foul weather. His signature request, "May I have your attention, please?" quiets the crowd quicker than a priest asking everyone to bow their heads in prayer.

If anyone is still talking when he continues with "This is Tim McCarthy for the Indiana State Police," they are immediately shushed by hoards of reverent fans. Truth be told, McCarthy's proclamations didn't always garner such respect. "After two games of making serious announcements, I could see that nobody was listening," he said. "I realized that no one wants to listen to a policeman telling them to behave themselves."

So, at the 1961 home opener, he added a pun to conclude his safety message: "The automobile replaced the horse, but the driver should stay on the wagon." Receiving cheers, and, more importantly, attention to his message, he hasn't looked back since. Well, he did backslide once in the mid-sixties and reverted to his straight-laced approach.

"When people came up to me after that game, they asked if the microphone went dead at the end of the announcement because they didn't hear my joke."

Tim, you are forgiven.

Today, not only do his announcements silence the crowd, but they also induce genuine cheers and applause. McCarthy is such an Irish icon that he has been immortalized (dare I say canonized?) on a CD titled *"May I have your attention please": Notre Dame Band with Tim McCarthy*.

Here are some of his favorites. (Feel free to laugh, or groan, when appropriate.)

1. Driving half lit is not very bright.

2. The reason we hammer at safety is to keep you from getting nailed.

3. Drunk drivers aren't very funny, but they can still crack you up.

4. No one relishes a pickled driver.

5. Anyone who tries to bolt through traffic is a real nut.

6. When you have congestion, try to keep a clear head.

7. Don't let your day go down the drain by forgetting today's safety plug.

8. If you drive when you're stoned, you may hit rock bottom.

9. If you horse around in traffic, you may get saddled with a ticket.

10. There have been so many drops of rain, there shouldn't be a drip behind the wheel.

Dunn Deal

Tefft

A philosopher once said, "Legend is the bridge to truth." But sometimes, it's the bridge that's the legend. Dunn's Bridge, just north of the tiny town of Tefft, has been the center of more than a little controversy for more than a hundred years.

The story begins in 1893 in Chicago, site of the World's Fair, also known as the Columbian Exposition. People in the Windy City, indeed the entire nation, were abuzz about a new amusement ride that would debut at the international event. George Ferris, folks say, had once scribbled his notion for this outrageous piece of machinery on a dinner napkin in Chicago after being challenged by a friend to design something that rivaled the Eiffel Tower. Many believe Ferris succeeded. His engineering feat thrilled the nation and lifted the spirits of the 2,000-plus people who sat in the wheel each trip.

That's not a misprint: 2,000 people per trip!

Ferris, with the help of Luther Rice, a Hoosier construction engineer, enjoyed great success with his ride for several years, but in 1906 the cost of maintaining the machine was so enormous that the wheel was dynamited and sold for scrap.

Where did the scrap metal go? Some say it went to Hoosier Isaac Dunn, who used some of the metal frame to construct a bridge across the Kankakee River. Well, that's what some folks say. The controversy continues. Some say the bridge is made from the original Ferris wheel, some say it isn't. Some say the story's all true; some say it's all malarkey. Some say it's half true. We could go round and round in circles on this and accomplish nothing. That's the way George Ferris would have liked it.

To get to the bridge, you have to approach it from upstream in Porter County, then cross the bridge by foot, which brings you to Jaspar County. It won't be the most exciting few minutes of your life, but you will be part of legend.

Rocky Start

Thorntown

In 1982 Bud Moody had a vision: Build it and they will pray. So the good reverend began a yearlong project constructing a prayer garden and chapel with stones he found at an abandoned rest stop.

As the tiny band of parishioners assisted Moody in his mission, nearby farmers and passing truckers stopped not only to gape but to gather rocks and donate money. No one really had any experience building anything like this, but that didn't stop the congregation from digging in.

Walnut Grove Church: A stone's throw from U.S. Highway 52.

When the prayer garden and chapel were complete, a church was also built to serve the tiny community. They had been conducting services in a small building in Thorntown, but now the Full Gospel Church had a new home.

The Walnut Grove Church has about thirty-five in the congregation, but Reverend Ryan Glauber feels he reaches the masses. "We have people from all over the country stop by and sign our prayer book in the chapel," says Glauber.

The stone chapel is adjacent to the Thorntown exit on U.S. Highway 52 and is visible from the road. Stop by, sign the book, and leave a few coins.

What a Card . . . Collection

Zionsville

If you ever meet insurance agent John Haffner of Zionsville and you offer him your business card, he'll take it. Not that he needs it. John once had ten million business cards in his basement. In boxes. In plastic bags. In three-ring binders. *Incredible.*

Ultimately, he sold that stash in fear that the next business card he would get would be from his wife's divorce lawyer. But while the magnitude of his collection has waned (he gave millions away), he still retains the cream of the cards and is comfortable boasting that he may have the largest sports and celebrity collection in the country.

Haffner spends at least an hour a day sending self-addressed, stamped envelopes to personalities and sports figures all over the world. Then each morning, he treks to the local post office to unlock his box and see what goodies have arrived.

While many of his requests are ignored, more are returned, often with a signed card. Haffner carefully catalogues each item, creating huge binders filled with various classifications: NFL football, college football, baseball, coaches. "I even started one with lacrosse coaches," says Haffner, "but so far it's a pretty slim book." Haffner still has binders filled with Walt Disney personnel, FBI agents, and museum employees. John ONCE had a book of call girl business cards. Mrs. Haffner requested we put the ONCE in big letters.

John also collects business cards from everyday people who have famous names. So if you're a plumber named George Clooney or a maid named Angelina Jolie, John Haffner is the guy to call.

Here's his card:

Sports Business Card Collector

John C. Haffner

P.O. Box 609
Zionsville, IN 46077
haf705490@AOL.com

Mooving Experience

Zionsville

Have you ever walked into a place, grabbed a bottle of milk off the shelf, and not paid the cashier? LEGALLY, I mean.

Even in Indiana, trust only goes so far, but that's exactly how far it goes at the Traders Point Creamery in Zionsville, an organic farm where the 130 cows are contented and the people are trusted. And it's the best chocolate milk I have ever had.

If you want to see a real organic farm (and the only commercial one in Indiana), I suggest an afternoon visit, when you can watch cows being milked, yogurt being made, and ice cream being packaged. Taste their award-winning cottage and fromage blanc cheese. Then, just take your stuff and throw some money (the correct amount is appreciated) in the antique milk can. And it's the best chocolate milk I have ever had.

City boys like me will learn that cows—not just bulls—have horns and that at five in the morning, people in Indiana are making more than doughnuts. You will also have your first taste of creamline milk, which means it is not homogenized, which also means it's twice as expensive, which also means I don't really understand that. And it's the best chocolate milk I have ever had.

The farm is owned by Jane and Fritz Kunz, who dedicated their family-owned 150 farm acres to the promotion of good health and tradition. The cows are grass fed. No antibiotics, chemicals, or hormones are ever used. And it's the best chocolate milk I have ever had.

You can buy these organic products at select local stores, but that kind of ruins the fun of seeing how an old-time dairy was run. The neatest part is watching the crystal bottles being filled with milk, then listening to the clanking as they wobble their way down the assembly line to be boxed for shipment.

On the farm there is also a 150-year-old barn that the Kunzes moved from northeast Indiana, all to add to the authenticity of your visit.

The farm is at 9101 Moore Road in Zionsville. Call them at (317) 773–1700. Sometimes they don't answer. You can call 'til the cows come home.

You probably already know about their chocolate milk.

INDEX

A

Add's Museum of All Sorts of Stuff,
257–58
Adrian Orchards, 21–22
Albanese Confectionery Group,
305–7
Alexandria, 54–57
Allen, Sandy, 182–83
American Heritage Village, 61–62
Assembly of God Church, 246
Atlanta, 57–58
Attica, 276–77
Auburn, 59–65
Auburn City Hardware, 63–64
Auburn Cord Duesenberg Museum,
59–60

B

Bainbridge, 198–99
Battle Ground, 278
Bedford, 202
bell farm, 215–16
Ben-Hur Museum, 288–89
Ben Schroeder Saddletree Factory,
163–65
Bendix Woods, 336–37
Bentcils, 4
Berne, 65–66
Bethel, 136–37
Bloomfield, 203
Blue Flash rollercoaster, 210–11

Blue Monkey Sideshow, 22–23
Boggstown, 138
Bourbon, 279
Bowersox, Kenneth, 202
bowling ball rosary, 309–10
Brick Chapel, 203–4
Bridgeport, 139
Bristow, 205–6
Brookston, 281
Brownsburg, 207–9
Bruceville, 210–11
Brush, Charles, 124
Buffalo Run Farm, Grill & Gifts,
239–40
Bundy Decoy, 114–15
Bunker Hill, 282
Burnside, Major General
Ambrose, 169
Buzz Bomb Memorial, 234–35

C

Caesars Indiana, 139
calliope museum, 148
Camp Atterbury, 220–21
Camp Chesterfield, 76–77
CANDLES Museum, 265–66
Carmel, 66–71
Carmel rock concert, 70–71
Carmel well, 67–68
Carnegie Library, 162–63
Cass County Carousel, 320–21

INDEX

Center Point, 211–12
Che Mah, 311
Chesterfield, 76–77
Chesterton, 284–85
Children's Art Gallery, 66–67
Children's Museum of Indianapolis, 14–16
Churubusco, 77–78
Circle City Copperworks, 17–19
Clinton Falls, 212–13
Cloverdale, 214–16
Cloverdale's house of bells, 215–16
Club Run Golf Course labyrinth, 122–23
Colgate clock, 160
Columbus, 75
Connersville, 140
Converse, 78–79
Corydon, 141–42
Court House Girls Calendar, 85–86
Covington, 286
Crawfordsville, 288–93
Custom Phone Shop, 42–43

D
Dale, 216–17
Dan Quayle Center, 98
Danville, 217–18
David Alan Chocolatier, 72
Davis, Don, 28–29
DeBrand Fine Chocolates, 72
Dillinger, John, 246–47, 300
Dillinger Museum, 247, 300
Dinosphere, 14–16
Dolly Mama's Toy Museum, 145–46
Don's Guns, 28–29
Dr. Cue, 214–15
Dr. Ted's Musical Marvels, 216–17

Dugger, 219
Dugger Coal Festival, 219
Dunkirk, 80
Dunn's Bridge, 339
Dutch Village Craft and Antique Mall, 112–13
Dyer's Moccasins, 150–51

E
East Chicago, 293–94
Edinburgh, 220–21
Elizabeth, 142–43
Elkhart, 81–82
Elletsville, 222–23
Elwood, 83–84
Eugene, 224–25
Evansville, 225–28
Exotic Feline Rescue Center, 211–12

F
Fair Oaks, 295–96
Fair Oaks Farms, 295–96
Farmland, 85–86
Fishers, 87–90
Forest Discovery Center, 185
Fort Wayne, 72, 90–92
Fortville, 145–48
Fountain County Courthouse, 286
Fountain Park Chautauqua, 330–31
Fourth Dimension Holographics, 253
Frankfort, 297–300
Franklin, 228–30
Fremont, 92–93
French Lick, 231
Friendship, 150–51
frog jumping championship, 56–57
Fungus Among Us, 87, 90

INDEX

G

General Lee car, 236–37
Genvea, 94–95
Ghyslain Chocolatier, Inc., 73
giant rocking chair, 282
Giant, The, 118–19
Glass Museum, 80
Glendale Mall Library, 34–35
Gobbler's Rock, 273
Godfroy, Chief Francois, 105–6
Goethe Link Observatory, 243
Goodwin Funeral Home, 297–98
Goshen, 96
Gosport, 232–34
Grabow Orchard and Bakery, 117–18
Gravity Hill, 248
Greencastle, 234–35
Greene County Viaduct, 262–63
Greenfield, 152
Greensburg, 153–54
Grissom, Virgil, 202
Gummi Army Guys, 305–7

H

Hagerstown, 155–56, 158–59
Hair Museum, 231
Hallmark Ornament Museum, 126–27
Hammond, 300
Happy Friday Guy, 108–9
Harris Sugar Bush farm, 204
Hegewisch Church, 304–5
Heidelberg Café, 9–10
Heltonville, 238–39
Hesston, 303–4
Hesston Steam Museum, 303–4
Highland, 304–5
Hobart, 305–7

Holiday World & Splashin' Safari, 260
Hoosier Boy, 180
Hoosier Orchid, 2–3
Hope, 157
Howard Steamboat Museum, 161
Huntington, 98

I

Indiana Basketball Hall of Fame, 171–73
Indiana Historical Radio Museum, 103
Indiana Rural Letter Carriers Museum, 157
Indiana Turtle Care, 176–77
Indianapolis, 1–51
Inland Aquatics, 266–67
Invasion of the Weird Trees, 133

J

J and J Collectibles, 232–33
Jasper-Pulaski Fish and Wildlife Area, 321–22
Jeffersonville, 74, 160–63
jelly jar museum, 107–8
Joe Palooka statue, 256–57
John Dillinger Museum, 300
John Wayne Museum, 208–9
Joybell Theater and Gift Shop, 252
Jug Rock, 261–62
Junky Joe's, 224–25

K

Kendallville, 99–100
Kentland, 308–9
Kentland Dome, 308–9
Key Strummers, 10–12

INDEX

Kipp Brothers, 31–32
Kittworks, 147
Knox, 309–11
Kokorno, 312–13
Koorsen Fire and Security, 7–9
Kramer, 276–77
Kruse Horsepower Museum, 61–62

L

Lafayette, 313–16
LaGrange, 74
Lake Village, 317–18
Lapel, 101–2
Le Studio des Parfums, 57–58
Lebanon, 72, 318–19
Lebanon Courthouse, 318–19
Lew Wallace Study and Museum, 288–89
Lewis, Matt, 16–17
Liberty, 169
Ligonier, 103
Limberlost, 94–95
Lincoln City, 239–40
Linkenhelt, Elmo, 334
Linton, 240–41
Logansport, 320–21
Loon Lake Lodge, 33–34
Lucent, 142–43
Luckey Hospital, 131–32
Lucky Point, 241–42

M

Madison, 73, 163–65
Marktown, 293–94
Martin Marietta Aggregates, 70–71
Martinsville, 73, 243
Martinsville Candy Kitchen, 73

Mary Rose Herb Farm and Retreat, 205–6
MC Axe and the Fireboys, 88–89
McCarthy, Tim, 337–38
McCordsville, 165–68
McCordsville Barber Shop, 165–67
Medaryville, 321–22
Medical History Museum, 30
Mentone, 104
Mentone Egg Festival, 104
Mid-America Windmill Museum, 99–100
Milan, 170–71
Milan Museum, 170–71
Milan Station Antiques & Collectibles, 171
Miller, Dennis "Denny", 334
Milltown, 245–46
Monon, 323–25
Monon Connection Museum, 323–25
Monticello, 326–27
Monticello United Methodist Church, 326–27
Montpelier, 105–6
Mooresville, 246–48
Morgantown, 249–50
mousetrap museum, 207–8
Mudlavia, 276–77
Mudslinger, 287
Muncie, 107–11
Mundt's Candies, 73
Museum of the Soldier, 121–22

N

Nappanee, 112–13
Nappanee Apple Festival, 113
Nashville, 250–53

INDEX

National Muzzle Loading Rifle
  Association, 151
Nettle Creek Valley Museum, 158–59
Never Too Late, 5–7
New Castle, 171–74
New Palestine, 174–77
Newburgh, 254
Newport, 255
Newport Antique Auto Climb, 255
Noah's Ark, 78–79
Noblesville, 114–17
Noblesville Veterinary Clinic, 116–17
Northeast Indiana's Baseball
  Association's Hall of Fame, 62
Northeastern Indiana Racing
  Museum, 62

O
Odyssey Map Store, 38–39
Ogden Dunes, 328
Ohio County Historical Museum, 180
Old Ben, 312–13
Old Jail Museum, 292–93
OneAmerica, 25–26
Oolitic, 256–57
Optical Repair Shoppe, 40–41
Oxford, 332–33

P
P. K. Distributors, 329–30
paintball, giant, 55
Party Shop, 126–27
Patch, Dan, 332–33
Pendleton117–19
Peru, 329–30
Pet Angel Memorial Center, 69
Philo T. Farnsworth Center for
  Television History, 62

Pierce, James "Babe", 334
Pinch, 119–20
pink elephant, 148–49
Plasterer, Eiffel, 97
Plump's Last Shot, 44–45
Plyley's Candies, 74
Portland, 121–22
Pratt Books and Other Fun Stuff, 153
Pumphrey, Craig and Paul, 142–43
pumpkin launcher, 222–23
Punkin Center, 257–58
Purdue Bug Bowl, 316
Purdue Marching Band, 301–2

Q
Quayle, Dan, 98, 172

R
Rainbow Christian Camp, 78–79
Randolph County Courthouse, 85–86
Recreational Vehicle/Manufactured
  Housing Museum, 81–82
Red Wolf Sanctuary, 181
Rees Harps, 179
Remington, 330–31
Republican, The, 217–18
Richmond, 178
Riddell, Roger, 244
Rising Sun, 179–81
Riverside Park, 320–21
Rock House, 249–50
Ropkey Armor Museum, 288–89
Round Barn Bed and Breakfast,
  167–68
Ryder, Bill, 12–14

INDEX

S

Salem, 184
Santa Claus, 258–60
Savage, Eugene, 286
Schimpff's Confectionery, 74
shagbark syrup, 267–68
Sharp, Zerna, 283
Sharpsville, 335–36
Shaw, Sam, 200–201
Shelbyville, 334
Shirk, Bill, 46–47
Shivaree Trough, 234
Shoals, 261–62
shoe tree, 245–46
Silvertowne, 129–31
Simpson Mortuary Museum, 254
Skunk Lady of Indiana, 299–300
Solsberry, 262–63
South Bend, 336–38
Spencer Lapidary, 83–84
St. Francisville Bridge, 269–70
Standard Oil gas station, 313–14
Starke County Historical
   Museum, 311
Starlight, 185
Stevens Museum, 184
Story, 250–51
Story Inn, 250–51
Story Still, 250–51
Stratton-Porter Home, 94-95
Summerplace, 335–36
Sun Aura Nudist Camp, 317–318
Super Jumbos, 50–51
Swiss Heritage Village, 65–66
Swiss Wine Festival, 188–89

T

Tarzan, 334
Tefft, 339
Terre Haute, 263–67
Thorntown, 340–41
Traders Point Creamery, 343–44
Trafalgar, 267–68
Trevlac, 186–87
Tuckaway, 48–49
Turner Doll Facotry, 238–39
Turtle Lady of New Palestine, 176–77
Turtle Town, 77–78
Twinrocker, 281

U

underwater pumpkin carving,
   110–11
Union City, 73
United States Vice Presidential
   Museum, 98
Upland, 122–23
USS LST Ship Memorial, 225–27

V

Vallonia, 187–88
Vevay, 188–91
Vincennes, 269–70

W

Wabash, 124
Wagon Wheel Liquor, 148
Wakarusa, 125–26
Waldron, 192–93
Walker, Charles, 202
Walnut Grove Church, 341–41
Warsaw, 126–29
Warsaw Biblical Gardens, 128–29

INDEX

Wayne County Historical
    Museum, 158
West Baden Hotel, 270–72
West Baden Springs, 270–72
West College Corner, 194–95
Whistle Stop Restaurant, 325
Whitewater Valley Railroad, 140
Wilbur Wright Birth Home and
    Museum, 155–56
Wild Winds Buffalo Preserve, 92–93
Wildlife Educational Services,
    212–13
Willard Library, 225–26
Willow by Greg Adams, 101–2
Winchester, 129–31
Wizard of Oz Museum, 284–85

Wolf Lake, 131–32
Wolf Park, 278
Woodruff Place Lawn Chair Brigade,
    36–37
WWII Victory Museum, 62

Y
Yellowwood State Forest, 273
Young, Myrtle, 90–92

Z
Zaharako's Ice Cream and
    Confectionery, 75
Zimmerman glass, 141–42
Zionsville, 341–44

About the Author

Dick Wolfsie has been a household name for twenty-five years. Okay, maybe not in your household but in his.

Dick taught high school and college before becoming a TV and radio talk show host. In Indiana alone, he's interviewed more than 15,000 people and done more than 5,000 hours of live broadcasting. He's not 100 percent sure those numbers are accurate, because, quite frankly, he's lost track.

He has worked for WISH-TV in Indianapolis for fifteen years, which is considered a long time for a TV reporter. Maybe they don't even realize he's still on every morning.

In this updated *Indiana Curiosities,* you will learn about some neat people and places that would have been in the first book if he hadn't gotten lost so often. He had better luck this time. That's why this book is a little thicker.

Dick lives in Indianapolis with his wife, Mary Ellen, Brett, his son, and his dog, Toby. By the way, Dick has written seven other books, more books than he has actually read.

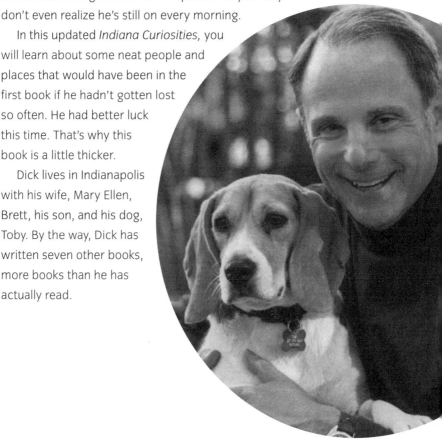